FLEUR DE LYS

The Kings and Queens of France

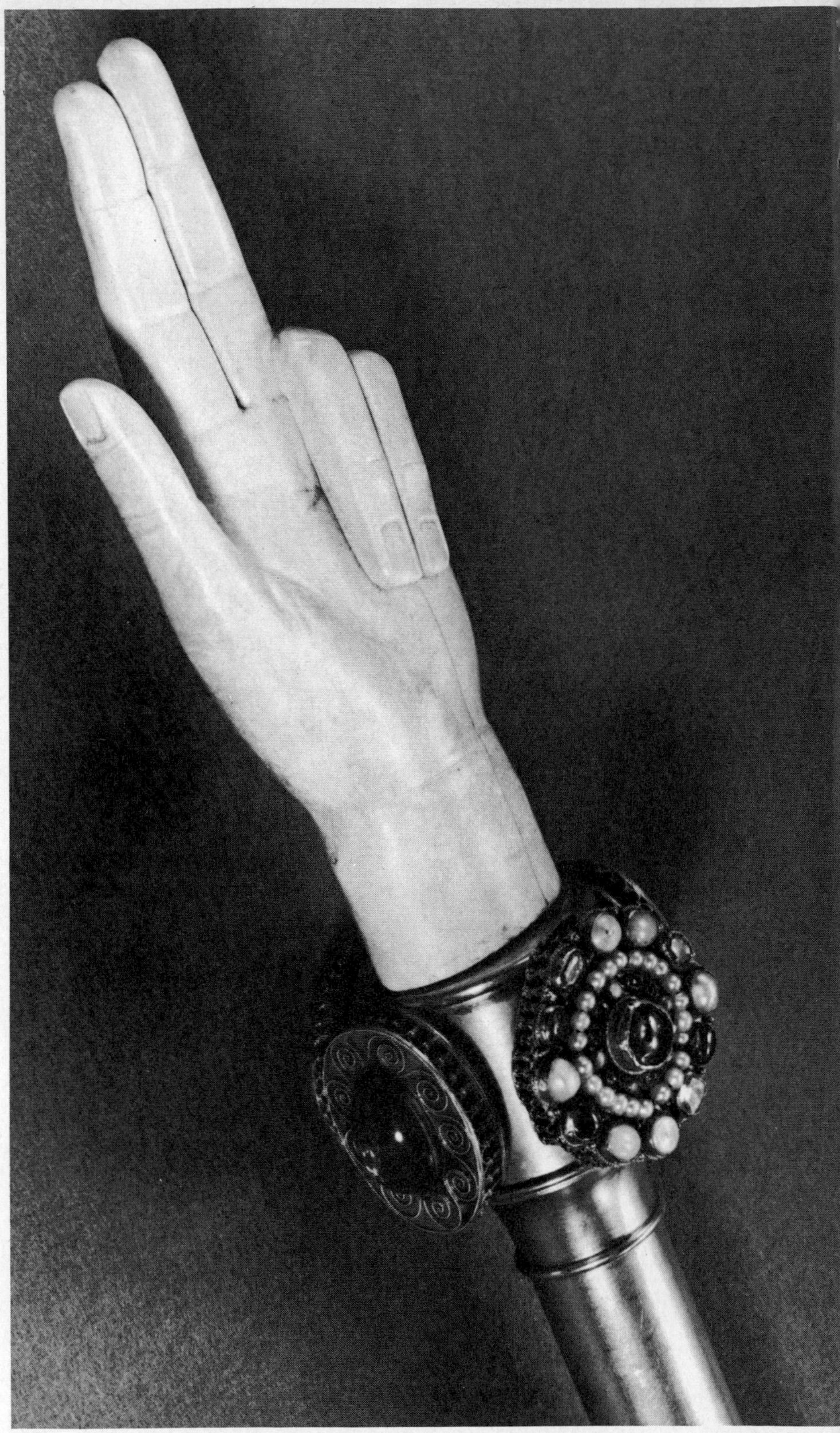

The 'hand of justice' used in the consecration service of the monarch, reset by Napoleon in 1804. The baton is capped with an ivory hand and encrusted round the wrist with precious stones. The three raised fingers symbolise both the crowned king and Christ in majesty. It was the symbol for power and the justice which the king undertook to provide for his subjects.

JOY LAW

Fleur de Lys

The Kings and Queens of France

McGRAW-HILL BOOK COMPANY
New York St. Louis San Francisco Dusseldorf Mexico Toronto

First published in Great Britain 1976
by Hamish Hamilton Ltd
90 Great Russell Street London WC1B 3PT

Library of Congress Cataloging in Publication Data
Main entry under title:

Fleur de lys.

1. France—Kings and rulers. 2. France—Queens.
I. Law, Joy.
DC36.6.F58 1976 944'.00992 75-28501
ISBN 0-07-036695-0

Designed by Patrick Leeson

Filmset by BAS Printers Limited, Wallop, Hampshire
Printed in Great Britain by Ebenezer Baylis & Son Ltd,
The Trinity Press, Worcester, and London

Dedicated to

Jennifer, Nicholas and Katie

Author's Note

My greatest debt is to the late Nancy Mitford who, through her work and friendship, infected me with her own love of French history, and who showed me how amusing and instructive the everyday activities of people in high places could be.

I should like to acknowledge the help of the staff of the London Library and the Royal College of Art Library; Miss June Lines; Mme Chantal Coural; Mme M-A Landon; the Reverend Canon Ian Dunlop; Miss Helen Thomson; Miss Caroline Tonson-Rye; Mr Christopher Elrington; Mr Desmond Seward, for suggesting possible sources of material for the Bourbons, and for allowing me to use his translation on page 184, Mrs Rhianna Forbes and Miss Lucy Norton for assistance in translation, and the latter for her permission to use her translation of the Memoirs of the Duc de Saint-Simon on pages 204–8, 211–14; Miss Beryl Smalley, who once attempted to teach me medieval history, and who has allowed me to quote her on page 39; and Mr Christopher Sinclair-Stevenson for his persistence, support and encouragement over a number of years.

I would not have been able to produce the book at all without the devoted assistance of Miss Susan Harris Browne, whose enthusiasm, methodical attention to detail and sheer hard work with both the text and the illustrations have been invaluable.
My gratitude to her.

Finally, I must thank my husband for his forbearance in the disruption of our family life and his practical adherence to the belief that the pursuit of happiness requires liberty.

Joy Law
September 1975

Contents

Full titles of the books and the exact sources are given on *pp. 252–6.*

List of Illustrations

SOURCES OF PHOTOGRAPHS: The list of illustrations above indicates where the originals of the illustrations are to be found. Museums and individuals listed there have supplied their own photographs; and works in the *Bibliothèque Nationale* and the *Archives Nationales* in Paris have been supplied by their respective *services photographiques,* unless otherwise credited below.

We are indebted to them, and to the following, for supplying or lending photographs and for permission to reproduce them:

Service de Documentation Photographique de la Réunion des Musées Nationaux, Paris: pp. 2, facing p. 97, 98 (both), 111, facing p. 112, 179, 191, 246 from the Musée du Louvre; pp. 159, 197, 201 (centre and right), 205, 218, 234, 251 from the Musée de Versailles. *Jean Roubier, Paris*: p. 25. *Ets J. E. Bulloz, Paris*: pp. 29, 130, 153, 200, 222, 229, 232. *Photographie Giraudon, Paris*: pp. 43 (top), 47, 49 (right), 62, 88, 139, 141 (right), 142, 143, 149, 151, 163, 181, 186, 195, 201 (left), 242. *British Library Board, London*: p. 43 (top). *Caisse Nationale des Monuments Historiques, Archives Photographiques, Paris*: pp. 56, 59, 69, 71, 75, 76, 79, 81, 82, 92, 99 (left), 102, 107, 152, 171, 251. *Giuseppe Malito, Cosenza*: p. 66. *Jeremy Whitaker, Hampshire*: pp. 84, 134, 135, facing p. 160. *Roger-Viollet, Paris*: pp. 91, 249. *Maison Cavenel, Amiens*: p. 101. *Service Départementale du Toursime, Préfecture d'Indre-et-Loire, Tours*: p. 110. *Fratelli Alinari sPa, Florence/Mansell Collection, London*: pp. 124 (left), 147, facing p. 161, 188. *Club Iris Photothèque*: p. 124 (right). *A. C. Cooper Ltd, London*: p. 129. *George Rainbird Ltd, London*: pp. 133, 141 (right), facing p. 160, facing p. 177. *Rodney Todd-White & Son, London*: pp. 156, 182. *Jean Arlaud, Geneva*: p. 178. *René Pérony, Pau*: facing p. 176. *John R. Freeman Ltd, London*: p. 228.

Anecdotes are the gleanings left over from the vast harvest field of history; they are details that have been long hidden, hence their name of anecdotes; the public is interested in them when they concern illustrious personages.

VOLTAIRE
Siècle de Louis XIV

The royal shield bearing three fleurs-de-lys from a document of Charles V, Paris, July 1364. It appears in a magnificently ornamented initial C. The fleur-de-lys was a symbol of great antiquity and had been used before its appearance on Hugh Capet's sceptre. It was probably Charles V who chose three in honour of the Trinity.

Prologue

Let anyone who would understand the fortunes of the French wander for days in the wooded valley of the Oise. There great forests still clothe the low rounded hills which border the widenings of the slow river, where it saunters through its pasturages and its marsh, with tall, delicate aspens in solemn lines to mark its passage. It is a flat river floor of half a league across, and about it the great woods of Compiègne and of Coucy, and all the others that still bear the name of their towns or castles, make a sheet of trees. That sheet of trees may have been a wider thing in the old days, but it remains for anyone who will visit it (and it is a countryside that will harbour a man for as long as he will, so broad is it and so deep) the memory of that landscape in which the fortunes of his country changed and re-arose.

But, in particular, the forest of Coucy and the depths of the tall trunks understand how the lords hunted there when the Emperor was still the Emperor, and before France was once again France. See how there still remain in fragments the lines of the Roman roads that led from town to town; all the towns that make up this countryside. Consider Paris, one hard day's ride away, two or three days' marches. Remember Laon on its impregnable horse-shoe hill upon the edge of those woods, overlooking the plains to the east and the north, and forming a bulwark and a stronghold for the last of the blood of Charlemagne.

Then, in your mind, see westward and southward the open land, Normandy and Anjou, the Island of France, the gardens of Touraine, Nevers, the high Morvan, the Champagne, crammed with Latinity, and the valleys of the Allier, of the Cher, and of the Vienne, leading upwards and southwards into those dead mountains of the centre which are the frontier against the south. Remember also the good lands that flank Brittany, and that make an approach and a barrier at once for that jealous, silent land. Do all this, and you will understand what happened when the Carolingians fell, and when, in one moment, a new line of kings that stood for Gaul re-arisen was accepted and crowned in the person of its ancestor.

France would be. The Germanies learning the Faith, and informed by the French, were still the Germanies: barbaric, lacking in stone and in letters; lacking in roads. The Latin speech had not followed in them the Latin rule, and the Church which had made them human had hardly welded them into Christendom. It was not possible that Gaul should any longer be confused with these, unless, indeed, they would consent to be ruled from Gaul. That, in their new-found faith and culture, they would not consent to. Yet the imperial line and the old name of Charlemagne, now wasted for nearly two hundred years, pretended to control the issue. But France knew itself again—that is, Gaul knew itself again, through the confusion of how many centuries; and a symbol must be found for France. The line of Charlemagne was exhausted. It could present for claimant to universal rule over the Germanies, as over Gaul, as over Italy, nothing that men respected, no one whom soldiers followed.

But in Gaul itself was a family and a man.

That Robert who had died at Brissarthe, and who had come, no man knew whence, but who was so strong, and who was called 'The Strong', had founded lineage. It was a man of his blood who had held Paris against the Normans. Men of his blood had claimed the crown and kingship once, and had been a part of the Empire, and had yet dropped the claim. But their great estate of land had grown and grown. Their command over many soldiers had grown therewith. They spoke in the Latin tongue; they were of us. And of all those who were of us they were the richest and, what is much more, the most captaining family of them. Of that great line Hugh was now the man. For a hundred years his father and his father's father and his father before him had been the true masters of those good river valleys, the Loire, and the Seine, and the Oise. If there was to be government, he, Hugh, must come.

Rheims of the Champagne, the town where Clovis, five hundred years before, had accepted the Faith and made a unity for Gaul, had in this moment for its great archbishop one Adalbéron, a man very subtle, and more learned than subtle; stronger in will than either in his learning or in his subtlety, and perceiving future things.

In those days there was between men a division. The great were very great. The mass of men were hardly free, and were all very small. The slaves that had worked for Roman lords in generations now half-forgotten, if they were no longer slaves, were still mean men; and the few that could ride by the day through their estates inland were great above all men—the great bishops, the great counts, the men of the palace, and the masters of the countryside.

These, then—the Empire now plainly in default, and wealthy Gaul, as it were, derelict, and the Germanies, in their barbarism, sheering off—counselled what they should do. They met in an assembly, going up the northern road from Paris to Senlis; and here there was great tumult. For each man came with his armed men about him, and confusedly they knew how mighty a thing was toward.

In that tumult it was Adalbéron who spoke: 'Charles of Lower Lorraine', he said, 'has many to speak for him, and he says that the throne should come to him by right of lineage. But there should not stand at the head of this kingdom any but he who is great. Hugh, the commander of armies, is known to you by his deeds, by his descent, and by the armed men in his troop, who are many. If you will have government, take him.'

In the further tumult that followed Adalbéron persuaded, and Hugh, coming from those who had saved Paris, and who had commanded armament in Gaul for now so long, was acclaimed by the great lords as king.

When the time came for the anointing and the crowning, and for this separation of France again from what was not France, this re-seizing of the nation to itself, Noyon was the town they chose.

Little Noyon, with its vast arcaded church, strong and Roman, amid the woods of the Oise, the altar before which Charlemagne himself had been crowned. To Noyon they came in the midst of those forests of the Oise, by that strict road of the Romans which bridged the river, and which is but one of the many that there meet, as in the centre of a wheel; for the dignity of Noyon, now so forgotten, lay in this—that men could come to it easily, even in those days of difficulty and of old arts forgotten.

In Noyon, then, was Hugh crowned.

He had no name but Hugh. Since, however, men must give names to a family as well as to a man, all the generations after him have remembered what his nickname was. For he had a nickname, this soldier and lord, and from his helmet or his hood he was called Hugh Capet, the man of the head covering—the man of the head or cap. And that is why this family is called Capetian: a little cause for a great thing.

A twelfth-century roof boss in the nave of the church at Chars showing the first four Capetian monarchs.

The Capets

THE CAPETS

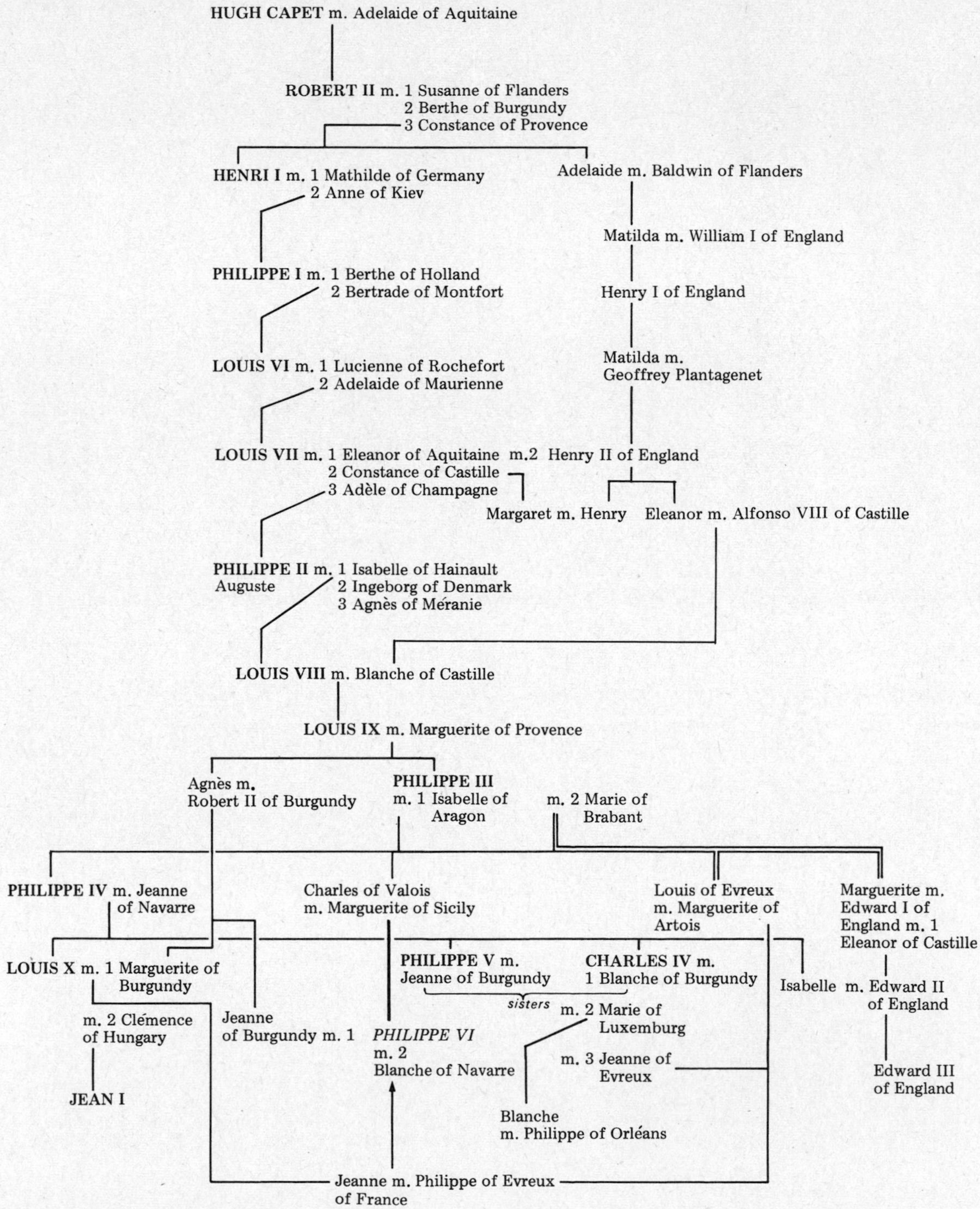

HUGH CAPET m. Adelaide of Aquitaine
ROBERT II m. 1 Susanne of Flanders
2 Berthe of Burgundy
3 Constance of Provence
HENRI I m. 1 Mathilde of Germany
2 Anne of Kiev
Adelaide m. Baldwin of Flanders
Matilda m. William I of England
PHILIPPE I m. 1 Berthe of Holland
2 Bertrade of Montfort
Henry I of England
LOUIS VI m. 1 Lucienne of Rochefort
2 Adelaide of Maurienne
Matilda m.
Geoffrey Plantagenet
LOUIS VII m. 1 Eleanor of Aquitaine m.2 Henry II of England
2 Constance of Castille
3 Adèle of Champagne
Margaret m. Henry
Eleanor m. Alfonso VIII of Castille
PHILIPPE II m. 1 Isabelle of Hainault
Auguste
2 Ingeborg of Denmark
3 Agnès of Méranie
LOUIS VIII m. Blanche of Castille
LOUIS IX m. Marguerite of Provence
Agnès m.
Robert II of Burgundy
PHILIPPE III
m. 1 Isabelle of
Aragon
m. 2 Marie of
Brabant
PHILIPPE IV m. Jeanne
of Navarre
Charles of Valois
m. Marguerite of Sicily
Louis of Evreux
m. Marguerite of
Artois
Marguerite m.
Edward I of
England m. 1
Eleanor of Castille
LOUIS X m. 1 Marguerite of
Burgundy
PHILIPPE V m.
Jeanne of Burgundy
CHARLES IV m.
1 Blanche of Burgundy
sisters
Isabelle m. Edward II
of England
m. 2 Clémence
of Hungary
Jeanne
of Burgundy m. 1
PHILIPPE VI
m. 2
Blanche of Navarre
m. 2 Marie of
Luxemburg
m. 3 Jeanne of
Evreux
Edward III
of England
JEAN I
Blanche
m. Philippe of Orléans
Jeanne m. Philippe of Evreux
of France

Hugh Capet

Hugh Capet was born about 946 at Paris and became king in May 987. He was proclaimed king at Noyon, on 1 July, 987, and consecrated on 5 July.
He married, in 970, Adelaide of Aquitaine (d. 1004–5).
He reigned for nine years and died, possibly from smallpox, aged about fifty, on 24 October, 996. He was buried at St Denis.

The Capetians had three great qualities of a peculiarly French character: they were adventurous, honest and sincere and they combined valour and loyalty with dexterity and patience.

Originally content to be Dukes of France only, they allied themselves with the Carolingians—the ruling house—rather than fight them. But in 987 the claimant to the throne, the last descendant of Charlemagne, was the Duke of Lorraine, and he was a vassal of the German Emperor. So Hugh thought the moment was ripe to press his claim to the throne.

An assembly of nobles met at Senlis, under the presidency of Adalbéron, the Archbishop of Rheims, who delivered himself of a fine electoral harangue on behalf of his candidate, as recorded by Richer (d. c. 998), a monk at St Remigius who was writing during Hugh and his successor's lifetime. Richer was of course politically biased in Hugh's favour but tells a good tale:

'Here we are met together once again in a body. Let us see that by our prudence and good faith hatred should not overcome reason, nor that affection should change the truth. We do not ignore the claims put forward by Charles [of Lorraine]'s supporters who maintain that the throne belongs to him by hereditary right. But the throne is not a hereditary right and we must elevate to it only those who not only have the advantage of birth but who also possess wisdom, and whose loyalty and high-mindedness are not in question . . . but why should we bow to a man who does not show the way to a true faith, one whom torpor has weakened, and who has, to his great shame, served a foreign king and who made a poor marriage with a woman from the ranks of his vassals?

If you think about it, you will see that Charles himself has brought about his own self-destruction. Nothing has caused his fall from his rank; it is by his own hand that he has fallen. Make therefore a choice that will bring well-being rather than ruin upon the country. If you wish it to be unhappy, choose Charles; if you want its prosperity, choose the glorious Duke of the Franks, Hugh. Choose as your leader the Duke, marked out by his actions, his nobility and his strength, a man in whom you will find not only the defender of the realm but the protector of your private interests too. Thanks to him, you will have found a father. Who has applied to him for help and been turned away? Who, deprived of succour by his own people, has not found it from him?'

This advice was favourably received and by general consent the Duke was elected to the throne.

Surrounded by his nobles, he published decrees and promulgated laws; he ruled most successfully, and acknowledged, with true piety, the good luck which accompanied all he did. To make certain of his succession, after consultation, he went to the Archbishop to discuss associating his son Robert with him on the throne. The Archbishop felt that it would be unreasonable to create two kings in one year but Hugh showed him a letter from Borel, Duke of Lower Spain, asking for help against the barbarians and said that if he or Robert should be killed in the ensuing war there must be a new king so that the army would have a chief. Moreover in the event of his death it would prevent dissension between the nobles, victory of the evil over the good and, by extension, the captivity of the whole nation.

The Archbishop, convinced, agreed to Hugh's wishes and as everyone was assembled for Christmas, he crowned Robert, son of Hugh, king in Ste Croix [at Orléans], amid the plaudits of the ranks and proclaimed him King of Western Gaul, from the Meuse to the Ocean.

Hugh was elected, though not without opposition. One of the barons, the Count of Périgord, raised an army to attack him. Hugh asked him, 'Who made you Count?' to be greeted with the reply, 'Who made you King?' But Hugh managed to establish primacy over the barons although he was only king in the sense of being obeyed in his own territories which consisted of Paris, Senlis, Orléans and Dreux—an area which could be ridden round on horseback in two or three days. However it was from this start that the Capetians set about uniting all the provinces of France.

Little is known about Hugh's character, though he was pious and more the diplomat than the warrior, as an earlier tale by Richer shows:

Otto [the German Emperor], anxious to receive his [Hugh's] homage, made everyone leave his room, placed his sword on a chair and gave orders that only the Duke [Hugh] and the Bishop, who was acting as interpreter, should be allowed in. As the King [Otto] spoke Latin it was necessary for what he said to be translated for Hugh. Hugh and the Bishop entered, and were graciously received. The King spoke kindly and spared Hugh recriminations, embraced him and called him friend. After a long discussion on the subject of an alliance, the King left the room, and when he returned, he asked for his sword. The Duke bent to pick it up and placed himself to carry it behind the King. This was why Otto had put the sword on the chair. He wanted it to be thought by all that the Duke had

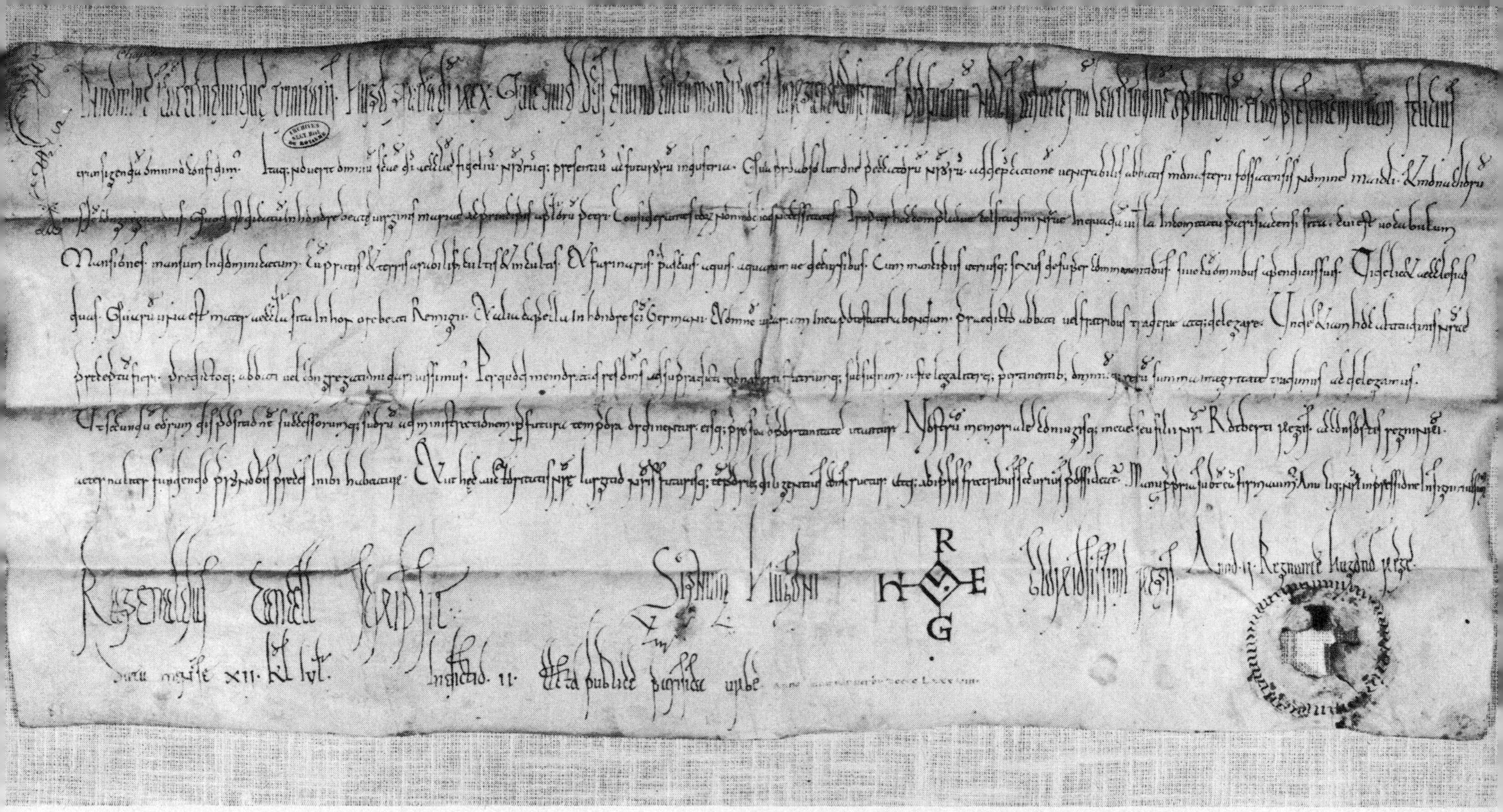

A document dated 20 June, 989 in which Hugh Capet made over Maisons-Alfort to the abbey of St Maur des Fossés in return for the prayers of the monks for his soul. The seal has been removed. It is the only original act of Hugh in the French National Archives.

Hugh's monogram: detail from the above.

held it thus previously but the Bishop, in the interests of the Duke, took it from his hands and himself carried it behind the King.

Hugh died shortly after his election, according to Richer,

covered in spots [probably pox or syphilis] at his château in the hands of the Jews [probably doctors].

but he had been strong enough to have his son crowned as his successor during his lifetime and many of his descendants were to reign over France.

Robert II

Robert II, the Pious, was born about 971 at Orléans. He was associated with the throne during his father's lifetime and became king on 24 October, 996.
He married, about 988, Susanne of Flanders (d. 1003); in 996 or 997, Berthe of Burgundy; and, about 1003, Constance of Provence (982–1032).
He reigned for thirty-four years and died, from unknown causes, aged about sixty, at Melun on 20 July, 1031. He was buried at St Denis.

Rather more is known about Robert, or at least his person, for his 'life' was written by Helgald, a monk of the abbey of Fleury-sur-Loire. Little is known of Helgald but he had been to the court and had met Robert so his description of his person is accurate even if his Life, *written* c. *1042, about ten years after Robert's death, is an act of piety.*

He was tall, and his hair was smooth and well-kept. He had a modest look, a gentle mouth, benign as if to bestow the kiss of peace, an imposing beard and high shoulders. When the crown was put on his head, one could tell that, from his parents and his grandparents, he was of royal descent; when he mounted the royal horse it was noticed that his toes practically reached his heels—thought to be miraculous by those who saw it. He prayed frequently and continually bent his knee; to sum up, he was a man who reached the highest level by his own merit. He was never vengeful, he loved simplicity and conversed, walked and ate with all. He was so devoted to holy readings that not a day passed but he read his psalter. He was gentle, graceful and had a civil and agreeable character, preferring to do good than to rely on good words. He was also well-versed in literature, for his mother had sent him to study with Gerbert at the schools in Rheims to be educated in liberal doctrines.

Richer confirms Helgald's assessment of Robert's character and explains the dissolution of Robert's first marriage, and the contraction of his second:

Robert was renowned for his energy and piety; he excelled both in military prowess and in his knowledge of divine and canon law; he studied literature and took part in the bishops' assemblies and took pleasure in discussing and arranging ecclesiastical affairs with them.

King Robert, at the age of nineteen, in the flower of his youth, repudiated his Italian wife Susanne, [widow of the Count of Flanders] because she was too old for him. The princess insisted on the restitution of her dowry and as the King refused to give it back she had recourse to methods other than prayer and to recover her goods put the prince to a good deal of trouble. When she saw she couldn't seize the château of Montreuil, which she had been given and where she wanted to live, she built another château nearby while

Robert's great seal of 997. 'King Robert, even when young, was wise and learned, and had a gentle eloquence and remarkable piety.'

Constance of Provence. Wash drawing of her tomb at St Denis, made for the Gaignières collection in the eighteenth century. Roger de Gaignières employed draughtsmen to record tombs and monuments, many of which have now been destroyed.

[baronial] quarrels kept the King busy. She hoped thereby to hinder navigation for the boats had to pass her property before reaching their destination.

Their divorce was thought ill of but only in private.

Robert, with advice, married Berthe on the ground that 'it is better to put up with a small evil in order to evade a greater one'.

Two years after Berthe left him Robert remarried. Ralph Glaber, another monk, writing about 1047–8, tells of the new wife:

Robert married Constance, as constant in heart as in name, and worthy of her position. A certain Hugh de Beauvais was anxious to sow discord between the King and his wife and succeeded in turning Robert against her. He hoped thereby to turn affairs to his own profit and he did in fact persuade the King to make him court chamberlain. But one day, when the King was out hunting, accompanied by Hugh who never left his side, Hugh was set upon by Foulque, the Queen's uncle, and his eyes were gouged out in front of Robert. The King was upset for a time but nevertheless managed to return to the Queen and re-establish a proper relationship with her.

Robert's piety seems to have increased with his marriage to Constance. Helgald tells of two incidents:

His queen, Constance, built a fine château and oratory at Etampes. The King, pleased with it, went there with the court for dinner and gave instructions that it should be open to the poor. One sat himself at the King's feet and was fed by him under the table. Seeing a gold ornament—what we call a fringe—hanging from the King's knee, he snipped it with his knife and made off quickly. When the time came to clear the room of beggars, the King commanded that those who had been given meat, food and drink should be reseated, and as he and the Queen got up from table, the Queen noticed that the King's gold ornament was missing. Disturbed, she cried out, 'Ah, my lord, what enemy of God has removed your device?' 'No one,' replied the King, 'has stolen it, but with God's help it will serve him better who has it than me.'

On the feast of the Last Supper he had collected together not less than three hundred paupers. With one knee on the ground, he gave each from his blessed hand vegetables, fish, bread and a coin. At the tenth hour he gave a hundred poor clerks a ration of bread, fish and wine, and handed each a dozen coins, whilst reciting, with both heart and voice, the Psalms. Then this humble king prepared a table for divine service, removed his clothes, covered his body with a hair shirt, and proceeded to wash the feet of twelve paupers, drying them with his hair and making them eat with him.

Robert and Constance's eldest son Hugh died young,

and after his death Robert decided he must choose from his remaining sons a worthy successor. He had already created Henri, Hugh's younger brother, Duke of Burgundy and he decided to put him on the throne. But the Queen, tormented by the spirit of contradiction natural to women, disagreed with her husband and Henri's following. She thought that the third son, Robert, was the most capable to take on the reins of government. And thus she sowed the seeds of discord between the two princes.

The King died in July [20 July, 1031] in his château at Melun. His body was taken to the church of St Denis and buried there. After his death, the quarrels between the Queen and her sons took on a new vigour.

Henri I

Henri I was born in April–May 1008, associated with the throne in 1027 and became king on 20 July, 1031.
He married Mathilde of Germany (d. before 1044) and, in 1051, Anne of Kiev (?1024–c. 1066).
He reigned for twenty-nine years and died, from unknown causes, aged fifty-two, at Vitry-en-Brie on 4 August, 1060. He was buried at St Denis.

Henri, Robert's son, continued the work of his father and grandfather in trying to bring the barons to heel and to centralise power within the monarchy but he laid up trouble for his successors when in 1032 he gave his brother, Robert, the Duchy of Burgundy—which did not revert to the crown until 1477.

Very little indeed is known about Henri except that he sent to Russia for a second wife:

By the niece of Henry, the Emperor of Germany, whom Henri had married, there was one daughter who died very soon. Her mother did not long survive her, and the King, who did not wish to remain without a wife, sent Gautier, Bishop of Meaux, to the King of Russia and asked him to send one of his daughters who was called Anne, which he did willingly. And when she arrived, the King sent his barons, and solemnly married her. And the lady, who led a holy life, thought more about spiritual life and the future than she did of temporal things. In the hope that she might benefit in the life hereafter she founded the church of St Vincent at Senlis. Lovingly and gloriously did she and the King live together and they had three sons, Philippe, Robert and Hugh.

Seal of Henri I from a charter dated 1035. This is the first example of a seal showing the king 'in majesty'—seated and holding the regalia.

At this time Paris was burnt and also about this time there was a great famine which lasted seven years. Philippe, the eldest of the three brothers, was anointed and consecrated during the lifetime of his father, by his command, since he was old and wretched. Henri died a year later and was buried at St Denis with his father and grandfather and other ancestors. This King Henri was very brave and a valiant fighter.

According to Orderic Vitalis (b. 1075), a monk of Anglo-French parentage who wrote a history of the Normans with a wealth of not always wholly accurate information, at the end of his life,

Henri asked for a potion from Jean, a doctor in Chartres who later and by accident was called the 'deaf'. The King hoped that this potion would prolong his life and improve his health. As however he indulged his fantasies rather than obey the instructions of his doctor he asked his chamberlain for water to assuage the thirst which tormented him while the medicine took its painful course. Before it could take effect he started drinking, unknown to his doctor, and unfortunately died the following morning.

Philippe I

Philippe I was born in 1052. He was associated with the throne, during his father's lifetime, at Rheims on 23 May, 1059 and became king on 4 August, 1060.
He married, in 1072, Berthe of Holland (d. 1093) who was repudiated in 1092, and, in that year, Bertrade of Montfort.
He reigned for forty-eight years and died, perhaps of malaria, aged fifty-six, at the château at Melun-sur-Seine on 3 August, 1108. He was buried at the monastery of St Benoît-sur-Loire.

No one has much good to say about Philippe I for he was physically gross and unattractive. Two English chroniclers, Henry of Huntingdon and William of Malmesbury, were far from flattering about Philippe or his son:

What is there to be said of Philippe, King of France, and his son Louis, who reigned in our day? Their belly was their god, and their ruin. They stuffed themselves to the point where they disappeared in rolls of flesh, unable to stand. No sooner had Philippe died of obesity than Louis, though a young man, at once expired from the same cause.

But what good can be said of them? Philippe was often defeated by his own men, and fled from the most paltry opponents. Louis was driven off the battlefield by King Henry [of England], and evidently terrorised by his own side again and again.

So far as concerned our own King, Philippe was a force neither for good nor ill, chiefly because he was preoccupied with his stomach rather than affairs of state.

Philippe's frequent brushes with the Church did not endear him to her servants who were the contemporary chroniclers. Moreover he had to contend with his vassal the Duke of Normandy invading and settling in England, although he was skilled at playing upon the family dissensions of William the Conqueror's heirs; he did what he could to curb his own 'turbulent barons', advising his son, according to Suger, to make sure that you never let the tower of Montlhéry out of your keeping. To tell the truth, that tower has made me old before my time. *He was also faced with the rising power of the burghers which made life internally troublesome for him, and he did not, as might have been expected, lead the First Crusade, (1096–99) preached by the French Pope Urban II, although it is less surprising as he was excommunicate at the time for having married Bertrade of Montfort—a subject which did excite his chroniclers. Orderic Vitalis, the monk of the abbey of Ouche who died in 1141 or 1142, says:*

About this time a scandal occurred which disturbed the kingdom. Bertrade of Montfort, the Countess of Anjou, was afraid that her husband Foulque le Réchin [restive or headstrong] would do with her as he had done with two other wives and repudiate her in her turn like a vile courtesan. Confident of her noble blood and in her beauty, she sent a man

Seal of Philippe I from a charter dated 6 January, 1082.

whom she trusted to Philippe, King of the French, to disclose to him her intentions. She would prefer to be the first to leave her husband and to find another than to be left by him and become an object of scorn to all. The voluptuous prince, having perfectly understood the meaning of this declaration, agreed to it, and when this lascivious woman abandoned her husband and went to France he gladly received her. He repudiated his own wife, the noble and virtuous Queen Berthe, the daughter of Florent, Count of Holland, who had borne him Louis and Constance, and married Bertrade, whom Foulque, the Count of Anjou, had had to wife for nearly four years.

The change of husband was not accomplished without difficulties. Foulque and Philippe quarrelled.

Between these two powerful rivals broke out a storm of threats, but the woman, clever and subtle, reconciled them and made peace between them so effectively that they met together at a splendid feast arranged by her. She sat them together at the table and that night she had beds for them made up in the same room.

The Pope was not at all satisfied with the marriage and when Philippe refused to break with Bertrade, they were excommunicated. But Philippe stood his ground and was reconciled to the Papacy in 1106 with a new Pope, Pascal II. Bertrade remained Queen until the King died, after which according to William of Malmesbury,

Bertrade, still young and beautiful, took the veil in the abbey of Fontrevault, always charming to men, pleasing to God, and like an angel.

Edifying deaths always gave chroniclers pleasure to record. Orderic Vitalis quotes the King himself:

I know that the Kings of France are buried in the church of St Denis but I have been too great a sinner for my body to lie alongside so great a martyr. I fear indeed that my sins have been so great that I shall be delivered up to the devil and that my end may not be that attributed to Charles Martel. I have always revered St Benoît; dying I call upon this father of these monks and I ask to be buried in his church by the Loire. He is filled with forgiveness and goodness; he welcomes sinners who wish to repent and to be reconciled to God within his rule.

Suger prefers funerals to 'concubines'; and Louis VI to his father:

In fact since he had as concubine the Countess of Anjou he did nothing any longer worthy of his royal majesty, but carried away by the violence of his lust for the woman whom he had made off with he did little but satisfy his passion for her. He ceased to care for the affairs of state nor in his excessive relaxation did he take care of his own body—actually well made and elegant. There was nothing to maintain the kingdom in its power except for the fear and love in which his successor and son was held. Barely sixty [he was fifty-six], the King expired and rendered up his last breath at Melun-sur-Seine in the presence of Louis.

The noble corpse of his royal majesty was carried to Notre Dame and the entire night was spent celebrating his funeral. The next morning his son had his funerary litter well clad with rich materials and all sorts of decoration and had it placed on the shoulders of the principal servants, while he himself displayed the sentiments of a true son as befitted such a prince. Sometimes on foot, sometimes on horseback, with the nobles who were there, he accompanied the litter in tears. What admirable grandeur of soul, for during the whole of his father's life neither during the repudiation of his mother nor even during the time of favours given outside marriage to the Angevin lady, did he take offence nor looked for, as is the case with other young people, an opportunity to make disorder in the kingdom, by aiming a blow at his authority.

Philippe was buried, as he asked, in the monastery at St Benoît-sur-Loire. After being neglected during the Revolution interest in his tomb was reawakened in 1830 when it was investigated. The report then was as follows:

Having shown there where its position might be between the balustrade of the altar and the choir, three feet from the first step of the sanctuary they took up sixteen square slabs, and then removed the earth beneath the tiling to a depth of fourteen or fifteen inches revealing stones of the same kind as the slabs. Considering the subsidence undergone by the church and the tiny space available for a close examination it was thought that these stones might be a second layer of tiling especially as it was probable that Philippe I was buried in a vault since there were no historical documents available. They set about to lift one of these stones and revealed a large human skeleton from which the solid parts appeared to have disintegrated and, from the bandages in which it was wrapped, to have been embalmed. It was thought that in view of the disintegration, and the solidity and age of the construction of the tomb that our conjectures were more than probable. So, pleased with progress so far, wishing to leave verification to more competent authorities, and out of respect for the royal ashes, we ordered the workmen to close the opening and tried to replace the stone we had lifted but because the groove was too narrow we could not do so and in spite of all precautions some loose earth fell into the tomb. So we did the best we could.

Later, 'more competent authorities' arrived to examine the tomb, and they decided that the skeleton was indeed that of Philippe I:

The King lay in a wooden coffin which seemed to be made of oak, as far as we could judge, as it had perished. He was placed by the entrance of the church, his head slightly raised, facing the altar, and his feet about a foot from the step to the sanctuary. He seemed to be very tall. Not all the stones were the same size which seemed to indicate a hasty burial taking place only at the moment itself, from which one could conclude that this prince wished to expiate his sins by a modest entombment—a sacrifice common to the nobles of the time. His tomb was seven feet long, thirty inches wide at the head and fifteen at the foot.

Inside, the shape of all his members were clearly distinguishable. His lower jaw was present in the head with the teeth in their cavities as white as ivory. Nothing remained of the upper jaw. His arms lay alongside his body. Although it maintained its shape the body had disintegrated, and was held together by a shell of linen, made up of embalmed bandages. There were remains of sweet-smelling herbs such as mint and others seemed to have been mixed with aromatics. The bandages wrapping the body from the shoulders to the feet were ornamented with a pattern of flowers and leaves in a coffee-coloured silk. Towards the stomach were found pieces of material thought to be silk or linen. Both the bandages and these scraps were dark brown, stained probably by the unguents and the decomposition of the body.

These facts, together with our information from before and after the Revolution, and since the tomb was in a church where the Benedictines performed their office night and day, lead us to the conclusion despite the absence of royal or religious insignia that this is truly Philippe I.

Louis VI

Louis VI, the Fat, was born in 1081 in Paris. He was associated with the throne in 1100 and acceded to it on 3 August, 1108. He was consecrated on that date at Orléans. He married, in 1104, Lucienne of Rochefort and repudiated her in 1107; and, in 1115, Adelaide of Maurienne (d. 1154).
He reigned for twenty-nine years and died, of dysentery, aged fifty-six, at Paris on 1 August, 1137. He was buried at St Denis.

Louis VI is fortunate in that his friend Suger, the Abbot of St Denis, produced shortly after the King's death a eulogistic life of him—indeed it might be called the first biography of a Capetian king. But although uncritical of his master, Suger did not write a wholly hagiographical work. Suger was the same age as the King and was a monk at St Denis when Louis was sent there in 1095 to be educated. He grew to be his great friend and counsellor. 'A propagandist of genius, he waved his wand over small beer and it turned into sparkling champagne.' An active and courageous man, Louis continued his father's policy of encouraging the English Normans to fight amongst themselves, he consolidated the royal domains and both defended and relied upon the church.

The glorious and renowned King of France, Louis, son of the magnificent King Philippe, was, even at the tender age of twelve or thirteen, good-looking and strong, and praiseworthy for his spiritual qualities as well as his physical elegance which augured well for the future of his kingdom and led to great hopes that he would protect the church and the poor.

Even at so young an age he displayed a mature attitude and scorned hunting and childish games. When he found himself troubled by the aggression of the lords of his realm, and especially by the illustrious King of the English, William, son of the even more renowned William, Conqueror of the English, feelings of a powerful sense of rightness fired him to prove his courage.

He threw off his inertia, embarked on the path of common sense, put idleness behind him and set out on an energetic career. William, an experienced warrior, master of Normandy, did all he could to extend the boundaries of the duchy and sought to wear down the illustrious young prince. The struggle between them was both similar and dissimilar: similar in that neither would cede to the other; dissimilar in that one had the strength of maturity and the other the weakness of youth: the one, opulent and open-handed distributor of the riches of England, recruited and paid his soldiers with great ease, while the other, kept short of cash by a father who only used the resources of his kingdom sparingly, was only able to raise his cavalry by skill and furious energy.

Louis, a veritable hero, young and gay, won all hearts; and was of such good character that some believed him to be simple, but he was hardly out of his teens when he showed himself to be a worthy and courageous defender of his father's kingdom, watching over the needs of the church and looking after the interests of peasants, workers and the poor—people who had long been neglected.

He had already [by 1126] become very fat and had great difficulty in moving his massive body; anyone else, however poor, would neither have wished nor been able, with so great a physical handicap, to expose himself to the danger of mounting a horse, but he, against the advice of all his friends, relied on his own undoubted courage and braved the heat of a June or August day which troubled the younger knights and scorned those who found the heat insupportable even though, in order to cross difficult or narrow paths in the marshes, he had to be held on by his servants.

For a long time the Lord Louis had been enfeebled by his obesity and the continual burdens of war had tired him but, although his body weakened, his mind was unimpaired. Even though he was sixty [actually fifty-four] he was so experienced and able that, had the weightiness of his body not incommoded him so greatly, he would have overcome his enemies everywhere. He complained incessantly and groaned to his friends, 'How miserable is man; knowledge and power together are hardly ever given to him.' Despite being so gross that he had to hold himself upright in his bed, he continued to fight the King of England, Count Thibaud and all his enemies so that those who witnessed his splendid actions or heard tell of them sang his praises while grieving for his physical debility. Worn out by his illness and hardly able to support himself because of a leg wound [at Livvy in 1128] he marched against Count Thibaud and burnt Bonneval—except for a monastery which he spared. His last expedition in which he took part was to lead his army against the château of St Brisson-sur-Loire. He destroyed it by fire, taking the tower and making captive its lord as a punishment for his depradations against the merchants. When he returned from this engagement he was taken violently ill yet again with diarrhoea and stomach-ache. A wise man, thinking of his own good, full of piety towards his soul and his maker, he assured his salvation through frequent confessions and fervent prayer. With all his heart he wished to be transported, in whatever manner, into the company of the martyr saints his protectors, Denis and his companions, and to lay his diadem and his royal dignity before their relics, to change his crown and regalia for a humble monk's habit and life.

In the meantime, terribly troubled by diarrhoea, he was cruelly tortured by his doctors, who in attempting to cure him, gave him drinks so unpleasant and bitter powders so disgusting that the most robust men would have refused them. But not he; in the midst of all his troubles, he never lost his natural gentleness or general friendliness, behaving as kindly as if he had not been indisposed.

Not wishing to make an ignoble end, he called to his side religious men, and confessed, and, to prepare himself for death, made ready to receive extreme unction. While the ceremony was taking place, the King suddenly got up, dressed himself and left the room to the astonishment of all, prostrating himself before the sacrament. There he divested himself of his royal power, gave up the reins of state, confessed to his sins, handed his

Seal of Louis VI from a charter dated Paris, 1108. 'Louis the Fat was huge, alike in body, energy and intellect.'

royal ring to his son Louis and gave away his worldly goods including a magnificent hyacinth [a reddish-orange semi-precious stone] which belonged to his grandmother Anne, daughter of the King of Russia.

After divesting himself in this way and taking communion he returned to his room and lay down on a plain covered bed. But feeling a little better, he had himself carried to Melun and thence to Béthisy, where he learned that Duke William of Aquitaine had died on his way to the shrine of St James at Compostela and had bequeathed to him his unmarried daughter Eleanor, together with all his property. King Louis accepted Eleanor and promised that he would give her in marriage to his son Louis.

The heat of that summer was extreme and more debilitating than usual. Lord Louis, sorely troubled by the heat, had himself taken to Paris but still suffered from dysentery and grew feebler daily. He had himself laid on a bed of cinders arranged in the shape of a cross and placed on a carpet where he died in the thirtieth year of his reign, aged sixty [fifty-six].

His body was wrapped in elaborate materials for burial, but then a strange thing happened. The King had told me [Suger] that he would like to be buried between the altar of the Holy Trinity and that of the saints. I asked the prior of St Denis if this could be arranged but the position was occupied by the tomb of King Carloman and it was not permissible to move the ashes of a dead king. However, by research and in the teeth of opposition from those who thought the place where we dug occupied, we found, as if by a miraculous dispensation, the exact spot where he wished to be buried to be empty and of his exact size both for length and breadth.

Louis VII

Louis VII, the Young, was born in 1120. He was associated with the throne in 1131 and became king on 1 August, 1137.
He married, in 1137, Eleanor of Aquitaine (1122–1204), whom he divorced; in 1154, Constance of Castille (d. 1160); and, in 1160, Adèle of Champagne (d. 1206).
He reigned for forty-three years and died, of a series of strokes, aged sixty, at Paris on 18 September, 1180. He was buried at the abbey of Barbeaux, Melun.

Louis VII was a gentle, bookish man, who was unfortunate in that his father married him young to Eleanor, the heiress of Aquitaine. Her territories were the duchy of Guyenne, Périgord, Limousin, Poitou, Angoumois, Saintonge, Gascony, the suzerainty of Auvergne and the county of Toulouse. He made the great mistake of taking her with him on the Second Crusade and her loose behaviour at Antioch caused a scandal.

On their return to France, and in the year after Suger, who had been regent during Louis's two-year absence, had died, he divorced her on grounds of consanguinity. Guillaume de Nangis writing later had no doubts about the greater virtues of Constance:

Louis went to Aquitaine with his wife, Eleanor, removed his garrisons there and brought his people out of that province. At Beaugency on the way back he repudiated his wife, swearing an oath that she was too closely related to him. Once the divorce was pronounced she returned to her lands and there married Henri, Duke of Normandy and Count of Anjou, and on this account violent disagreement broke out between him and King Louis.

The King took in marriage Constance, daughter of the Emperor of Spain, a lady distinguished for her impeccable morals. She was consecrated queen in Orléans by Hugh, Archbishop of Sens, which was taken very badly by Samson, Archbishop of Rheims, who complained that the right to consecrate kings and queens of France belonged to him, wherever he might be.

Ives, Bishop of Chartres, learned in law and legal procedure, opposed him both with arguments and precedents, saying that the consecration did not belong to him exclusively as of right and that he could find no written authority for such a claim.

Louis of course soon found himself faced with a king on the English throne whose lands in France exceeded his own but it is doubtful if he could have prevented Eleanor's marriage to Henry Plantagenet. Walter Map records Louis's reply to an Englishman boasting of England's wealth:

The King of England lacks for nothing: he has men, horses, gold, silken materials, precious stones, fruit, beasts—in fact everything, whereas we in France have only bread, wine—and good humour.

Eleanor of Aquitaine, Louis VII's first wife, with her second husband, Henry II of England, returning from Gascony, 1260. Manuscript drawing by Matthew Paris.

Seal of Louis VII.

Seal of Constance of Castille. The silver matrix for the seal was found in her tomb at St Denis when the tomb was despoiled in 1793.

Suger's continuator carries on the story of Louis's marriages and the intermarriages of all their children:

The King, wishing to live according to the divine law which requires a man to marry a woman and that they should be of one flesh, and wishful to have an heir to rule France after him, took as wife Constance, daughter of the King of Spain. After a time of living together the King had of her a daughter whom they called Margaret, and with the dispensation of the church she was married to Henry, the son of Henry [II] of England and his wife, Eleanor.

Henry died before he could inherit the English throne and Henry II was succeeded by Richard.

Later Queen Constance was delivered of a daughter called Adelaide [who was affianced to but did not marry Richard of England] but died giving birth to her [1160]. The whole kingdom was saddened by her death but the King, consoled by his courtiers, soon forgot his affliction and decided to take another wife, repeating to himself that it is better to marry than to burn. So, for his own health and that of the kingdom, he married Adèle, daughter of Thibaud, Count of Blois.

Walter Map also recounts a charming tale of this courteous king, who spent the long years of his reign quietly consolidating the Capetian heritage:

It was his custom when he felt sleep overcoming him to take his rest upon the spot. Once when he was sleeping in a shady grove accompanied by only two soldiers, the others having gone hunting, he was found by Count Thibaud who reproached him for thus sleeping alone as being improper for a king. The King replied: 'I sleep alone in safety since no one wishes me ill.' A simple reply and the words of a man with a clear conscience.

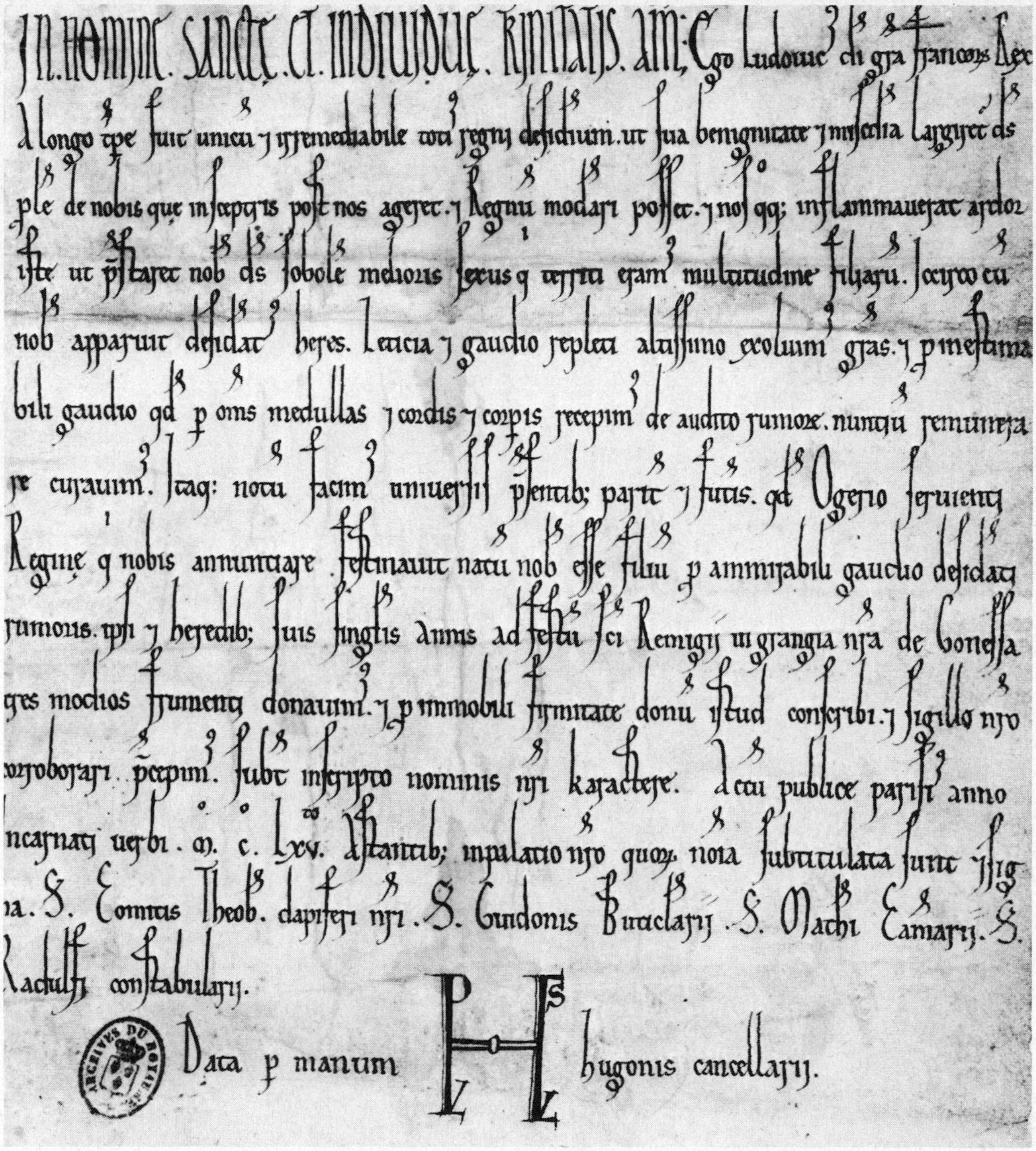

Document giving the order for a reward to be given to the messenger, Oger, who brought Louis VII the news of the birth of a son (Philippe Auguste) to his third wife, Adèle of Champagne. Paris, 22 August, 1165.

Philippe II

Philippe II Auguste was born on 21 August, 1165 at Gonesse, near Paris. He was associated with the throne on 1 November, 1179 and became king on 18 September, 1180. He married, in 1180, Isabelle of Hainault (d. 1190); in 1193, Ingeborg of Denmark (1175–1236), whom he repudiated the same year; and, in 1196, Agnès of Méranie (d. 1201).
He reigned for forty-two years and died, from malaria, aged nearly fifty-eight, at Mantes on 14 July, 1223. He was buried at St Denis.

Rigord, a contemporary, who was a monk at St Denis, wrote:

Philippe, King of the French, was born in 1165 in August. His nickname of 'God given' was correct; for his father, the saintly Louis, seeing that his three wives had given him a large number of daughters but no male heir, eventually, with Queen Adèle, his wife, had recourse to prayer. He did not ask God to give him a son as a right due to his merits but as a favour. 'Have pity on me, O Lord,' he prayed, 'and give me a son to mount the throne and to rule the French so that my enemies may not say "Your hopes are deceived; your alms and prayers have been in vain".'

Such were the prayers of the King, the clergy and the people of the realm that God gave Louis a son. Before his birth Louis had a vision in a dream. It seemed to him that Philippe, his son, held a chalice full of human blood and offered it to the nobles, and drank from it himself. He confided his dream to Henri, Bishop of Albano, exhorting him to tell no one until after his death; after which the Bishop told a number of clergy.

A contemporary canon of St Martin, Païeu Gâtineau, has left us this portrait of the king who tried but failed to learn Latin, and who founded the royal archives:

Philippe was a handsome strapping man, with a pleasant face, bald, with a high colour, and inclined to like food, drink and women. He was generous to his friends, and mean to those who displeased him. A skilful engineer, a faithful Catholic, prudent in counsel, firm in word, a speedy and fair judge, he was lucky in battles. He was fearful for his life, easy to rouse . . . easy to appease, hard on the evil barons and wishful to sow discord among them. Not one of his adversaries died in prison. He liked to employ lesser men

Statue of Philippe II at Rheims cathedral from the bay on the left of the rose window in the north transept, before 1233.

and to subdue the arrogant and he only bore grudges for a short time. He was the defender of the church and succourer of the poor.

Two examples of his ready wit are told by the chroniclers:

One day, while entering the chapter in connexion with an election to the bishopric, holding the pastoral cross, Philippe walked down the ranks of the canons, and saw amongst them a very thin sad-looking man. 'Here,' he said, 'take this staff, so that you may become as fat as your brothers.'

A strolling player asked him for help, claiming relationship. 'How are you related to me?' asked Philippe, 'in what degree?' 'I am your brother, seigneur, descended from Adam, the first man; but alas his heritage was inequitably shared out and I received nothing.' 'Ah, well, come back tomorrow and I will give you that which is justly due to you.' The next day Philippe sent for him in front of the whole court and gave him a farthing. 'Here,' he said, 'is the just portion that I owe you. When I have given as much to each of our brothers, descended from Adam like you and me, I shall be lucky if I am left with a single coin for myself.'

Philippe was a good organiser and liked Paris which he did his best to improve.

In 1183 King Philippe, in response to requests from many of his subjects and the advice of his counsellors, dealt with the lepers who lived outside the walls of Paris and bought from them a market which he had transferred to the city. In order to maintain the beauty of the place and the comfort of his courtiers he had two buildings erected, commonly called Les Halles, so that the merchants, in bad weather, could sell their wares without having to worry about the rain and to protect their goods from theft at night.

One day King Philippe was walking about his palace in Paris, thinking of affairs of state, when he looked out of a window which gave on to the Seine and which enabled him to watch the river traffic and saw the horsedrawn carts coming from the city with mud on their wheels emitting the most stinking smell. The King could not bear it and thenceforward set about devising a scheme which was as difficult as it was necessary and the expense of which had beaten his predecessors. He called together the burghers and provost of the town and gave instructions that the roads should be paved with solid and durable stone so that Paris should not lose its good name. It had originally been called Lutèce or muddy because of its pestilential bogs but the inhabitants, shocked by the name had rechristened it Paris after Priam the King of Troy's son, for we read that the first King of the Franks was Pharamond, son of Marcomir son of Priam—not the King of Troy but a descendant of his son Hector.

Philippe, like so many of the Capets, had wife trouble. His first wife died in 1190. So, according to Rigord:

Eighteenth-century drawing of Isabelle of Hainault's black marble tomb from Notre Dame, Paris from the Gaignières collection.

Calvary and descent from the cross from the Ingeborg Psalter made in the Ile-de-France for the Queen, c. 1195.

Philippe sent Stephen, Bishop of Noyon to visit Canute, King of Denmark to ask for the hand of one of his sisters. Canute was pleased and sent Ingeborg, the most beautiful of his sisters, laden with gifts to Philippe who was at Arras. There she became his wife and was crowned queen but—O wonder—the very same day, the King, doubtless at the instigation of the devil, or according to some, as a result of witchcraft, took violently against this long-awaited bride and a few days later, having persuaded his barons and clergy that the degree of consanguinity between them was too high, repudiated her.

When Richard succeeded his brother Henry on the throne of England he and Philippe were on good terms. Indeed they went on the Third Crusade in 1190 together, during which the malaria that killed Philippe first attacked him. Guillaume le Breton, who was Philippe's court chaplain and who was sent to Rome several times on his behalf, once to arrange for a divorce from Ingeborg, wrote a long poem about Philippe's life:

Philippe, surrounded by only a small company, was taken with a high fever accompanied by a most troublesome shivering and took to his bed at Accaron. Violent sweating, and a high temperature wrought havoc with his bones and in all his members so that his fingernails and the hair from his head fell out and it was thought he had been given a deadly poison. But divine providence spared him for us so that France did not have to mourn the loss of this prince whose care had given to her the benefits of a long peace. But he languished for a long time and his convalescence was lengthy and as he could not cure himself completely he decided, at the request of his nobles, his friends and on the advice of his doctors, to return to his country and go back to the place of his birth; but before leaving he gave to five hundred knights, out of his own purse, the sums necessary to keep them for three years as well as taking care to see they had ten thousand footmen, wishing that they should all work with the same zeal and faithfulness to fight in his place for the Holy Sepulchre.

At this time many enemies menaced France. On his return from the crusade in 1191 Philippe and Richard Coeur-de-Lion fell out and the French king found himself at odds with the English. He set about recapturing for the French crown Normandy, Maine, Anjou, Touraine and Poitou.

In July the King in spite of public opinion and his own word recalled the Jews to Paris, but six months later he was well punished. The King of England appeared unexpectedly and surprised the King of France with a large army.

The Emperor of Germany, Otto IV, thinking Philippe too occupied with the English foe—John by now—decided to invade France, but Philippe defeated their combined forces at Bouvines in 1214. After midday the King was exhausted, removed his armour and took some rest, when, according to Philippe Mouskes:

Philippe ate, in a fine gold dish, a soup with wine which warmed him greatly.

An anonymous chronicler seems to think Philippe's meal was interrupted for at this point Brother Guérin came to tell him not only that the enemy was approaching but that the French rearguard was already at blows with the allied van:

Brother Guérin arrived and found the King dining on bread and wine. 'What are you doing?' he asked. 'Well,' said the King, 'I'm having dinner.' 'All right but you had better get armed for the enemy will not put the battle off until tomorrow. He is upon us. Look.'

The battle of Bouvines was a great victory for France and the universal delight after it was the first great national celebration. Guillaume le Breton tells of the journey to Paris:

Who can recount, imagine or depict with the pen on parchment or tablets the joyful welcome, the hymns of triumph, the endless dancing of the people, the sweet singing of the clerks, the melodious sounds of warlike instruments, the decoration of the churches, the solemn sanctuaries, inside as well as outside, the streets, the houses, the thoroughfares in all the towns and all the villages hung with tapestries and silks covered with flowers, plants and green leaves; the inhabitants of each sex, all ages and all classes running together from all over the place to take part in so great a triumph? Peasants and the harvesters interrupted their work, hung round their necks their scythes, their mattocks and their nets (for it was harvest-time) and pushed forward in a crowd to see Ferrand [the Count of Flanders, taken prisoner at the battle] in chains, he who so recently had frightened them by his strength. Peasants, old women and children were not afraid to jeer at him, profiting by punning on his name which could apply equally well to a horse as to a man. Furthermore, by a marvellous coincidence, the two horses which dragged the prisoner in a cart were of the kind whose colour gave rise to the name. They shouted out that he was *ferré*, that he could kick no more, he who previously swollen with grossness raised his hoof against his master. This happened along the whole length of the journey to Paris. The Parisian burghers, and above all the throng of students, clergy and people went in front of the King, singing hymns and canticles, showing by their actions the happiness which filled their souls. The day was not long enough to contain their happiness so that they celebrated all night and moreover for seven consecutive nights they had illuminations so bright that night was turned into day. The students especially held numerous banquets, singing and dancing without cease.

Not all the chroniclers spoke well of Philippe. Gilles de Paris, a friend of Guillaume le Breton, was highly critical of him personally, though less so of him as King of France:

Yes, there is no doubt that no one, unless he were evil-minded or an enemy, could deny that for our time Philippe was not a good prince. Certainly under his rule the realm was strengthened and royal power advanced. If only he had drunk from the source of divine mildness a little more moderation, if he had had a little more paternal love, if he had been as approachable, as amenable, as patient as he was intolerant and passionate, as calm as he was active, as prudent and circumspect as he was anxious to satisfy his lusts, the realm would have been in better condition. O France, torn apart by the extortioners of your prince, you have had to undergo cruel laws and terrible times . . . but look about you; other kings who rule in their fashion are even worse. They impose upon the poor as on the church an even more despotic yoke. Remember that you are governed by a prince of good will, and do not complain, in paying obedience to him, that you are not weighed down under the sad rule of Richard Coeur-de-Lion nor downtrodden by the harsh tyranny of a German king.

In 1224 Guillaume le Breton added a piece about Philippe's death to his second, prose, work. The Vie de Philippe Auguste *endorses the modern view that Philippe was a great king; powerful and secure enough on the throne not to need to have his son consecrated during his own lifetime and the midwife to an emergent French nationalism:*

In the year 1223 the noble Philippe, King of the French, died at the château called Mantes. A man of great skill and courage, noble in deeds, greatly renowned, a winner of battles and distinguished in gaining victories which redounded to the glory of France as well as enriching the royal treasury. He successfully defeated those who attacked him and his realm, and overcame many a noble and powerful prince who opposed him or his country. He was a loyal and devoted protector of the church and upheld her in all things. He looked after the church of St Denis above all others in the country, on account of his great love for it, and often showed his great affection for it. From his earliest youth he was a loyal and loving Christian and as a young man, the sign of the cross embroidered on his shoulders, he set out across the sea to deliver the Holy Sepulchre. Later in his decline into old age, he did not spare his eldest son, sending him twice to fight the heretics in Albi which was very costly.

During his life and at the time of his death he made generous grants in various places to the poor. He was buried in St Denis, with the honours and dignity befitting to so great a prince.

Philippe II's will, St Germain-en-Laye, September 1222. It is the oldest extant French royal will, and may be in the King's own hand. In it he refers to Ingeborg of Denmark as his 'very dear wife' and he left her 10,000 livres. On his death he is reputed to have said: 'Who knows how many knights have obeyed my slightest wish at court; will I find a single one today who has the courage to prepare my lodgings?'

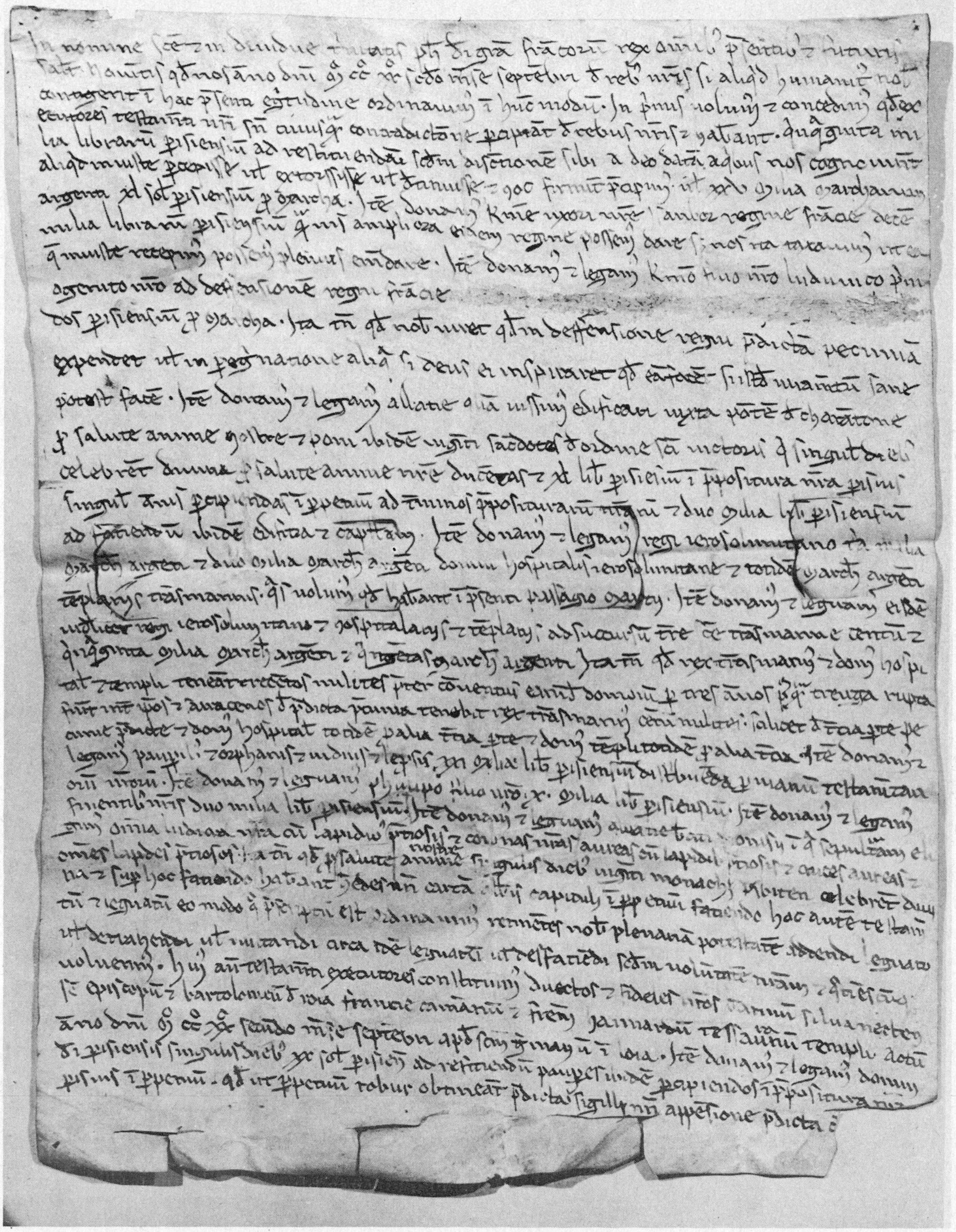

Louis VIII

Louis VIII was born on 5 September, 1187 in Paris. He acceded to the throne on 14 July, 1223 and was consecrated at Rheims on 6 August, 1223.
He married, in 1200, Blanche of Castille (before 1188–1252).
He reigned for forty months and died, of dysentery, aged thirty-nine, at the château of Montpensier, Auvergne, on 8 November, 1226. He was buried at St Denis.

Louis VIII, before he came to the throne, led an expedition to England at the instigation of the barons who wished to get rid of John. Two-thirds of them went over to Louis who failed to take Dover and who was beaten by William Marshal and Fawkes de Breauté at Lincoln. On John's death and the accession of Henry III, the barons, who had no quarrel with him, left Louis who made his peace and returned to France.

When the barons of England revolted against their king, John, because of some customs he had initiated and which he refused to obey himself despite his oath, the common people, peasants and a large number of towns allied themselves with the barons. They, fearing they were not strong enough to fight John to the finish, sent messengers to Louis, the eldest son of the French king, seeking his aid and promising him the kingship of England when they had dethroned John. Louis, having received hostages from them, sent them a large number of knights. In September, some gentlemen from Brabant and Flanders ran into a storm and were drowned in their attempt to bring succour to the King who had promised them great wealth in return for their help. The enemies of the King were delighted by this accident and were spurred on by it in their revolt saying that the hand of God showed itself in their favour.

Simon de Montfort asked Louis to abandon his idea of going to England to fight against John and asked his father Philippe to stop him. But he failed and therefore returned to England to try and establish peace, if possible, between the barons and the King. While this was happening, Louis, who had fitted out a fleet, crossed to England and was joyfully welcomed there by the people who had sent for him and received their homage.

Louis returned to France and collected reinforcements,

and having assembled as large a number of foot as horsemen [in 1217] went back to England, very displeased with a number of the barons who, despite their oaths, in his absence had abandoned him and gone over to the new king [Henry III]. While they were besieging Dover, Thomas, Count of Perche, who had gone to his help was killed at Lincoln by the English. When Louis heard this, seeing the treachery and perfidy of the English, he set fire to his siege machines and took himself and his army to London. There he found himself betrayed by the English barons, the target of the hatred of the whole country

Seal of Louis VIII.

and all doors closed against him. So he made a settlement and returned to France. He would have achieved admirable victories had he been served with the loyalty that was his due.

Louis VIII went in person to Languedoc to help put down the Albigensian heresy. Nicolas de Bray reports on his return journey—and death:

The King advanced upon Provence, and all the towns, fortresses and castles as far as Toulouse ceded to him without a fight. The King was in a hurry to return to France. The day before All Saints' Day, as he was returning home, he was seized with a mortal illness and the following Sunday he died. He was during his life a good Catholic and of saintly behaviour. He was not concupiscent and was attached only to the legitimate wife to whom he was married. So one might say that Merlin's prophecy was fulfilled: 'The peaceful lion will die in the belly of the mountain', [a pun on the word Montpensier—where he died]. No other French king had died there. His body was taken thence to St Denis and buried with his father, Philippe Auguste.

Guillaume de Puyslaurens amplifies the scene at his deathbed:

His illness was of a kind, it was said, that it would be cured by using a woman. So that the prince could benefit from the embrace of a young woman, a nobleman found and sent into his room during the day while he was asleep, a pretty, selected virgin from a good family who was told how she should behave. She was to say she was not there to debauch him but to cure his illness. When the King awoke and saw her he asked what she was doing there and she replied as she had been told to. 'Ah no,' said the King, 'it will not be so, young woman. I will not commit mortal sin for whatever reason.' He sent for the noble-

Tomb effigy thought to be of Blanche of Castille at St Denis. It is known that the Queen's tomb in black marble from Tournai was erected in the abbey she founded at Maubuisson, near Pontoise, and this tomb is known to have gone from Maubuisson to St Denis.

man and told him to see the girl honourably married. And so this prince conducted himself so well that he would not avoid, even if he had been able to, death through sin.

The notes on the exhumation of Louis's body in 1793 read:

The body of Louis VIII, father of St Louis, who died on 8 November, 1226, aged forty, was virtually decomposed. There was a cross carved in low relief on the stone lid of his coffin. Only a fragment of decayed wood remained of his sceptre, and his diadem, made of a band of cloth of gold surmounted a skull cap the satin of which was well-preserved. The body was wrapped in a winding sheet or shroud of cloth of gold of which some pieces were still intact. Under this the body was covered and sewn in thick leather which retained all its suppleness. It was the only body amongst those exhumed in St Denis to have been so treated, and was probably treated in this way to avoid decomposition on the journey from Montpensier in the Auvergne where he died on his return from the crusade against the Albigensians.

Louis IX

Louis IX, St Louis, was born on 25 April, 1214 at the château of Poissy. He became king on 8 November, 1226 and was consecrated at Rheims on 29 November.
He married, in 1234, Marguerite of Provence (1221–1295).
He reigned for forty-three years and died, of the plague, aged fifty-six, at Carthage on 25 August, 1270. He was buried at St Denis.

Louis IX succeeded to the throne at the age of twelve. He was fortunate in having as his mother Blanche of Castille, a regent of energy, guile and intelligence. She reigned for eight years until, on his majority, she presented him with a country in good order and she presented the country with a king whose piety and concern for justice earned him not only the universal love and regard of his subjects but also canonisation twenty-seven years after his death.

According to Geoffroy de Beaulieu, some aspects of saintliness did not come altogether easily to Louis:

With the Queen his wife's consent, they abstained from sexual relations with each other for the whole of Advent and Lent, and on certain of the great feast days. In addition, in preparation for the solemn days on which he wished to take communion, he was continent for several days both before and after out of reverence for the holy mysteries.

If on any of his continent days it happened that he had to visit the Queen for any reason and to linger with her, and he found himself moved by carnal desire on account of the proximity of his wife and his human frailty, he would get out of bed and walk around the room until his rebellious flesh was quiescent.

It seems that, according to Robert de Sorbon, Louis's form of dress did not please his wife:

'Madam,' said the King to the Queen, 'it would please you would it if I dressed myself more modishly?' The Queen replied that it would and that she wished he would. The prince replied, 'All right, I will do it for you since the laws of marriage decree that the man must please his wife, and vice versa. But this law which makes me bow to your wishes works both ways and you have agreed to accede to mine as I to yours. Therefore I wish you to give me the pleasure of wearing simpler clothes. You wear mine and I will wear yours.' This the Queen refused to do, so that she had to allow her husband to dress in his habitual style.

Fra Salimbene, a Franciscan visiting France, tells of the King's appearance and a feast he gave, in the year he set out to lead the Seventh Crusade:

In the year 1248 about the feast of Pentecost or somewhat later, I went down from Auxerre to the convent of Sens, for the provincial chapter of our order in France was to be held there and the Lord Louis was to come thither.

Now the King was spare and slender, somewhat lean and of a proper height, having the face of an angel and a mien full of grace. And he came to our church, not in regal pomp, but in a pilgrim's habit, with the staff and scrip of his pilgrimage hanging at his neck, which was an excellent adornment for the neck of a king. And he came not on horseback but on foot.

When he came into our church and had made a most devout genuflexion, he prayed before the altar and as he departed from the church and was yet standing on the threshold, I was by his side; and behold the treasurer of the cathedral at Sens sent him a great living pike in water, in a vessel of fir-wood, wherein nursling children are washed and bathed: for in France the pike is esteemed a dear and precious fish. And the King thanked not only the sender, but him who brought the gift.

The King took on himself all that day's cost and ate together with us in the refectory. This then was our fare for that day: first, cherries, then most excellent white bread; and choice wine, worthy of the King's royal estate, was placed in abundance before us; and after the wont of the French, many invited even the unwilling and compelled them to drink. After that we had fresh beans boiled in milk, fish and crabs, eel-pasties, rice cooked with milk of almonds and cinnamon powder, eels baked with most excellent sauce, tarts and junkets and all the fruits of the season in abundance and comely array. And all these were laid on the table in courtly fashion, and busily ministered to us.

In the same year, leaving the country once more in the care of his mother, Louis embarked on the Seventh Crusade. Joinville (b. 1224–5) joined the Crusade in 1248 and wrote a Life of St Louis *full of the intimate as well as heroic deeds of the King:*

When the King heard that the standard of St Denis was on shore he strode quickly across the deck of his ship, and in spite of all that the legate, who was with him, could say, refused to be parted from the emblem of his sovereignty, and leapt into the sea, where the water came up to his armpits. He went on, with his shield hung from his neck, his helmet on his head, and lance in hand, till he had joined his people on the shore. When he had reached land and scanned the enemy, he asked who they were, and was told they were Saracens. He put his lance under his armpit, and holding his shield before him, would have charged right in among them if certain sagacious men who were standing round him had allowed it.

Three times the Saracens sent messages by carrier-pigeon to the Sultan, to say that the King had landed; but they never received any message in return, because the Sultan was incapacitated by the sickness which had taken hold on him. Assuming therefore that their lord was dead, the Saracens abandoned Damietta. The King sent a knight to find out if they had really left the city. He returned to inform the King that he had been into the

Group of statues by Pierre de Montereau from the tympanum of the Red Door of Notre Dame, Paris. Louis IX, crowned, is on the left. Christ is blessing the Virgin who is being crowned, and Marguerite of Provence kneels on the right. This part of the cathedral was built about 1270 and the figures are therefore the earliest known statues of St Louis and his wife. It is doubtful if they are true portraits; they are more likely to be representations of royal personages.

Sultan's palaces, and could affirm that the report was true. His Majesty immediately sent for the legate and all the bishops who were with the army, and they one and all joined in chanting *Te Deum laudamus*. Afterwards the King mounted his horse, the rest of us followed his example, and we all went and encamped before the city of Damietta.

Louis was captured at the battle of Mansourah and Blanche was regent for a further four years, until her death in 1252. Louis was ransomed and continued the campaign.

It was while he was in Saida that the King received news of his mother's death. He was so prostrated with grief that for two whole days no one could speak to him.

Madame Marie de Vertus, a very good and pious lady, came to tell me that the Queen was plunged in grief, and asked me to go to her and comfort her. When I arrived there, I found her in tears. So I said to her that the man who said one can never tell what a woman will do spoke truly. 'For,' said I, 'the woman who hated you most is dead, and yet you are showing such sorrow.' She told me it was not for Queen Blanche that she was weeping, but because of the grief the King was showing in his mourning over the dead, and also because of her own daughter—later Queen of Navarre—who was now left in the sole guardianship of men.

Queen Blanche had treated Queen Marguerite so harshly that, in so far as she could help it, she had not allowed her son to be in his wife's company except when he went to sleep with her at night. The palace in which the young King and his wife had most liked to live was at Pontoise, because there the King's room was on an upper floor and the Queen's room just below it. They had so arranged matters that they had managed to meet and talk together on a spiral staircase that led from one room to the other. They had also arranged that whenever the ushers saw Queen Blanche approaching her son's room they would knock on the door with their rods, and the King would run quickly up to his room so that his mother might find him there. Queen Marguerite's gentlemen of the bedchamber did the same when Queen Blanche was going to her daughter-in-law's room, so that she might find the young Queen safely installed within.

On their return journey:

we had another adventure at sea. One of the lay sisters in attendance on the Queen was so careless that, after putting her mistress to bed, she took the kerchief the Queen had been wearing round her head, and threw it down near the iron stove on which the Queen's candle was burning. After this good soul had gone to bed in the cabin where the women slept, below the Queen's bedroom, the candle went on burning till its flame was low enough to set the kerchief alight, and from there the fire passed to the cloths that covered the Queen's clothing.

The Queen woke to find her cabin all in flames. She jumped out of bed quite naked, picked up the kerchief, and threw it all burning into the sea, and then extinguished the fire on the cloths. The men in the long-boat behind the ship cried softly: 'Fire! Fire!' I raised my head and saw the kerchief still burning brightly on the calm sea. I put on my tunic as quickly as I could, then went and sat with the sailors.

While I was there my squire, who had been sleeping at the foot of my bed, came and told me that the King was awake, and had asked where I was. 'I told him,' said he, 'that you were in your cabin; and the King said to me: "You're lying".' As we were speaking, the King's clerk, Maître Geoffroy, suddenly came up to us. 'Don't be afraid,' he said to me, 'everything's all right.' 'Maître Geoffroy,' said I, 'go and tell the Queen the King is awake, and ask her to go to him to set his mind at rest.'

Next day, the constable of France, the King's chamberlain, Pierre, and Gervais, master of the royal pantry, said to the King: 'What happened in the night that we heard talk of fire?' I for my part kept silent, but the King replied: 'It was some sort of accident about which the seneschal is apparently more reticent than myself. However, I will tell you how it chanced that we all narrowly escaped from being burnt last night.' So he told them what had happened, and then said to me: 'Seneschal, I order you from now on not to go to bed till you have seen to putting out all fires, except the main fire in the ship's hold.

And take note that I shall not go to bed either till you come back to tell me this has been done.' I performed this duty as long as we were at sea; and the King never went to bed till I had gone back to him.

Louis's concern for his kingdom, his piety and charm, allied to a period of prosperity and peace in France, endeared him both to his contemporaries and posterity. Joinville continues:

After the King's return from oversea he lived with such a disregard for worldly vanities that he never wore ermine or squirrel fur, nor scarlet cloth, nor were his stirrups or his spurs gilded. His clothes were made of camlet or grey woollen cloth; the fur on these and on the coverings of his bed was either deerskin, hare skin, or lambskin. He had such sober tastes in food that he never ordered any special dish for himself, but took what his cook prepared, and ate whatever was put before him.

When minstrels in some nobleman's service arrived with their viols to entertain him after dinner, the King would always wait till they had finished singing before he would let grace be said. Then he would rise, and the priests would stand before him to say grace. On occasions when we paid him an informal visit, he would sit at the foot of his bed. If some predicant friar or Franciscan in the company happened to speak of a book he might like to hear read the King would say: 'Don't read it to me. There's no book so good after meals as free and friendly conversation, when everybody says just what it pleases him to say.' Whenever strangers of some importance came to dine with the King, they always found him the best of company.

I will now speak to you of his wisdom. There were times indeed when men were heard to declare that no one on his council was so wise as the King himself. That this was so was apparent from the fact that when anyone consulted him on a certain matter he would not say: 'I will take advice on this question'; but if he saw the right solution clearly and plainly he would answer without reference to his council, and at once. That, so I have heard, is how he answered all the prelates of his realm in the case of a petition they once presented to him.

The King had so deep a love for Our Lord and His sweet mother that he punished most severely all those who had been convicted of speaking of them irreverently or of using their names in some wicked oath. Thus I saw him order a goldsmith of Caesarea to be bound to a ladder, with pig's gut and other viscera round his neck, in such a quantity that they reached up to his nose. I have also heard that, since I came back from oversea, he had the lips and nose of a citizen of Paris seared for a similar offence; but this I did not see for myself. The saintly King used to say: 'I would willingly allow myself to be branded with a hot iron on condition that all wicked oaths were banished from my realm.' I spent over twenty-two years in his company without ever hearing him swear by God, or Our Lord's mother, or His saints. When he wished to emphasize any statement he would say: 'Indeed it was so,' or 'Indeed it is so.'

Polychrome statue of Louis IX of 1307 believed to have been executed from a drawing from the life, in the church at Mainneville, Eure.

The King asked me once if I washed the feet of the poor on Maundy Thursday. I replied that I did no such thing, for I thought it unbecoming. He told me I should not disdain to perform such an act, seeing that Our Lord had done so. 'I suppose,' said he, 'you would be very unwilling to follow the example of the King of England, who washes the feet of lepers, and kisses them.'

Before he went to bed the King used to send for his children and tell them of the deeds of good kings and emperors, at the same time pointing out that they should take such men as an example. He would also tell them of the deeds of wicked princes, who by their dissolute lives, their rapacity, and their avarice had brought ruin on their kingdoms. 'I'm drawing your attention to such things,' he would say, 'so that you may avoid them, and not make God angry with you.'

Louis left careful instructions about correct behaviour for his eldest son:

Dear son, since I desire above all that you should be well instructed in all things, I hope to teach you what is right in these notes for I have sometimes heard you say that you learn more from me than from anyone else.

Dear son, first of all, you must love God with all your heart and all your strength, for without so doing nothing is of any use.

If Our Lord sends you any trials or illnesses or other things, you must suffer them gladly, and you must thank Him and bear them in good part, for you must believe that He sends them for your good. And you must believe that you have deserved them, and more had He so wished because you have loved and served Him too little and you have gone against His wishes.

Dear son, if you succeed to the throne, make sure that you have the qualities which befit a king. Be so just that you never deny justice to anyone on any account. If there is a dispute between a poor man and a rich man, uphold the poor against the rich until such time as you know the truth of the matter—and then do justice.

If you should be involved in a dispute with another man, uphold that man's cause even before your own council. Give no appearance of favouring your own case until you know the whole truth of the affair, for otherwise your counsellors may hesitate to speak against you, a situation you should wish never to arise.

If you should discover that you are in wrongful possession of any land or revenue, even if possession of it was acquired by your ancestors, surrender it forthwith, no matter how great its value. If the case is so involved and obscure that the truth of it cannot be disentangled, seek the advice of honest men, and then make such an agreement that your soul and the souls of your ancestors shall not go guilty in the matter. And even if men shall say to you that your predecessors made all the restitutions necessary, exert yourself to find out whether there is not yet some restitution to be made for the good of your soul and the souls of your ancestors.

Dear son, you must love and honour your mother, and listen carefully to her advice and be inclined to believe her good counsel.

Love your brothers and always look after their interests. Act as a father to them for their good, but watch out that on account of love, you do not stray from the path of virtue or do anything that you should not.

Louis was greatly loved by his people and had all the private virtues required for sanctity. Joinville:

This saintly man loved Our Lord with all his heart, and in all his actions followed His example. This is apparent from the fact that as Our Lord died for the love He bore His people, even so King Louis put his own life in danger, and that several times, for the very same reason. It was danger too that he might well have avoided.

The great love King Louis bore his people is shown by what he said, as he lay dangerously ill at Fontainebleau, to his eldest son, my Lord Louis. 'My dear son,' he said, 'I earnestly beg you to make yourself loved by all your people. For I would rather have a Scot come from Scotland to govern the people of this kingdom well and justly than that you should govern them ill in the sight of all the world.' This upright King, moreover, loved truth so well that he would never consent to lie to the Saracens with regard to any covenant he made with them.

He was so temperate in his appetite that I never heard him, on any day of my life, order a special dish for himself, as many men of wealth and standing do. On the contrary, he would always eat with good grace whatever his cooks had prepared to set before him. He was equally temperate in his speech. I never, on any single occasion, heard him speak evil of any man; nor did I ever hear him utter the name of the devil—a name in very common use throughout the kingdom—which practice, so I believe, is not pleasing to God.

He used to add water to his wine, but did so reasonably, according as the strength of the wine allowed it. While we were in Cyprus he asked me why I did not mix my wine with water. I replied that this was on the advice of my doctors, who had told me that I had a strong head and a cold stomach, so that I could not get drunk. He answered that they had deceived me; for if I did not learn to mix my wine with water while I was still young, and wished to do so in my old age, gout and stomach troubles would take hold on me, and I should never be in good health. Moreover, if I went on drinking undiluted wine when I was old, I should get drunk every night, and it was too revolting a thing for any brave man to be in such a state.

I have sometimes seen him, in summer, go to administer justice to his people in the public gardens in Paris, dressed in a plain woollen tunic, a sleeveless surcoat of linsey-woolsey, and a black taffeta cape round his shoulders, with his hair neatly combed, but no cap to cover it, and only a hat of white peacock's feathers on his head. He would have a carpet laid down so that we might sit round him, while all those who had any case to bring before him stood round about. Then he would pass judgment on each case, as he often used to do in the wood of Vincennes.

In 1270 Louis set out again for the Holy Land and died of the plague at Tunis shortly after his arrival. Louis IX was canonised in 1297. Nearly five centuries later Voltaire endorsed his canonisation:

Louis IX appeared to be a prince destined to reform Europe had she been so capable; to secure a triumphant and well-ordered France and to be the model for all men. His piety, that of an anchorite, did not minimise his virtues as a king. His wisdom over money matters did not prevent him from being generous. He knew how to combine profound political ability with scrupulous justice and he is perhaps the only king to merit this praise. Prudent and resolute in his counsel, fearless in his battles but not carried away by them, he had the compassion of a man who had always been unhappy. It is not given to man to go further towards true virtue.

Philippe III

Philippe III, the Bold, was born on 1 May, 1245 at the château of Poissy. He became king on 25 August, 1270 and was consecrated at Rheims on 15 August, 1271.
He married, in 1262, Isabelle of Aragon (1247–1271) and, in 1274, Marie of Brabant (d. 1321).
He reigned for fifteen years and died, of malaria, aged forty, at Perpignan on 5 October, 1285. His body was buried at St Denis and his entrails in Narbonne cathedral.

Philippe III was severely brought up by his pious and strict father. Geoffroy de Beaulieu:

After the devotions which followed meals, the King [Louis IX] returned to his room with his children, and when the priest had sprinkled holy water over the bed and the room, he sat the children round him and proceeded to discuss edifying matters for their instruction.

Joinville recounts how nervous Philippe was of his father:

A little later on the King beckoned to his son, the Prince Philippe, and to Thibaut. Then, seating himself at the entrance to his oratory, he patted the ground and said to the two young men: 'Sit down here, quite close to me, so that we shan't be overheard.' 'But, my lord,' they protested, 'we should not dare to sit so close to you.' Then the King said to me, 'Seneschal, you sit here.' I obeyed, and sat down so close to him that my clothes were touching his. He made the two others sit down next, and said to them: 'You have acted very wrongly, seeing you are my sons, in not doing as I commanded the moment I told you. I beg you to see this does not happen again.' They assured him it would not.

Guillaume de Nangis says that

Philippe, good King Louis's son, was worthy of honour and praise. Although he was not literate, he was handsome, gentle and good-humoured towards men of the church.

It is difficult to discover from contemporary chroniclers what Philippe looked like but the face on his tomb at St Denis, executed between 1299 and 1307 by Pierre de Chelles and Jean d'Arras, is thought to be a reasonably life-like portrait. The monument on his tomb in Narbonne was described thus in 1718:

Instead of representing him with a sad face, long nose and big lips, the effigy showed a smiling face, gentle and open, which was much more in keeping with descriptions of his character. One could even see the traits of a bold man.

Philippe lived to put his father's principles into practice, according to Guillaume de Nangis—a cleric himself, of course:

Philippe did not forget what his father commanded for he fulfilled his last wish and employed the counsel of wise men. He followed the advice of the Abbot of St Denis, a man of high religious principles in the flower of his wisdom and let him supervise the affairs of his kingdom in his father's style.

After his wife died, he wished to do penitence and he wore a hair shirt and coat of mail to mortify and chastise his flesh. He fasted and abstained from meat, and did all he could to avoid the sins of human flesh, and did so until the day of his death, so that one could say he lived more a monk's life than that of a knight. He was full of good words and spoke reasonably; he was wise amongst his barons and without arrogance or pride. His realm benefited from his virtues all the days of his life.

Philippe married in 1274 the young and energetic Marie of Brabant, who contrived to upset Pierre de la Broce, the King's powerful and greedy favourite:

The King Philippe decided to marry and take a wife. Various young women of suitably high lineage and parentage were proposed. Among the women mentioned was Marie, daughter of the Duke of Brabant, who was of good repute. So the King agreed to marry her and sent messengers to her. When the Duke Jean heard the news he was very happy and received the messengers with such ceremony as he could and he sent his sister laden with jewels and rich accessories as befitted her rank. The King married her and welcomed her with much love.

A pair of kneeling figures representing Philippe III and Isabelle of Aragon from the cathedral at Cosenza, Calabria. They form part of a funerary monument erected for Isabelle who died there as a result of a fall from a horse on her return from the Tunisian crusade on 28 January, 1271. The monument was erected between 1271 and 1276 and may therefore have been from life. The features of the King resemble those on his tomb effigy at St Denis *(see page 69)**.*

Seal of Marie of Brabant.

Pierre de la Broce, the King's high chamberlain, was very angry and disturbed that the King should love his wife so much and was displeased. He thought that his own position with regard to the King was threatened and that he might be toppled from the great height to which he had risen. So he sought daily for ways in which to disrupt the love between the King and the Queen, taking no account of the place he had come from nor the low estate from which he had arisen. For when he came to King Louis's court, he was a poor surgeon and he was born in Touraine. He had climbed so high that King Philippe made him his chamberlain and did nothing without his advice. Neither the barons nor the prelates made any headway at court unless they gave him lavish presents and rich gifts. This they found displeasing and they were indignant that he should have so much power with the King over them. He asked that Pierre de Baray, the cousin of his wife, should be appointed Bishop of Bayeux, and the King at once acceded to his request. The chapter of Bayeux dared not oppose the appointment. The King gave in marriage his sons and his daughters as he directed.

Pierre de la Broce hoped to get his revenge on the new Queen when two years later Philippe's eldest son [Louis] *by his first wife, Isabelle of Aragon, was taken mysteriously ill. The King was enjoying his great pleasure—hunting—in the forest of Vincennes, when the boy died rather suddenly. An anonymous chronicler tells the story:*

Some people said the King's son had been poisoned and even the King was suspicious. So he sent the Abbot of St Denis and the Bishop of Bayeux—cousins of the famed Pierre de la Broce—to Germany to ask the advice of a wise woman renowned for her ability to tell fortunes. What the wise woman said I do not know for when the King asked the

Bishop on his return, he replied that he could not answer because she had replied to him in the confessional. The King was very angry and said he had not sent the Bishop to hear her confession. So he sent other messengers to the woman and they asked her again. She replied that if anyone had maligned the Queen to the King he should not be believed for she was a good woman and intended only good to him and his family.

Philippe III, who went on the crusade with his father, brought King Louis's bones home to be buried at St Denis. He inherited his father's tremendous prestige, but became involved in a conflict with Aragon which ended in military disaster for the French and death, at Perpignan, for the King himself. He had nevertheless increased the territorial boundaries of France, Toulouse by legacy, Navarre and Champagne by marriage.

His death was mourned by an anonymous chronicler:

He died by the will of Jesus Christ; it was a pity he died when he did because he had become wonderfully wise for his age and a man of impeccable morals.

Dante had little love for the Capets, reserving his most bitter hatred for Philippe IV, but he puts Philippe III into Purgatory in the mountain hollow where the souls of kings and rulers who neglected their duties for selfishness are placed and cannot find anything harsher to say of him than:

That snub-nosed one, who seems close in counsel with him that has so kindly a mien [Henri III of Navarre], died in flight and deflowering the lily; look there how he is beating his breast. The other see, who, sighing, hath made a bed for his cheek with the palm of his hand. Father and father-in-law are they of the plague of France; they know his wicked and foul life, and hence comes the grief that pierceth them so.

Tomb effigy of Philippe III at St Denis. The marble tomb was erected between 1298 and 1307 and is by Pierre de Chelles. It still has traces of paint on it. It is possible that the head was modelled from a death mask. Philippe was 'virtuous, rich, generous, gay, right-minded and courageous'.

Philippe IV

Philippe IV, the Fair, was born in 1268 at Fontainebleau. He became king on 5 October, 1285 and was consecrated at Rheims on 6 January, 1286.
He married, in 1284, Jeanne of Navarre (1271–1305).
He reigned for twenty-nine years and died, of a stroke, aged forty-six, at Fontainebleau on 29 November, 1314. He was buried at St Denis.

Philippe IV presents a problem; historians have argued that he was either a great king or a weak man given to relying on his counsellors too closely. Contemporary chroniclers have left very few descriptions of his person. Most however agree that he was handsome and kind; William the Scot, a monk of St Denis:

Philippe was decorous in body because of the elegance of his limbs and his agreeable appearance which were worthy of his royal calling. He did not lack learning, he had an affable aspect and was straightforward in his behaviour and habits. He was gentle and humble and did not lend an ear to improper conversation. He was sedulous and devoted in obeying the dictates of religion, abstaining on the second and fourth day from meat and on the sixth day from fish and milk, contenting himself with bread only. He mortified his flesh with a hair shirt and underwent chastisement at the hands of his confessor. The seemliness of his heart and mouth sustained him even through the adversities of his reign.

Despite the dearth of anecdotes about Philippe his long reign was of central importance to the monarchy. As a result of his need to raise money he instituted new taxes and devalued the currency, arrested the Jews and seized their goods, hunted down the Templars, fifty-four of whose knights were condemned to be burned at the stake; he also expelled the Lombard bankers and then called them back to extort more money from them. His preoccupation with finance brought him into conflict with the church and it was during his reign that the Papacy moved its seat in 1309 from Rome to Avignon, where it remained subject to French influence until 1377. But he remained popular with his people for he succeeded in increasing the mystical power of the crown, and increased both the efficiency of the central administration and the extent of the royal domain. He could not, however, foresee that none of his three sons would produce surviving male issue or that the

Tomb effigy of Philippe IV at St Denis. 'The most handsome man in the world, tall, well-proportioned, a wise and good man who loved hunting.'

Miniature from the Livre de Dina et Kalila, *1313 showing Philippe IV enthroned, with his three sons Louis (X), Philippe (V) and Charles (IV), his daughter Isabelle (Queen of England) and his brother Charles of Valois.*

Philippe IV's armour.

marriage of his daughter Isabelle to Edward II of England would lead to the start of the Hundred Years War or to the end of the Capetian dynasty within fourteen years of his death.

Guillaume de Nangis reports his last illness and death:

Philippe suffered from a lengthy illness, the cause of which escaped the doctors and was a great surprise to them especially as neither his pulse nor his urine indicated that it was mortal. He was eventually taken to Fontainebleau where he had been born. There, a few days later, seeing the moment of his death approaching, with wisdom and care he made his dispositions with regard to his house and domestic affairs. He invested his youngest son Charles, to whom he had given nothing, with the county of La Manche and its environs. Applying himself with even more zeal to the health of his soul he stopped the tax called the *maltôte* of which he had heard speak and which greatly displeased him. Finally, after having read his will with great care, he gave his eldest son, already King of Navarre, wise advice and threatened him with divine and paternal retribution if he failed to follow it. He took the last sacrament with admirable fervour and devotion.

Louis X

Louis X, the Quarrelsome, was born on 4 October, 1289 in Paris. He acceded to the throne on 29 November, 1314 and was consecrated on 29 August, 1315 at Rheims. He married, in 1305, Marguerite of Burgundy (1290–1315) and, in 1315, Clémence of Hungary (c. 1293–1328).
He reigned for eighteen months and died, of a pulmonary infection, aged twenty-six, at the château of Vincennes on 5 June, 1316. He was buried at St Denis.

Even less is known about Louis X's person than about his father and he reigned for only eighteen months. He, with his brothers, Philippe (later Philippe V) and Charles (later Charles IV), had been involved in an unsavoury matrimonial scandal.

Joinville offering his book to Louis X in 1309 before his accession. This manuscript illumination comes from an early fourteenth-century copy of the Vie de St Louis.

Louis was married to Marguerite, a grand-daughter of Louis IX, Philippe and Charles were married to sisters Jeanne and Blanche, the daughters of Otto of Burgundy and Mahaut of Artois.

Two of the girls were accused of adultery and the third of connivance by their sister-in-law, Isabelle of England. Guillaume de Nangis reports their punishment:

The young Marguerite, and Blanche, wife of the younger brother Charles, were, as their faults deserved, repudiated by their husbands for having committed adultery with the two brothers Philippe and Gautier d'Aunay. Stripped of all their temporal honours, they were imprisoned, so that in strict seclusion, deprived of all human consolation, they should end their days in misfortune and misery. As for the two lovers, not only had they infamously soiled the beds of their lords who had complete trust in them as their most personal servants but they were odious traitors as was proved by the livery that they and some of their servants wore. Even more culpable in this action were the young women of the weaker sex who were seduced by their paramours. Ten days after Easter, at Pontoise, the men confessed to having committed this crime over three years, in various places and at sacred times. They were made to suffer ignominious torture and a fitting death to expiate such foul deeds, and they were flayed alive in full public view. Their genitals were removed, their heads struck off and, skinned, they were hung on the public gibbet by their shoulders and elbows.

Those of their accomplices found to be innocent were acquitted.

Marguerite was not so lucky. Louis X wanted to remarry, and Marguerite was quietly suffocated in prison. His second wife was Clémence of Hungary, who after under a year of marriage produced a baby who died, and then retired to a convent. Louis died suddenly, and as it happened, without an heir. Despite rumours of poison, Guillaume de Nangis reports it in a very matter-of-fact way:

Louis, spending several days in the royal palace in the forest of Vincennes, was taken with a violent fever and died on 5 July [June] leaving Queen Clémence pregnant of a boy and a single girl, Jeanne, by his first wife. In Paris, at the Louvre on the 15th day of November, Queen Clémence was brought to bed of a boy who died five days later.

Hugh de Boville, Louis X's chancellor, asking for the hand of Clémence of Hungary for his king. A manuscript illumination from the Grandes Chroniques de France, c. *1450.*

Tomb effigy, 1327–9, of Louis X at St Denis.

Jean I

Jean I was born on 14–15 November at the Louvre in Paris and died on 19–20 November, 1316.

Tomb effigy, 1327–9, of Jean I from his father's tomb at St Denis.

Philippe V

Philippe V, the Tall, was born in 1294 in Lyons. He was regent from 5 June, 1316 until he became king on 19–20 November, 1316 and he was crowned on 9 January, 1317 at Rheims.
He married, in 1307, Jeanne of Burgundy (c. 1293–1329).
He reigned for four years and died, of dysentery, aged twenty-eight, at Longchamp on 3 January, 1322. He was buried at St Denis.

Philippe V was married to Jeanne, Blanche of Burgundy's sister who was also involved in the scandal of the Tour de Nesle:

She had been suspected in the early days, removed from her husband and imprisoned at Dourdan, but after an enquiry was declared innocent by the *Parlement* in Paris. She was reconciled to her husband.

Philippe, of whom we know little personally, reigned only for a short time, and also left no son:

The King standardised the units of measurement for wine, grain and all commodities, but,

Philippe V, 1317. This miniature manuscript illumination is believed to be drawn from the living king. The text is part of the Vie et Miracles de St Denis, *by William the Scot.*

taken ill, he was not able to complete the work he had proposed. He was also intending to unify the coinage, and as an undertaking of this sort involved huge expense, it was said that by misleading information he extorted a fifth of his subjects' wealth. To this end he sent his servants round the country, but the bishops and nobles, as well as the major cities of the realm, who had had for many years the right to mint their different coins, objected to this measure. So the messengers returned to the King without having concluded successful negotiations.

In the same year, towards the beginning of August, the King was attacked by dysentery and a quartan fever, neither of which the doctors could cure and which kept him in bed for five months. Some people said his illness was caused by the curses heaped on him because of the burdens and taxes he laid on them. However, during his illness the exactions were minimal if not wholly discontinued.

As his illness continued, to help him recover the Abbot and monks of St Denis walked, barefoot, carrying Our Lord's cross and nail and the arm of St Simeon, to Longchamp where Philippe lay. Philippe received the holy relics with piety and humility and as soon as he had touched them felt remarkably better, which is why it was announced that he was cured. But persistent and entrenched maladies return easily and because the King did not look after himself properly, his illness returned. That is why it was reported that he said, 'I know that I was cured by the goodwill and prayers of St Denis, and that my fall is due to my evil rule'. On the 3rd of the following January he died and Charles, his brother, succeeded to the throne without argument or opposition.

Seal of Jeanne of Burgundy. This seal is rather more elaborate than those of preceding queens. Jeanne is shown standing crowned, with her dress in elegant folds, against a richly embroidered backcloth held up by angels. She holds a sceptre in one hand and a flower in the other. The shield on the left bears the arms of France, that on the right those of Burgundy.

Tomb effigy of Philippe V at St Denis.

Charles IV

Charles IV, the Fair, was born in 1295. He acceded to the throne on 3 January, 1322 and was crowned on 21 February, 1322 at Rheims.
He married, in 1307, Blanche of Burgundy (c. 1296–1326); in 1322, Marie of Luxemburg (1305–1324); and, in 1325, Jeanne of Evreux (d. 1371).
He reigned for six years and died, from unknown causes, aged thirty-three, at the château of Vincennes on 1 February, 1328. His body was buried at St Denis; his entrails at Maubuisson.

Charles IV was less ruthless in ridding himself of an unfaithful wife but no less successful:

After the death of Philippe, Charles his brother thus obtained the crown. He then discovered that his marriage to Blanche, who was in prison at Château Gaillard for her

The bishops of Paris and Beauvais, with other clerics debating Charles IV's marriage to Blanche of Burgundy. Manuscript illumination from the Grandes Chroniques de France, *c. 1450.*

Tomb of Jeanne of Evreux, companion to that of her husband Charles IV, from the abbey at Maubuisson.

adultery, was invalid because of the spiritual relationship between him and Blanche's mother, who had held him at his christening, and for which the sovereign pontiff had not given dispensation. Delighted, Charles wrote to the Pope to arrange the matter as suited him. So the Pope told the Bishops of Paris and Beauvais and Geoffroy du Plessis, the protonotary of the court of Rome, to set up a working party and to announce their findings to the court of Rome. So in 1322, having heard their findings, the Pope announced in a public consistory that the marriage was null and void. The King, no longer married and fearing that so noble a throne should remain without an heir, married Marie, daughter of the former Emperor Henry and sister of the King of Bohemia.

In 1324 the Queen of France died, and the King took in marriage Jeanne, daughter of the late Count of Evreux, his first cousin, for she was the daughter of his uncle. In the same year, the Queen being pregnant was taken to Neuchâtel, near Orléans, because it had been predicted by sorcerers of both sexes that it was in that spot that she would be most likely to give birth to a boy. But God, wishing to show them to be mistaken, ordained otherwise, for the baby was a girl.

Charles's and his brothers' failure to have a living male heir and the marriage of their sister to Edward II of England whose son Edward III was 15 in 1327 on his accession after his father's murder, was to pose problems for the French crown for a hundred years:

In 1327 Charles sent messengers to the new King of England [Edward III] asking him to come and do homage for the duchy of Aquitaine. But the King of England, saying that on account of the recent death of his father he was not sure that he should go so far from his country and fearing, not without reason, secret enemies, excused himself, and the King of France accepted this.

Charles's death evoked the usual pious sentiments:

This year on Christmas day about midnight King Charles was attacked by a grave illness and having suffered for a long time died on the eve of the Purification of the Virgin [1 February] at the château of Vincennes near Paris.

And so ended the Capets.

Tomb effigy of Charles IV at St Denis.

The Valois

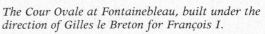

The Cour Ovale at Fontainebleau, built under the direction of Gilles le Breton for François I.

THE VALOIS

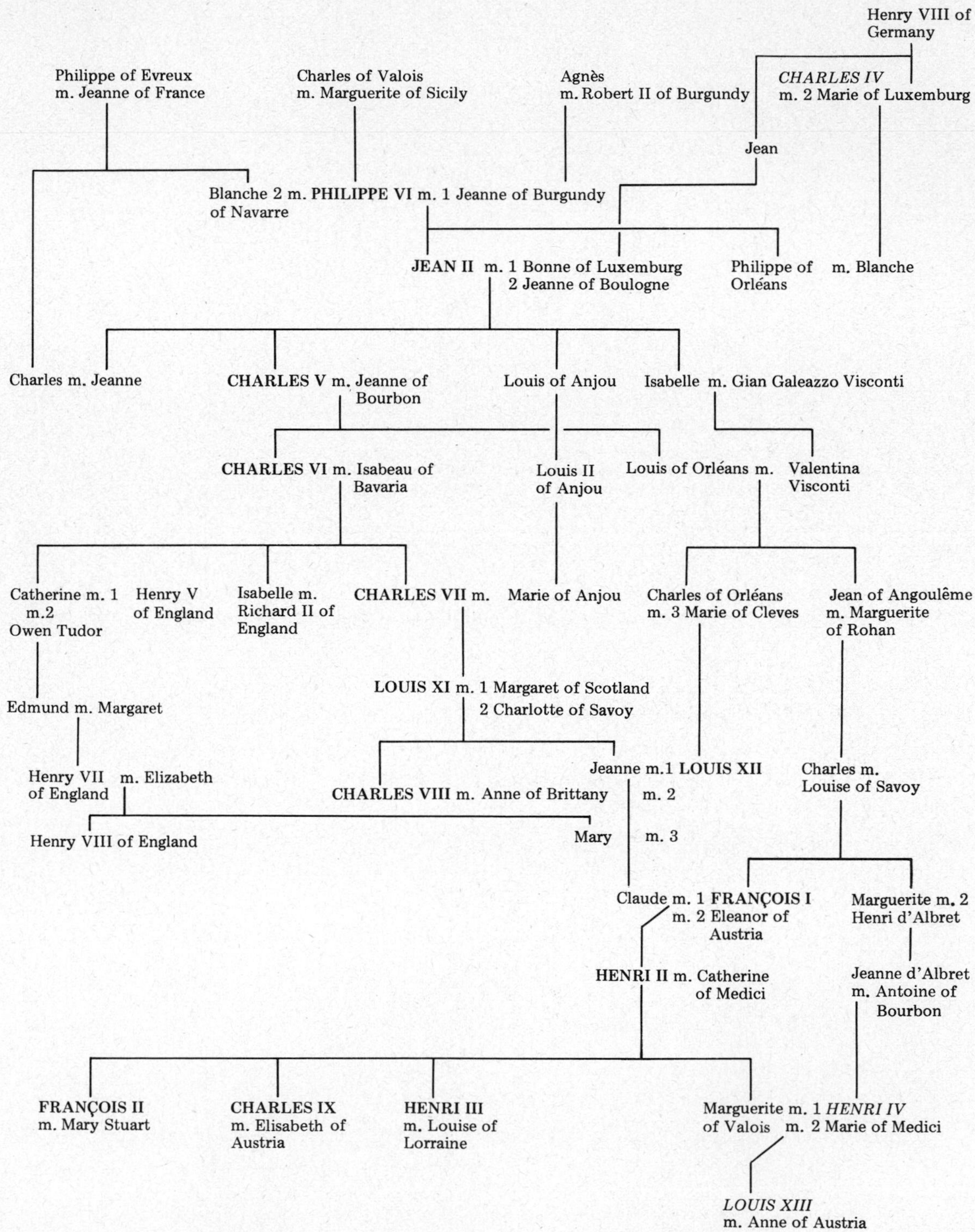
Henry VIII of Germany
Philippe of Evreux m. Jeanne of France
Charles of Valois m. Marguerite of Sicily
Agnès m. Robert II of Burgundy
CHARLES IV m. 2 Marie of Luxemburg
Jean
Blanche 2 m. **PHILIPPE VI** m. 1 Jeanne of Burgundy
of Navarre
JEAN II m. 1 Bonne of Luxemburg
2 Jeanne of Boulogne
Philippe of Orléans
m. Blanche
Charles m. Jeanne
CHARLES V m. Jeanne of Bourbon
Louis of Anjou
Isabelle m. Gian Galeazzo Visconti
CHARLES VI m. Isabeau of Bavaria
Louis II of Anjou
Louis of Orléans m. Valentina Visconti
Catherine m. 1 Henry V of England
m.2 Owen Tudor
Isabelle m. Richard II of England
CHARLES VII m. Marie of Anjou
Charles of Orléans m. 3 Marie of Cleves
Jean of Angoulême m. Marguerite of Rohan
Edmund m. Margaret
LOUIS XI m. 1 Margaret of Scotland
2 Charlotte of Savoy
Henry VII of England m. Elizabeth
CHARLES VIII m. Anne of Brittany
Jeanne m.1 **LOUIS XII**
m. 2
m. 3
Charles m. Louise of Savoy
Henry VIII of England
Mary
Claude m. 1 **FRANÇOIS I**
m. 2 Eleanor of Austria
Marguerite m. 2 Henri d'Albret
HENRI II m. Catherine of Medici
Jeanne d'Albret m. Antoine of Bourbon
FRANÇOIS II m. Mary Stuart
CHARLES IX m. Elisabeth of Austria
HENRI III m. Louise of Lorraine
Marguerite of Valois m. 1 *HENRI IV*
m. 2 Marie of Medici
LOUIS XIII m. Anne of Austria

Philippe VI

Philippe VI was born in 1293 and acceded to the throne on 1 April, 1328. He was crowned at Rheims on 29 May, 1328.
He married, in July 1313, Jeanne of Burgundy (d. 1348) and in 1349, Blanche of Navarre (d. 1398).
He reigned for twenty-two years, and died, from an unspecified illness, aged fifty-seven, at Nogent-le-Roi on 22 August, 1350. His body was buried at St Denis, his entrails in the church of the Jacobins, Paris and his heart at Châtreux de Bourgfontaine, Valois.

From Hugh Capet onwards the French kings succeeded each other from father to son. The Salic Law did not allow women to succeed to the throne, so that if the king had no son, the crown had to pass to his nearest male relation. Thus, although Philippe IV had three sons, none of them had surviving male issue and on the death of the third, Charles IV, his cousin, the first Valois, Philippe VI, a nephew of Philippe IV, ascended the throne and was recognised by the French as their legitimate king. But his second cousin, Edward III of England, whose mother was Isabelle, sister to the last three French kings, believed he had as legitimate a claim, and this claim precipitated the Hundred Years War.

When Philippe acceded to the French throne, a year after Edward became King of England, he required homage from Edward for the duchy of Aquitaine. Sir John Froissart recounts the occasion:

It is hardly necessary to say that King Philippe received the young King of England with all honour and dignity, and so did all the kings [of Bohemia, Navarre and Majorca], dukes and counts who were present there. Many discussions were held and arrangements proposed and I believe that King Edward paid homage with words and a kiss only, without putting his hands between the hands of the King of France, or of any other prince or prelate delegated by him. The King of England refused on that occasion, on the advice he was given, to proceed further with his homage without first returning to England to see and study the earlier charters which would throw light on the matter and show how and in what respect the King of England should declare himself the man of the King of France.

The King of France, seeing that his cousin the King of England was young [16], understood this reasoning perfectly and did not try to press him then.

But despite formal homage, Edward III took an army to France to substantiate his claim to the throne by force. The French army still relied on its cavalry, but it was no match for Edward's bowmen, and for the French the battle of Crécy was a disaster.

King Philippe bestirred himself and had all the penthouses in Paris removed to make it easier for his men to ride through the streets.

Portrait drawing of Philippe VI, probably copied from a window, from the Recueil d'Arras, *a collection of fourteenth- and fifteenth-century portraits.*

When the people of Paris saw that their King was leaving, they were more alarmed than ever. They came and knelt before him, saying: 'Beloved sire and noble king, what are you about to do? Will you abandon your good city of Paris in this way? The enemy are only five miles from us. When they hear that you have gone, they will be here in an instant, and we shall have no one to defend us against them. Sire, we beg you to stay and help protect your loyal city.'

The King answered: 'My good people, you have nothing to fear. The English will come no nearer. I am going to St Denis to be with my soldiers, for I mean to march against the English and fight them, whatever the outcome.'

King Philippe pursued the enemy, and arranged for the last crossing of the Somme to be defended.

Having given these orders, King Philippe, who was eager to come up with the English and engage them, left Amiens with his whole force. At about noon he reached Airaines, which the King of England had quitted in the early morning. The French found that large quantities of provisions had been left behind. There was meat on the spits, there were loaves and pies in the ovens, barrels and kegs of wine, and many tables ready laid, for the English had left in great haste.

The French king settled in to Airaines for the night, not expecting the English to cross the river. Next morning he

was riding rapidly forward when news was brought to him of the English crossing and Godemar's defeat. He was extremely angry, for he had been expecting to find the English on the bank of the Somme and fight them there. He halted in open country and asked his marshals what was the best thing to do. They replied: 'Sire, you cannot cross the river yourself because the tide is in again now.' So the King turned back in fury and took up his quarters in Abbeville with all his people.

The English moved on to Crécy and the King of France prepared for battle. It took place on Friday, 25 August, 1346.

There is no one, even among those present on that day, who has been able to understand and relate the whole truth of the matter. This was especially so on the French side, where such confusion reigned. What I know about it comes chiefly from the English, who had a good understanding of their own battleplan, and also from some of Sir John of Hainault's men, who were never far from the King of France.

The English, who were drawn up in their three divisions and sitting quietly on the ground, got up with perfect discipline when they saw the French approaching and formed their ranks.

Seal of Jeanne of Burgundy.

It must be stressed that the French lords—kings, dukes, counts and barons—did not reach the spot together, but arrived one after another, in no kind of order. When King Philippe came near the place where the English were and saw them, his blood boiled, for he hated them. Nothing could now stop him from giving battle. He said to his marshals: 'Send forward our Genoese and begin the battle, in the name of God and St Denis.'

He had with him about fifteen thousand [perhaps 6000] Genoese bowmen who would sooner have gone to the devil than fight at that moment, for they had just marched over eighteen miles, in armour and carrying their crossbows. They told their commanders that they were not in a state to fight much of a battle just then. These words came to the ears of the Count of Alençon, who grew very angry and said: 'What is the use of burdening ourselves with this rabble who give up just when they are needed!'

While this argument was going on and the Genoese were hanging back, a heavy storm of rain came on and there were loud claps of thunder, with lightning. Before the rain, huge flocks of crows had flown over both armies, making a deafening noise in the air. Some experienced knights said that this portended a great and murderous battle.

Then the sky began to clear and the sun shone out brightly. But the French had it straight in their eyes and the English at their backs. The Genoese, having been marshalled into proper order and made to advance, began to utter loud whoops to frighten the English. The English waited in silence and did not stir. The Genoese hulloa'd a second time and advanced a little farther, but the English still made no move. Then they raised a third shout, very loud and clear, levelled their crossbows and began to shoot.

At this the English archers took one pace forward and poured out their arrows on the Genoese so thickly and evenly that they fell like snow. When they felt those arrows piercing their arms, their heads, their faces, the Genoese, who had never met such archers before, were thrown into confusion. Many cut their bowstrings and some threw down their crossbows. They began to fall back.

Between them and the main body of the French there was a hedge of knights, splendidly mounted and armed, who had been watching their discomfiture and now cut off their retreat. For the King of France, seeing how miserably they had performed, called out in great anger: 'Quick now, kill all that rabble. They are only getting in our way!' Thereupon the mounted men began to strike out at them on all sides and many staggered and fell, never to rise again. The English continued to shoot into the thickest part of the crowd, wasting none of their arrows. They impaled or wounded horses and riders, who fell to the ground in great distress, unable to get up again without the help of several men.

So began the battle between La Broye and Crécy in Ponthieu at four o'clock on that Saturday afternoon.

The King of France was in great distress when he saw his army being destroyed piecemeal by such a handful of men as the English were. He asked the opinion of Sir John of Hainault, who was at his side. 'Well, sire,' Sir John answered, 'the only advice I can give you now is to withdraw to some place of safety, for I see no hope of recovery. Also, it will soon be dark and you might just as easily fall in with your enemies and meet disaster as find yourself among friends.'

The King, shaking with anger and vexation, made no immediate reply, but rode on a little farther as though to reach his brother the Count of Alençon, whose banners he could see at the top of a small rise. The Count was launching a very well-ordered attack on the English, as was the Count of Flanders from another quarter. They moved their forces along the flank of the archers and reached the Prince of Wales's division, which they engaged fiercely for a long time. King Philippe would gladly have joined them had it been possible, but there was such a throng of archers and men-at-arms in front of him that he could not get through. The farther he advanced, the smaller his numbers grew.

The lateness of the hour harmed the French cause as much as anything, for in the dark many of the men-at-arms lost their leaders and wandered about the field in disorder only to fall in with the English, who quickly overwhelmed and killed them. They took no prisoners and asked no ransoms, acting as they had decided among themselves in the morning when they were aware of the huge numbers of the enemy.

Late in the evening, as it was growing dark, King Philippe left the field in despair,

Tomb effigy of Blanche of Navarre at St Denis.

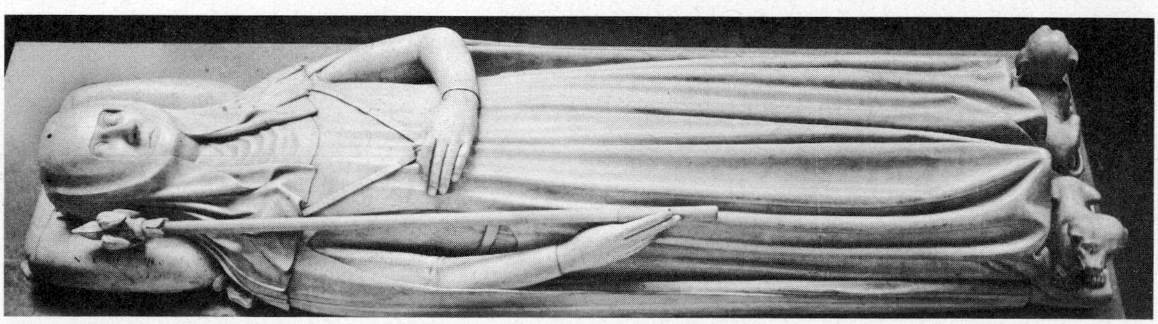

Tomb effigy of Philippe VI by Beauneveu at St Denis. This was probably begun in 1364 from a death mask at St Denis.

accompanied by five lords only. The King rode lamenting and mourning for his men until he came to the castle of La Broye. He found the gate shut and the drawbridge up, for it was now fully night and pitch-dark. He called for the captain of the castle, who came to the look-out turret and shouted down: 'Who comes knocking at this hour?' 'Open your gate, captain,' King Philippe answered. 'It is the unfortunate King of France.'

The captain came out at once, recognizing the King's voice and having already heard of the defeat from fugitives who had passed the castle. The drawbridge was lowered and the King entered with his whole troop, but he was warned that it would be unwise to stay shut up inside there. So he and his men took a drink and left the castle again at about midnight, taking guides with them who knew the country. They rode so hard that by daybreak they reached Amiens, where the King stopped and lodged in an abbey, saying he would go no farther until he had news of the fate of all his army.

It must be said that fearful losses had been inflicted on the French and that the kingdom of France was greatly weakened by the death of so many of her brave nobility. If the English had mounted a pursuit, as they did at Poitiers, they would have accounted for many more, including the King himself. But this did not happen. On the Saturday they never once left their lines to pursue the enemy, but stayed on their positions to defend themselves against attack.

Jean II

Jean II, the Good, was born on 26 April, 1319, at Gué-de-Maulny, near Le Mans, and acceded to the throne on 22 August, 1350. He was crowned at Rheims on 26 September of that year.
He married on 28 July, 1332, Bonne of Luxemburg (d. 1349) and, on 19 February, 1350, Jeanne of Boulogne (c. 1326–1361).
He reigned for ten years intermittently and died, aged nearly forty-five, at the palace of the Savoy in London on 8 April, 1364. He was buried at St Denis.

Jean II inherited the war from his father but did nothing to improve French military strategy or tactics. Froissart records the battle of Poitiers, 19 September, 1356, at which Jean was taken prisoner and sent into captivity in England.

You read earlier in this chronicle about the battle of Crécy, and heard how unfavourable fortune was there to the French. At Poitiers similarly it was unfavourable, fickle and treacherous, for the French were at least seven to one in trained fighting-men. But it must be said that the battle of Poitiers was fought much better than Crécy. There were incomparably more fine feats of arms than at Crécy, though not so many great lords were killed. The King of France remained on the field from beginning to end, like the brave knight and stout fighter he was. He had shown his determination never to retreat when he commanded his men to fight on foot and, having made them dismount, he did the same and stood in the forefront of them with a battle-axe in his hands, ordering forward his banners in the name of God and St Denis. So, in good order, the King's main division came face-to-face with the English.

Later in the battle

the French were so overwhelmed by their enemies that in places there were five men-at-arms attacking a single knight. Round the King of France himself there was a great jostling and turmoil, with everyone struggling to take him prisoner. Those who were near enough to recognize him cried: 'Surrender, surrender, or you're a dead man!' There was a knight there from St Omer called Sir Denis de Morbecque who had been with the English for five years because he had been banished from France in his youth after killing a man in a family feud. He had become a paid retainer of the King of England. Fortunately for this knight he found himself near to King Jean during the scuffle to capture him. He forced his way through the press, for he was a big, strong man, and said in good French, by which he attracted the King's attention better than the others: 'Sire, give yourself up!' Seeing himself in this desperate plight and feeling that resistance was useless, the King looked at him and said: 'To whom shall I surrender? To whom? Where is my cousin, the Prince of Wales, the Black Prince? If I could see him, then I would speak.' 'Sire,' replied Sir Denis, 'he is not here. But surrender to me and I will take you to him.' 'Who are you?' the King asked. 'Sire, I am Denis de Morbecque, a knight from Artois. But I serve the King of England because I have been exiled from France and have forfeited all my possessions.' Then, as I was informed, the King answered, or probably answered: 'I surrender to you,' and gave him his right-hand glove. The knight took it with delight. But there was still a great commotion round the King, with each man clamouring: 'I took him! I took him!' and neither the King nor his young son Philippe could move a step forward.

The Prince of Wales, who had been like a raging lion under his battle helmet, and had revelled in the fighting and the rout of the enemy, was hot and exhausted towards the end of the day. The Prince asked his two marshals if they had any news of the King of France. They said no, nothing definite. They thought he must have been either killed or captured, since he had certainly not left the battlefield. The Prince then turned anxiously to the Earl of Warwick and Sir Reginald Cobham and said: 'Please go out again and ride about until you have found out the true position.' The two commanders mounted their horses and rode them up a hillock from which they had a view all round. They saw a great mob of men-at-arms on foot moving very slowly towards them. In the midst of it was the King of France in grave danger, for English and Gascons had got hold of him, having snatched him away from Sir Denis de Morbecque, who was no longer near. The strongest were shouting: 'I took him, he's mine!' The King, who understood their eagerness to get possession of him, attempted to end this dangerous situation by saying: 'Sirs, sirs, take me in a gentlemanly way, and my son with me, to my cousin the Prince, and stop this brawling over my capture. I am a king, and great enough to make each one of you rich.' These words satisfied them for a moment, but soon the brawling broke out again and they came to blows at every step they took.

Seeing the crowd in the distance, the two commanders decided to go towards it. They spurred up to it and said: 'What's happening? What's going on here?' Someone answered: 'It's the King of France, and a dozen knights and squires squabbling to get him.' Wasting no more words, the two knights pushed their horses through the crowd and ordered every man there to stand back and stay back, if he valued his life. No one dared to disobey this order, so they drew well away from the King and the two barons, who sprang to the ground and bowed humbly before him. He was indeed glad to see them, for they had delivered him from great danger.

That evening the Prince of Wales gave a supper for the King of France and most of the captured counts and barons. The Prince seated King Jean and his son Philippe at a high table, lavishly provided, and the rest of the nobles at other tables. He himself served in all humility both at the King's table and at the others, steadfastly refusing to sit down with the King in spite of all his entreaties. He insisted that he was not yet worthy to sit at the table of so mighty a prince and so brave a soldier as he had proved himself to be on that day. He constantly kneeled before him, saying: 'Beloved sire, do not make such a poor

Jean II returning to captivity in London, 1362. Manuscript illumination from the Grandes Chroniques de France, *1370–80.*

meal, even though God has not been willing to heed your prayers today. My royal father will certainly show you every mark of honour and friendship in his power, and will come to such a reasonable understanding with you that you and he will always remain firm friends. In my opinion, you have good cause to be cheerful, although the battle did not go in your favour, for today you have won the highest renown of a warrior, excelling the best of your knights. I do not say this to flatter you, for everyone on our side, having seen how each man fought, unanimously agrees with this and awards you the palm and the crown, if you will consent to wear them.

King Jean was taken with his servants to England to be imprisoned there:

News of their arrival was brought to the King and Queen of England who were at Eltham, a very fine royal manor about seven miles from London. Some of the household knights were immediately sent down to Dover, where the King of France had remained since his arrival. They greeted him with all possible respect, telling him that King Edward was delighted that he had come. The next morning King Jean mounted his horse and rode with all his followers to Canterbury, which they reached at dinner-time. After spending two days at Canterbury, he rode on towards London and, travelling in short stages, came to Eltham where the King and Queen of England were waiting to receive him with a great company of knights and ladies. He arrived on a Sunday in the afternoon, and between then and supper there was time for much dancing and merriment.

It would be impossible for me to record all the honours with which the King and Queen of England received King Jean, but finally he left Eltham and entered London. There he was welcomed by people of all conditions, who came out in companies to meet him, greeting him with the greatest respect. Amid a great playing of musical instruments he was escorted to the palace of the Savoy, which had been got ready for him, and where he was lodged with the members of his family and the French hostages.

King Jean spent the rest of the winter there cheerfully and sociably. They held several big entertainments and parties together, dinners, suppers and so forth, either at the Savoy or at the palace of Westminster situated near by, to which the King of France went privately whenever he liked by boat along the Thames.

He returned to France on being ransomed by money put up by Gian Galeazzo Visconti of Milan in return for the hand of Jean's daughter Isabelle, but voluntarily went back to England when he discovered that his second son, the Duke of Anjou, whom he had left as a hostage, had escaped and he died there.

Charles V

Charles V, the Wise, was born on 21 January, 1337 at the château of Vincennes. He acceded to the throne on 8 April, 1364 and was crowned at Rheims on 19 May.
He married, on 8 April, 1350, Jeanne of Bourbon (1338–1378).
He reigned for four years as regent and then sixteen years as king, and died, aged forty-three, from gout, at Beauté-sur-Marne, near Vincennes, on 16 September, 1380.
His body was buried at St Denis and his heart at Notre Dame, Rouen.

Jean's son, Charles, became regent during his father's captivity. He was the first heir presumptive to bear the title of dauphin. Dauphiné had been sold to Philippe VI in 1349 on condition that the title of dauphin would be borne by the sovereign or his heir.

During his father's captivity Charles had called a meeting of the Estates General in Paris to discuss defence. Their leader, Etienne Marcel, who advanced popular ideas of democracy against the monarchy, at one point forced Charles to wear the colours of Paris—red and blue—in his hat. But Etienne Marcel's alliance with Charles the Bad of Navarre was unpopular and cost him his life. Charles V, a scholarly man, left the fighting to his commanders and was fortunate in being able to call on the services of Bertrand du

OPPOSITE: *The young Louis IX, crowned, holding the sceptre in his right hand, turning his head towards his mother, Blanche of Castille. A page from a thirteenth-century* Bible moralisée.

OVERLEAF: *Portrait of Jean II, distemper on wood. School of Paris, about 1360, or possibly by Gérard d'Orléans. It is the first known painted portrait of a king of France. It belonged to Charles V, his son, and eventually found its way into the possession of Roger de Gaignières, on whose death in 1717 it was reserved for Louis XV by the regent.*

Guesclin, a professional soldier.

When the King of France heard of the retaking and destruction of Limoges, he was greatly angered and his heart ached for the sufferings of its inhabitants. It was therefore decided by the council of the nobles and prelates, strongly supported by the common feeling of the whole kingdom, that it was a necessity for the French to have a supreme commander, with the title of constable. After full consideration, Sir Bertrand du Guesclin was unanimously chosen, provided he was willing to accept, as the worthiest and most suitable man for the post, as well as the most gallant and successful leader fighting at that time in the service of France.

Du Guesclin made objections but

the King answered and said: 'Sir Bertrand, you cannot excuse yourself on those grounds. I have neither brother nor cousin nor nephew, nor count, nor baron in my kingdom who would refuse to obey you. If any did, it would anger me so much that he would soon hear about it. So take the post with an easy mind. I beg you to.'

Charles V was called the Wise not only because he was wise and prudent, but also because he was a scholar and fond of knowledge. Not strong physically, he deemed it wiser to direct his army and the affairs of state from the château of Vincennes rather than risk capture in the field.

*He was a brilliant administrator who set about rebuilding France, though he was a man of some austerity as Christine de Pisan (1364–*c.* 1430), a poet and writer at the court of France at the time, points out:*

He was long-waisted and well-built, straight and broad-shouldered, with slim hips. He had thickset, well-developed arms and beautiful limbs, as finely proportioned in body as could be. He had a good shaped face—a bit long, with a broad forehead and big arched eyebrows; his eyes were beautifully shaped, well-set and chestnut in colour, and had a steady gaze. He had a long nose, but too small a mouth and firm lips. He was quite heavily bearded and had high cheek bones. His hair was neither blond nor black but light brown. He had very pale skin and since he was very thin I think that his pallor was due to the results of illness rather than a natural characteristic. His features and manners were wise, controlled and composed at all times in all states and in every movement. He was never hot-tempered, never intemperate. In all his actions and bearing and everything he did he was full of wisdom and comported himself as a noble prince. He had a fine manly voice with a good timbre and, certainly, I do not think any rhetorician in the French language could have improved on his splendid, well-ordered and well-arranged manner of speaking.

Amongst other virtues to be praised in people King Charles loved very much that of chastity, which he himself upheld in word, deed and thought and wished that it should

Statues of Charles V, and Jeanne of Bourbon, French school, c. *1375, from the Augustinian convent, Paris.*

Charles V with his sons, Charles (VI) and Louis, his wife, Jeanne of Bourbon and their daughters, Marie and Isabelle. Manuscript illumination of 1374 from the Rational des divins offices *by Guillaume Durand, translated by Jean Golein, from a copy of the book owned by Charles V.*

Tomb effigy of Charles V by Beauneveu at St Denis. The King ordered it in 1364 sixteen years before he died. It shows him as a young man of twenty-seven.

be thus with all those near to him and his servants, as much in demeanour as in habits, words, deeds and all things. He was faithful in marriage and in word and action was honest and chaste according to God's way, as the Queen and her children and the servants of her court were. He allowed no man from his court, however noble and powerful he might be, to wear clothes that were too short or outrageous, nor were women permitted to wear dresses which constricted them too tightly nor that were too full either. He ordered all his nobles to take care that their women bore themselves in such a manner that no one should have any cause of displeasure from them.

He thought sobriety a cardinal virtue and preferred food and drink to be nourishing rather than elaborate. He was also fussy about his clothes, and liked them neat but not gaudy.

Charles VI

Charles VI, the Well-loved, was born on 3 December, 1368 at Paris. He acceded on 16 September, 1380 and was crowned at Rheims on 4 November.
He married, on 17 July, 1385, Isabeau of Bavaria (1371–1435).
He reigned for forty-two years, and died, insane, aged fifty-three, at the hôtel de St Pol, Paris on 22 October, 1422. He was buried at St Denis.

Charles VI was only twelve when he succeeded and his uncles ruled badly for him. It was hoped that he would be another Charles the Wise but alas he was insane.

His marriage arrangements throw a kindlier light on him, though he was to be betrayed by the young Bavarian lady.

On his death-bed King Charles V of France of happy memory had desired that, if a suitable match could be found, his son Charles should be married to some German lady.

The Duchess of Brabant, who had a talent for this kind of thing, pointed out to the King's uncles and his council when at Cambrai that the young lady [Isabeau, daughter of Duke Stephen of Bavaria] was the daughter of a great nobleman in Germany, the most powerful of the Bavarians, and that strong alliances with the Germans would result.

It is the custom in France for any lady, however great her family may be, whom it is intended to marry to the King, to be seen and examined by ladies in a completely naked state, to decide whether she is fit and properly formed to bear children. Besides this, the lady lived in a country as far distant as Bavaria and it was not known, once she had been brought to France, whether she would be to the liking of the King.

The Duchess, who was very experienced in such things, instructed the young Bavarian lady daily in manners and behaviour, although she was graceful and sensible by nature and had received a good upbringing, though she knew no French. The Duchess of Hainault could not leave her with the clothes and outfit she had come with, for they were too simple by French standards.

She had her dressed, bejewelled and equipped as lavishly as if she had been her own daughter. When everything was perfect and it was time to set off, they made good progress until they came to Amiens.

The King of France and his council were also there. The King could hardly sleep for eagerness to see his prospective bride, and he kept asking the Lord of La Rivière: 'When am I going to see her?' The ladies had some good laughs when they heard about this.

On the Friday, when the young lady had been dressed and adorned as befitted her, the three duchesses led her before the King. As she came up to him, she sank in a low curtsey at his feet. The King went towards her and, taking her by the hand, raised her up and looked at her long and hard. With that look love and delight entered his heart. He saw that she was young and beautiful and was filled with a great desire to see her and have

Statue of Charles VI when still dauphin by an unknown artist, c. 1376, from the buttress of the north tower of the cathedral at Amiens.

her. Then said the constable of France: 'This lady is going to stay with us. The King cannot take his eyes off her.'

The King married Isabeau who was given a stately and lavish entry to Paris:

At twelve o'clock on the Tuesday about forty of the most prominent citizens of Paris, all dressed identically, came bringing the Queen's present through the streets of Paris. It was carried on a litter of beautiful workmanship by two strong men disguised as savages. The litter had a canopy of fine silk crêpe, through which could be seen the treasures which it contained. They went at once to the King's room, which was open and ready for their reception. They were expected, and those who bring gifts can always be sure of a welcome. They placed the litter on two trestles in the middle of the room, then knelt before the King, saying:

'Most dear and noble sire, to celebrate the joyous arrival of your Queen, your burgesses of Paris offer you all the precious objects on this litter.'

'Many thanks, good people,' replied the King. 'It is a handsome and costly present.'

The burgesses rose to their feet and stepped back. Then, with the King's permission, they left him. When they had gone, the King said to Sir Guillaume des Bordes and to

White marble tomb effigy of Isabeau of Bavaria by Pierre de Thury, 1424–9, at St Denis.

Montaigu, who were with him:

'Let us have a closer look and see what the presents are.'

They went up to the litter and looked into it. This is what it contained: there were four gold pots, four large gold goblets, four gold salt-cellars, twelve gold cups, twelve gold bowls and six gold dishes. The whole of this plate weighed seventy-five pounds in solid gold.

Meanwhile other citizens of Paris, richly dressed all in similar clothes, waited on the Queen, taking her present on a litter which was carried to her room and commending the city and its inhabitants to her. The present consisted of a ship made of gold, two large gold flagons, two gold comfit-dishes, two gold salt-cellars, six gold pots, six gold goblets, twelve silver lamps, two dozen silver bowls, six large silver dishes, two silver basins. The whole, both gold and silver, weighed a hundred and fifty pounds. The present was carried into the Queen's room on a litter, as I said, by two men, one of them dressed as a bear and the other as a unicorn.

Charles, when young, was high-spirited and gay. At twenty, according to Froissart, he enjoyed his life.

The King stayed for more than twelve days in Montpellier. All that he saw there, the aspect of the town and of the married ladies and the young ladies, the style they lived in and the amusements which were provided for him and his court, were very greatly to his liking. To tell the truth, the King was still completing his education, for at that time he was young and lighthearted. So he danced and danced the whole night long with the lively ladies of Montpellier. He gave splendid banquets and suppers for them and presented them with gold rings and clasps, to each according to his estimation of her worth.

The King enjoyed himself for about a fortnight at Montpellier. When he had put everything in order with the help of his inner council and had removed several injustices by which the inhabitants had been oppressed, he took affectionate leave of the ladies and set out one morning for Lymous, where he dined, and then lodged for the night at St Hubert. After his morning drink the next day he went on to Béziers, where he received an enthusiastic welcome. The King spent three days at Béziers in revels and parties.

Soon afterwards, it was decided that the King should leave Toulouse and make his way back to France. He left the city one morning after his drink and lodged that night at Castelnaudary, then pressed on until he reached Montpellier, where he had a joyous welcome. He relaxed there for three days, for this was the town which had pleased him so much, with its maids and its ladies; yet he very much wanted to get back to Paris and see the Queen. It so happened that, while chatting idly with his brother, the Duke of Touraine, he said: 'Brother, I wish that I and you were in Paris at this moment, leaving all our followers here, just as they are. I feel a great desire to see the Queen, and you no doubt to see your Duchess.' 'Sire,' replied the Duke, 'we aren't in Paris. It's too far off to get there just by wishing it.' 'You are right,' said the King. 'Yet I have an idea that I could soon really be there if I wanted to.' 'By hard riding, then,' said the Duke. 'That's the only way. So could I, but it would be a horse that would take me.' 'All right,' said the King. 'Which of us will get there first, I or you? Let's have a bet on it.' 'It's a bargain,' said the Duke, who was quite ready to exert himself to win the King's money.

They made a wager of five thousand francs on which of them would reach Paris first, both to start at the same time on the next day. Each was to take only one servant with him, or a knight in place of a servant, for that was how it turned out. No one raised objections to the wager, and they both got on their horses as arranged. With the King was the Lord of Garencières as his sole attendant. The Duke of Touraine had the Lord of La Viefville with him. Those four keen young men continued riding night and day or, when they felt like it, had themselves taken on in carriages to give themselves a rest. Of course they made several changes of horses.

So the King of France and his brother of Touraine rode forward with all their energy, each striving to win the other's money. Think of the discomforts those two rich lords endured through sheer youthful spirits, for they had left all their household establishments behind. The King took four-and-a-half days to reach Paris, and the Duke of Touraine only four-and-a-third; they were as close to each other as that. The Duke won the bet because the King rested for about eight hours one night at Troyes, while the Duke went down the Seine by boat as far as Melun, and from there to Paris on horseback. He went to the hôtel de St Pol, where the Queen and his own wife were, and asked for news of the King, not knowing whether he had arrived ahead of him or not. When he learnt that he was not there yet, he was very pleased indeed and said to the Queen: 'Madam, you will soon be hearing something of him.' He was quite right, for not long after the King came in too. When his brother saw him, he went to meet him and said: 'Sire, I've won the bet. Have the money paid to me.' 'Yes, you have won,' said the King. 'You shall be paid.'

Then they described their whole journey to the ladies, saying where they had started from and how, in four-and-a-half days, they had come all that way from Montpellier, which is a good four hundred and fifty miles from Paris. The ladies treated the whole thing as a joke, but they did realise that it was a great feat of endurance, such as only the young in body and heart would have attempted. I should add that the Duke of Touraine insisted on being paid in hard cash.

But Charles was suffering from insanity and its first manifestation was in August 1392:

The King had been overloaded with councils. Apart from this unforeseen work, he was not at all well and had not been so all the year, but had been suffering from head-pains, eating and drinking little, and almost every day afflicted with heats and fevers. He was disposed to these, by the nature of his constitution, and very harmful to him they were.

I was told that as he was riding through the forest of Le Mans, he was given a solemn warning which ought to have caused him to reflect and to call his council together before going farther. There suddenly came towards him a man with bare head and feet dressed

Christine de Pisan offers her book on Charles V to Charles VI. Manuscript illumination of c. 1405 *from her* Œuvres.

in a mean smock of white homespun and looking more nearly mad than sane. He dashed out from between two trees, boldly seized the reins of the King's horse, stopped him short and said: 'King, ride forward no farther. Turn back, for you are betrayed.' These words struck home into the King's mind, which was already weakened, and afterwards had a very much worse effect, for his spirits sank and his blood ran cold. At this, men-at-arms came up and beat savagely on the man's hands, which were holding the reins, so that he let go and was left behind.

So the King of France was riding in the sun over the sandy plain, on the hottest August day that has ever been known before or since. He was wearing a black velvet jerkin, which made him very hot, and had on his head a plain scarlet hat and a string of large milky pearls which the Queen had given him when he said good-bye to her. Behind him was riding a page who wore a Montauban helmet of burnished steel which glittered in the sun. Behind him came another page carrying a gilded lance on which was fixed a silk banner, the distinguishing mark of the King. The lance had a broad head of fine, gleaming steel.

Then, as they were all riding along like this, the page carrying the lance forgot what he was about or dozed off, as boys and pages do through carelessness, and allowed the blade of the lance to fall forward on to the helmet which the other page was wearing. There was a loud clang of steel, and the King, who was so close that they were riding on his horse's heels, gave a sudden start. His mind reeled, for his thoughts were still running on the words which the madman or the wise man had said to him in the forest, and he imagined that a great host of his enemies were coming to kill him. Under this delusion, his weakened mind caused him to run amok. He spurred his horse forward, then drew his sword and wheeled round on to his pages, no longer recognizing them or anyone else. He thought he was in a battle surrounded by the enemy and, raising his sword to bring it down on anyone who was in the way, he shouted: 'Attack! Attack the traitors!'

The longer he raged about, the weaker he grew. A Norman knight, of whom he was very fond, came up behind him and flung his arms round the King as he still waved his sword, and gripped him tight. While he was being held, all the others came up. His sword was taken from him and he was lifted from his horse and laid very gently on the ground and stripped of his jerkin to cool him. His three uncles and his brother went to him, but he had lost all recollection of them and gave no sign of affection or recognition. His eyes were rolling very strangely, nor did he speak to anyone.

That evening the doctors were very busy and the great lords very troubled. The doctors were sent for and closely questioned. Their reply was that the King had been sickening for this illness for some time past. The next day, the King's uncles went to visit him and heard that he was very weak. They asked how he had slept. His attendants said, hardly at all; he did not seem able to get any rest. 'Bad news,' said the Duke of Burgundy.

The King's insanity resulted in, as usual, a struggle for power, and in addition to having the English to fight, civil war broke out.

Queen Isabeau of Bavaria was a wicked woman, who did not like France and did all the harm she could. And the French fought amongst themselves instead of uniting against the English as they had under Charles V and du Guesclin. On the one hand there was the Duke of Orléans, brother of the King, who wanted to save the heritage of his nephews. And on the other, there was his cousin the Duke of Burgundy, Jean the Fearless, who reckoned to get the throne for himself. One night Jean the Fearless had the Duke of Orléans killed by assassins hidden in a deserted street.

The adherents of the Duke of Orléans swore to be revenged. They had as their leader the Duke of Armagnac and they were called the Armagnacs on this count, while the partisans of the Duke of Burgundy were known as the Burgundians. The Armagnacs were for France but the Burgundians were a bad lot. And they had on their side the butchers and the skinners at Paris who perpetrated a lot of crimes.

As the Armagnacs and the Burgundians fought without respite, Henry V, the King of

White marble tomb effigy of Charles VI by Pierre de Thury, 1424–9, at St Denis.

England, thought that the moment was ripe to take possession of France. He invaded with an army, and as at Crécy and Poitiers the French chivalry went out to meet them. But always rash, they threw themselves upon the English archers with their horses. It was raining, the ground was sodden and the horses fell. So once again the English massacred the French who could no longer count on the skill of a du Guesclin and who went into battle as if to a party.

The disaster of Agincourt in 1415, at which ten thousand Frenchmen lost their lives, ought to have reconciled the two parties. Not at all; they tore each other to pieces with even more fury than before. The butchers and the skinners handed Paris over to the Burgundians, and they murdered a large number of Armagnacs. Those who could escape did so with the dauphin who had to travel around France until the day that Joan of Arc had him consecrated at Rheims.

Meantime the Armagnacs and the Burgundians were never more detested nor more fought against. The Armagnacs said that Jean the Fearless was a traitor who wished to sell France to the English and they murdered him at the bridge of Montereau to punish him for killing the Duke of Orléans. In revenge, the Burgundians went over to the enemy, and the new Duke of Burgundy with Queen Isabeau, signed the most shameful treaty of French history. Remember that date—1420. The Treaty of Troyes was intended to make Englishmen of the French for ever. At the death of the poor demented Charles VI, Henry V of England was to become King of France.

Charles was himself persuaded to agree to this:

Charles by the grace of God, King of France, to our dear and well-beloved cousin Charles, Duke of Lorraine, greetings and happiness. We inform you that we have given instructions to all our people and vassals that they should recognise after our death our dear and well-beloved Henry, at present King of England, as our heir and regent of France as King of the realm of France.

Charles VII

Charles VII, the Victorious, was born on 22 February, 1403 at the hôtel de St Pol, Paris. He acceded on 22 October, 1422 and was crowned at Rheims on 17 July, 1429. He married, on 18 December, 1422, Marie of Anjou (1404–1463). He reigned for thirty-eight years, and died, from tubercular disease of the jawbone followed by septicaemia, aged fifty-eight, at the château of Mehun-sur-Yèvre, near Bourges on 22 July, 1461. He was buried at St Denis.

Henry V of England married Charles's sister Catherine, but he died before Charles, leaving a son of only ten months. Charles VII, Charles VI's son, was therefore desperate to be crowned although the presence of English armies made it temporarily impossible. He was so impoverished that it was a great treat for his court to eat chicken, and he had been so reduced by the English that they jeeringly called him the 'King of Bourges' after the largest city still left in his hands.

And then a miracle happened.

When the realm was afflicted with tribulation on all sides and was weakened and impoverished by the wars it had undergone, as if by divine providence there appeared a young maid, called Joan born in Domrémy, near Vaucouleurs. This maid, by her good advice and a miracle by God, affected by compassion for the horrors going on, went to talk to Robert Baudricourt of Vaucouleurs and persuaded him and his companions to take her to the King to whom she could offer help. She recognised him although he was more poorly dressed than his courtiers. 'I salute you, noble King,' she said, 'and God give you a good life.' Charles denied that he was King. 'Ha,' she said, 'useless to hide yourself; you are the very noble King of France.' At this the King took heart and had her examined by his counsellors. She told them that she had come to restore the King to his kingdom on God's orders. And that she would chase the English out of France and deliver the city of Orléans. That done, she would have Charles crowned at Rheims. She spoke with such conviction that it was as if she was divinely inspired. And when she was interrogated about difficult points on the Catholic faith, she answered with equal conviction, so much so that she convinced many. The council therefore decided that it would be good for Charles to try his fortune in battle but he, like a sage and prudent prince, did not wish to rush into adventure. So he took himself to his prayers asking God to tell him if He had truly sent the maid. He kept her with him for six weeks, asking everyone's opinion but all found in her no evil, only humility, virginity and devotion. When he asked Joan for a sign she told him she would give him one outside Orléans and nowhere else since these were her orders from God. So Charles decided he would let her go to Orléans, his first charge being that she should take food to the inhabitants.

And at Blois they put food into carts and arrayed themselves in battle order. On the

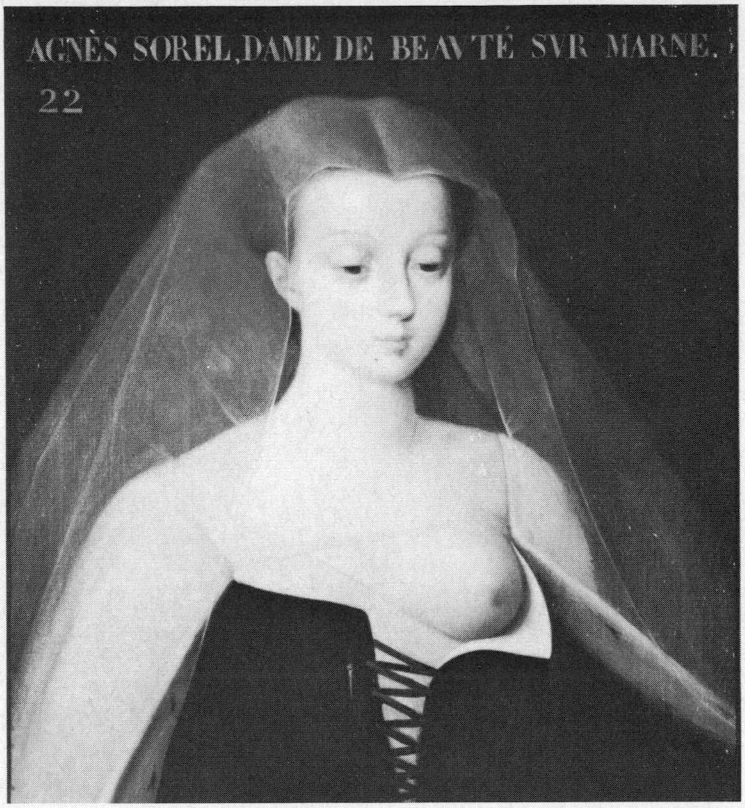

Agnès Sorel by an unknown artist of the French school, fifteenth century.

next day they set out for Orléans. Joan carried a white satin standard with Our Lord sitting on the arc showing his wounds with two angels at either side holding a fleur-de-lys.

Now I will tell you how Joan proved herself in battle. There is in Touraine a church dedicated to St Catherine at a spot greatly venerated in those parts. Joan, being with the King, just before they set off for Orléans told Charles that there was an old sword covered on all sides with fleurs-de-lys. And Joan asked the King to send an armourer to go and fetch it. Charles was astonished at this and asked her if she had ever visited the church. 'He who told me of it was not a man; it was God Himself, for I have never been there in my life,' she replied. At which the King sent an armourer to fetch it. There, in the church of St Catherine, amongst other old armour, he found it and brought it back to Charles who gave it to Joan who used it and none other for the rest of her life.

The English were duly chased out of Orléans and out of France and the story of the burning of Joan as a heretic has become as much English as French history. Charles spent the rest of his reign rebuilding French confidence and strengthening the monarchy, and when he died he left a stronger nation and the English in possession of Calais only. The Hundred Years War was over.

Charles, from being the sickly dauphin who could barely afford chicken, was called in

Marble bust of Marie of Anjou from the recumbent statue erected on Charles VII's tomb in 1463.

later life 'the pillar of Christianity' and was one of Europe's most powerful sovereigns. His private life, however, continued to evoke unfavourable comment.

Charles VII was short, but healthy and agreeable-looking. His shoulders were wide but his legs were surprisingly thin. In a long gown he nearly achieved elegance but in the short clothes which he habitually wore—he liked green material—the extreme thinness of his legs, swollen at the thigh and slightly knock-kneed, made him appear deformed. He ate and drank sparingly, which kept him in good health, and he was in fact rarely ill since he scrupulously followed the diet prescribed by his doctors.

He indulged himself, not only when young, but also at an age when it was no longer suitable and was encouraged to do so by his hangers-on who thought thereby to keep in his good books and profit by so doing. At the time of the truce between him and the English [1444] he enjoyed the favours of a young woman of great attractiveness who was known as 'the beautiful Agnès'. He did not have her to himself nor she him, for he simultaneously kept a bevy of women given to all sorts of frivolity. Alas, this gaggle of concubines bore heavily on the impoverished state of the kingdom, for wherever the King went, he took them along in great style and luxury, spending limitless sums on them, and very considerably more than he spent on the Queen. She could not fail to be aware of what graces and favours were spent on them for they were often lodged in the same building but she had to suffer these ills in silence, for she dared not utter a word. It was not only risky for the Queen to complain of the favourite; when one of the curs at the court wanted to blacken the name of a good man and excite the King's anger against him, he only needed to say that he had spoken ill of the beautiful Agnès. Agnès died of dysentery at the early age of twenty-eight, after, so they say, having borne the King two [actually four] girls and was buried in a superb tomb paid for by the King at the abbey of Jumièges.

Charles was buried with the usual stately pomp and ceremony, as is recorded in the Secret History of Louis XI, King of France, otherwise called the Scandalous Chronicle, *which is published in some editions of Philip de Comines's* Memoirs, *and appears to be contemporary with it:*

On Thursday, the 6th day of August, 1461, the body of the late King Charles VII was brought from Mehun with great solemnity, to the church of Notre Dame in the Fields, without the gates of Paris; and the next day the clergy, nobility, officers, citizens, and abundance of the populace repaired thither, and conducted it from thence to Paris, with a great deal of pomp, ceremony, and respect, as is usual upon such occasions. The funeral procession was thus regulated. Before the corpse were borne two hundred wax-candles weighing four pounds each, adorned and painted with the arms of France, and carried by two hundred inferior persons dressed in long mourning robes and black caps. The body was borne in a litter by the salt-porters of Paris, which was lined and covered with a rich cloth of gold, valued at one thousand two hundred crowns of gold; and upon the top of it was placed the effigies of the late King Charles dressed in his royal robes, with a crown on his head, holding in one hand a sceptre, and in the other a regal truncheon; and in this state was carried to the great church of Notre Dame in Paris; all the bell-men of the city clothed also in black, and bearing on each side of their gowns the arms of France, marching before it; and after them came those that bore the candles, adorned and painted with the same arms, before the litter. After the litter came the Duke of Orléans and the Count of Angoulême as chief mourners, accompanied by the Counts of Eu and Dunois; Monsieur Jean Jouvenelles des Voinins, knight and chancellor of France, and the master of the horse; all clothed in deep mourning, and mounted on horseback. Next to them all the officers of the household to the late King, on foot, by two and two, dressed in deep mourning also; and close to the litter rode six pages in black upon six fine horses covered all over with black velvet, which was a very dismal and melancholy sight to behold. And

OPPOSITE: *Detail of a portrait of Charles VII, c. 1451, by Fouquet. 'So Charles was crowned and anointed King of France with the help of the Pucelle who carried a war standard in her hands and who had cause for joy that he was crowned and anointed in the traditional place, by her efforts alone.'*

OVERLEAF: *Portrait of Charles VIII, c. 1495, attributed to Perréal. Oil painting on the wooden binding of* Oraisons à Notre Seigneur et la Sainte Vierge.

there was such an universal concern and lamentation for his death, that scarce a dry eye was left in the whole city; nay, it is reported that one of his pages took his master's death so to heart, that for four whole days together he neither ate nor drank anything. The next day, which was the 9th of August, his body was removed from the church of Notre Dame, in Paris, about three in the afternoon, and carried with the above-mentioned pomp and ceremony to St Denis, where it was deposited, and where it now lies.

Louis XI

Louis XI was born on 3 July, 1423 at the Bishop's Palace, Bourges. He acceded to the throne on 22 July, 1461 and was crowned at Rheims on 15 August.
*He married, on 24 June, 1436, Margaret of Scotland (1418–1445) and, on 14 February, 1457, Charlotte of Savoy (*c. *1445–1483).*
He reigned for nearly twenty-two years, and died, from a series of strokes, aged sixty, at the château of Plessis-les-Tours on 30 August, 1483. He was buried at Notre Dame de Cléry.

According to the Scandalous Chronicle*:*

Towards the end of this month our most gracious sovereign Louis XI was crowned King of France at the city of Rheims by the Archbishop Jouvenel, where he was attended by the greatest part of the nobility of his kingdom.

Upon the last day of this month of August, the King set out from an hotel named Les Porcherons, which was in the suburbs near the gate of St Honoré, in order to make his public entry into Paris; upon which the whole body of the nobility, clergy, and gentry came out to pay their homage to him, and welcome him to their city; amongst whom were the Bishop of Paris, the whole university, the court of *Parlement*, the mayor of Paris, all the officers of the exchequer, and the provost of the merchants, with the aldermen in their damask robes lined with sables; and the mayor and aldermen, after they had saluted and paid their respects to the King, presented him with the keys of the city gates, through which he was to make his entry, which he very graciously returned; and then the way was ordered to be cleared to make room for others to approach His Majesty, and pay their compliments to him, of which number he made a great many knights on the spot. As the King passed through the gate of St Denis, he found, near the church of St Ladre, a herald mounted on horseback and clothed in the city livery, who presented him with five ladies on the part of the city, richly dressed, and mounted on five fine horses, sumptuously accoutred with rich furniture, on which were embroidered the city arms; and these five ladies were habited after a sort of manner representing the five letters of Paris, and every one of them made a speech to the King, which was prepared for them beforehand.

There was a very great appearance at the King's public entry into Paris, both of his own nobility, and of foreign princes and noblemen, and a great number of persons of note and distinction; who, in honour of the day, and to augment the splendour and magnificence of the triumphal entry, had bestowed vast sums in rich and costly furniture, with which their horses were caparisoned: some of their housings were of the richest cloth of gold, made after different fashions, and lined with sables; others were of crimson velvet, lined with ermine or rich damask, embroidered with gold and silver, and hung round with great silver bells, which were of considerable value; and upon the horses rode fine young pages, the very flower of youth and beauty, richly dressed, and wearing an embroidered scarf over their shoulders, that hung down to the crupper, which made a very noble and gallant show.

The Parisians, on this occasion, caused a very fine ship to be cast in silver, which was borne aloft upon men's shoulders, and just as the King made his entry through the gate of St Denis, it was placed upon the drawbridge near the said gate, to represent the city arms. In it were placed three persons representing the three estates of the kingdom; and in the stern and the poop sat two more personating justice and equity; and out of the scuttle, which was formed in the shape of a fleur-de-lys, issued a king dressed in royal robes, and attended by two angels. A little farther, at the fountain of Ponceau there were wild men that played the parts of gladiators, and near them were placed three handsome wenches stark naked, representing mermaids with lovely hard white bubbies, a glorious sight, sporting and singing gay enlivening airs, which were humoured and accompanied with the melodious harmony of soft music. And to comfort and refresh the people, there were several pipes in the said fountain that ran milk, wine, and hippocras, of which every one drank what he pleased.

Louis XI as dauphin, after years of misunderstanding, intrigued against his father and conspired against him with the barons who found the king had become too powerful. He fled to the court of Philippe, Duke of Burgundy. When his father heard this, he is reputed to have said: 'The Duke of Burgundy has taken in a fox who will eat his hens.' A fair prophecy, for after Louis came to the throne, he found himself at odds with his rebellious subjects who allied themselves with Burgundy and whom he defeated at Montlhéry. But Louis thought war chancy and expensive and preferred guile and patient negotiation to achieve his ends. In an attempt to solve his differences with Philippe of Burgundy's son, Charles the Rash, he went to meet him at Péronne. The Duke promptly took him prisoner. Louis had been imprudent but was caught. He gained his freedom by agreeing to give Charles what he wanted, and promptly broke his promises. 'He who has success likewise

A limestone head of Louis XI from Toul, Meurthe et Moselle.

has honour' was a phrase he used. He continued fighting sporadically with Charles, but on his death in 1477, the great duchy finally reverted to the King for lack of a male heir, and in 1480 Anjou and Maine reverted to the French crown too. Louis left France the richer by eleven provinces.

Philip de Comines, Lord of Argenton, wrote his first six books between 1488 and 1494 and the remaining two probably between 1497 and 1501, but they were not printed until 1649, when Louis XIV took the first proof off the royal press. His portrait of Louis XI was from the life:

The chief reason that induced me to enter upon this subject, is the observation I have made of the many fallacies and circumstances in the world, especially in servants towards their masters; and I have always found that proud and stately princes who will hear but few, are more liable to be imposed on than those who are open and accessible: but of all the princes that I ever had the honour to know, the wisest and most dexterous to extricate himself out of any danger or difficulties in time of adversity, was our master King Louis. He was the most humble in his conversation and habit, and the most painful and indefatigable to win over any man to his side that he thought capable of doing him either much mischief or good; though he was often refused, he would never give over a man that he once undertook, but still pressed and continued his insinuations, promising him largely, and presenting him with such sums and provisions as he knew would satisfy his ambition; and for such as he had discarded in the time of peace and prosperity, he paid dear for their recovery when he had occasion for them again; but when he had once reconciled them, he retained no pique to them for what had passed, but employed them freely for the future. He was naturally kind and indulgent to persons of indifferent condition; and morose to such as he thought had no need of him. Never prince was so conversable, nor so inquisitive as he, for his desire was to know everybody he could; and indeed he knew all persons of any authority or worth in England, Spain, Portugal, and Italy, in the territories of the Dukes of Burgundy and Brittany, and in his own country; and by those qualities he preserved the crown upon his head, which was in much danger by the enemies he had created to himself by his inadvertency upon his accession to the crown. But above all, his great bounty and liberality did him the greatest service. And yet, as he behaved himself wisely in time of distress, so when he thought himself a little out of danger, though it were but by a truce, he would disoblige the servants and officers of his court by mean and trifling ways, which were little to his advantage; and as for peace, he could hardly endure the thoughts of it. He spoke slightly of most people, and rather before their faces, than behind their backs, unless he was afraid of them, and of that sort there were a great many, for he was naturally timorous. When he had done himself any prejudice by his talk, or was apprehensive he should do so, to make them amends whom he had injured, he would say to the person whom he had disobliged, 'I am sensible my tongue has done me a great deal of mischief; but, on the other hand it has sometimes done me good; however, it is but reasonable I should make some reparation for the injury.'

And he never used those kind of apologies to any person, but he did something for the person to whom he made it, and it was always considerable.

It is certainly a great blessing for any prince to have experienced adversity as well as prosperity, good as well as evil, and especially if the good outweighs the evil, as it did in our master. I am of opinion that the troubles he was involved in in his youth, when he fled from his father, and resided six successive years in the court of the Duke of Burgundy, were of great service to him; for there he learned to be complaisant to such as he had occasion to use, which was no little improvement. As soon as his coronation was over, and he began to be a little settled in his kingdom, his mind was wholly bent upon revenge; but he quickly found this inconvenient, repented by degrees of his indiscretion, and made sufficient reparation for his error, by regaining those he had injured upon very dear terms. Besides, I am very confident that if his education had not been different from the usual education of such princes as I have seen in France, he could not so easily have worked himself out of his troubles; for they are brought up to nothing but an idle kind of vanity, both in their apparel and discourse. They have no knowledge of letters, no wise man is suffered to come near them, to improve their understandings; they have stewards and governors that manage their business, but they do nothing themselves: nay, there are some upstart ridiculous Frenchmen who, though they have but a very slender income, will take a pride to bid you, 'Go to his servants, and let them answer you'; thinking by such answers to imitate the state and grandeur of a prince; and I have seen their servants manage them at such a rate, that all the world might see they were sots; and if afterwards they came to apply their mind to business, and would willingly have managed their own affairs, they began so late that they could make nothing of it. And it is certain that all those who have performed any great or memorable action, worthy to be recorded in history, began always in their youth; and this is to be attributed to the method of his education, or some particular blessing from God.

The King had extricated himself out of all his troubles and wars with the great lords of his kingdom, by large presents, and larger promises; was sensible of many false steps he had made; and for the future was resolved to put nothing to a venture that he could gain otherwise. Many were of the opinion it was from his fear and cowardice that this cautious way of acting proceeded; but several persons, who, upon the strength of that imagination durst presume to provoke his anger, found themselves strangely mistaken, and their fancy very ill-grounded, as the Count of Armagnac and others, who paid dear for that opinion; for he knew very well how to distinguish between the appearance and reality of danger: and this I dare boldly say in his commendation, and if I have said it before, it is not unworthy to be repeated, that in my whole life I never knew any man so wise in misfortunes.

Later on:

Our King sent the King of England three hundred cart-loads of the best wines in France as a present, and I think the carts made as great an appearance as the whole army. Upon the strength of the truce several of the English came into the town, where they behaved themselves very imprudently, and without the least regard to their prince's honour; for they entered the town all armed, and in great companies, so that if the King of France could have dispensed with his oath, never was there so handsome an opportunity of cutting off a considerable number of them; but His Majesty's design was only to entertain them nobly, and to settle a firm and lasting peace, that might continue during his reign. The King had ordered two large tables to be placed on each side of the street, at the entrance of the town gate, which were covered with a variety of nice dishes of all sorts of food most proper to relish their wine, of which there was great plenty, and of the richest that France could afford, and abundance of servants in the king's livery to wait and attend on them, but not a drop of water did the English call for. At each of the tables the King had placed five or six jolly drinking companions, persons of rank and condition, to entertain those that had a mind to take a hearty glass.

Those English which were within sight of the gate saw the entertainment, and there were persons appointed on purpose to take their horses by the bridles, and lead them to the tables, where every man was treated handsomely, as he came in his turn, to their very great satisfaction. When they had once entered the town, wherever they went, or whatever they called for, nothing was to be paid; they were liberally furnished with all that they wanted, and they had whatever they had a mind to call for, without paying for it, according to the King of France's orders, who bore all the expense of that entertainment, which lasted three or four days.

Pierre de Bourdeille, Seigneur de Brantôme, who wrote at the end of the sixteenth century, quotes a letter to Monsieur de Bressuire from Louis, in which he reckoned he had his priorities right for he says of it, 'spoken by a brave and valiant king':

I have been informed that the English army in Normandy and elsewhere is dispersed for this year. And as I can tell that you have nothing to do where you are at the moment I am planning to come back to hunt the boar so that I do not miss the season while waiting for the next to take and kill the English. Let me have your news and tell me what is happening to you. At all costs, do not move and let me know if you need me.

Brantôme also has another anecdote which shows Louis in a more attractive light than is usual:

One day he met a young scribe who came to him as he was in a hurry to have something written. Seeing his writing case hanging from his belt the King commanded him to write. As he fumbled in the case to get out his pen two dice fell out at the same time. The King asked what purpose the 'pills' served. 'Sire,' replied the scribe, 'it is a remedy against the plague.' 'Get on with you,' said the King, 'you are a pleasant bawd—a word he often

A late fifteenth-century drawing of Charlotte of Savoy from the Recueil d'Arras.

used—but I'll employ you.' He took him into his service for the King was fond of a ready wit and fast reply.

Louis shut himself away in the last years of his life at the château of Plessis-les-Tours (now in the suburbs of Tours), where he led a strange miserly existence, dressed in fustian and wearing a fur-lined cap hung with leaden medallions. He was ruthless in punishing his enemies and lived there surrounded by his prisoners and his fears. Comines tells us of his last days:

He [the King] began now to decline in age, and to be subject to infirmity; and as he was sitting at dinner one day near Chinon, he was seized on a sudden with a fit that took away his speech. Those who were about him took him from the table, held him to the fire, shut up the windows; and though he endeavoured to get to them for the benefit of the air, yet imagining it for the best, they would not suffer him to stir. It was in March, 1480, when this fit seized upon him after this manner, which deprived him of his speech, understanding, and memory. It was your fortune, my Lord of Vienne, to be present at that time and act the part of a physician; for having ordered him a clyster, and caused the windows to be opened to give him fresh air, he came a little to himself immediately, recovered his speech and his senses in some measure, and mounting on horseback he returned to Forges, for he was taken with this fit in a small village about a quarter of a league off, whither he went to hear mass. He was diligently attended, and made signs for everything he wanted; among other things, he desired the official of Tours to come and take his confession, and made signs that I should be sent for, for I was gone to Argenton, about ten leagues off.

Upon my return I found him at the table. He made signs that I should lie in his chamber; he understood little that was said to him, and his words were not intelligible; but he felt no manner of pain. I waited on him above a month at the table, and in his chamber as one of the gentlemen of the bedchamber, which I took for a great honour, and it gave me great reputation. At the end of two or three days he began to recover his speech and his senses; and he fancied nobody understood him so clearly as myself, and therefore would have me always attend him. He confessed himself to the official in my presence, for otherwise he could not have understood what he said; there was no great matter in his confession, for he had been at confession a few days before; because whenever the kings of France touch for the king's evil, they confess themselves first, and he never missed touching once every week; and if other princes do not the same, I think they are highly to blame; for there are always great numbers of people to be touched.

On the other hand, he remembered that his father, King Charles, in the last fit of which he died, took a fancy that his courtiers had a mind to poison him, to make way for his son; and it made so deep an impression upon him, that he refused to eat, and by the advice of his physicians, and all the chief of his favourites, it was concluded he should be forced; and so after a great deliberation, they forced victuals down his throat, upon which violence he died. King Louis, having always condemned that way of proceeding, took it very heinously that they should use any violence with him, and yet he pretended to be more angry than he was; for the great matter that moved him was an apprehension that they would govern him in everything else, and pretend he was unfit for the administration of public affairs, by reason of the imbecility of his senses.

He would also see all letters and dispatches as they arrived, and couriers arrived every hour; they shewed him the originals, and I read them to him: he would pretend to understand them, take them into his own hand, and make as if he read them to himself, when, in truth, he did not understand one syllable of them: yet he would offer now and then at a word, and make signs what answers should be given; but little business was dispatched during his illness, the greatest part hanging in suspense till we could see what would be the event; for he was a prince that required all things to be done with the utmost nicety and exactness. This indisposition continued about a fortnight, at the end of which he recovered his speech and senses pretty well; but he remained very weak, and in great fear of a relapse, for naturally he was not apt to put confidence in his physicians.

His indisposition continued for about a fortnight, he recovered a little but shortly afterwards:

The King sent for me back to him, to Beaujeu, in Beaujolais: I was amazed to find him so weak and wondered how he had strength enough to bear the fatigue of travelling so well as he did; but his great spirit carried him through all difficulties.

The King returned to Tours, and kept himself so close, that very few were admitted to see him; for he was grown jealous of all his courtiers, and afraid they would either depose, or deprive him of some part of his regal authority. He removed, from about him, all his old favourites, especially if they had any extraordinary familiarity with him; but he took nothing from them, only commanded them to their posts or country seats: but this lasted not long, for he died shortly after. He did many odd things, which made some believe his senses were a little impaired; but they knew not his humours. As to his jealousy, all princes are prone to it, especially those who are wise, having many enemies, and have oppressed many people, as our master had done: besides, he found he was not beloved by the nobility of the kingdom, nor many of the commons; for he had taxed them more than any of his predecessors, though he now had some thoughts of easing them, as I said before.

In the first place, nobody was admitted into Plessis-du-Parc, which was the place where he kept himself, but his domestic servants and his archers, which were four hundred, some of which kept constant guard at the gate, while others walked continually about, to prevent its being surprised. No lord, nor person of quality was permitted to lie in the castle, nor to enter with any of his retinue; nor, indeed, did any of them come in, but the Lord of Beaujeu, the present Duke of Bourbon, who was his son-in-law. Round about the castle of Plessis he caused a lattice, or iron gate to be set up, spikes of iron planted in the wall, and a kind of crowsfeet, with several points, to be placed along the ditch, wherever there was a possibility for any person to enter; besides which, he caused four watch-houses to be made, all of thick iron, and full of holes, out of which they might shoot at their pleasure, and which was very noble, and cost above 20,000 francs, in which he placed forty of his crossbow-men, who were to be upon guard night and day, with orders to let fly upon any man that offered to come near before the opening of the gate in the morning. He also persuaded himself that his subjects would be mighty fond of divesting him of his power, and taking the administration of affairs upon themselves, when they saw their opportunity; and, indeed, there were some persons about the court, that consulted together how they might get in, and dispatched those affairs which at present hung in suspense; but they durst not attempt it, and they acted wisely; for the King had provided against everything. He often changed the gentlemen of his bedchamber, and all the rest of his servants, alleging that nothing was more delightful to nature than novelty. For conversation, he kept only one or two with him, and those of inferior condition, and of no great reputation; who, if they had been wise, might well think, as soon as he was dead, the best they could expect would be to be turned out of all their employments; and so it happened.

The Scandalous Chronicler *finishes the story:*

On Monday the 25th August the King fell very ill at Montils, near Tours, and in two hours' time lost his speech and his senses, and the news of his death came to Paris on Wednesday the 27th of the same month; upon which the mayor and aldermen ordered the city gates to be shut up, and a strong guard to be placed at each of them, that none might go out or in without being examined, which made the common people cry out that the King was dead; but it was a false alarm, for His Majesty was only in a fit, out of which he presently recovered, and lived till Saturday the 30th of August and then died about six or seven in the evening of the same day.

As soon as he was dead his body was embalmed, and buried in the church of Notre Dame de Cléry, at Montils, having in his lifetime ordered it should be so, and positively commanded the dauphin not to bury him in the church of St Denis, where three Kings of France his illustrious predecessors were interred. He never gave any reason for it, but some people were of opinion it was for the sake of the church, which he had liberally endowed, and out of a singular veneration for the Blessed Virgin, who was worshipped there after a more solemn manner than in any other place in the kingdom. The King had during his whole reign, by evil advice, committed great injustice in his kingdom, and so miserably oppressed and harassed his people, that the very reflection of his tyrannical usage of them stung him to the heart, and almost drove him to despair; so that when he lay upon his death-bed he sincerely repented of all his sins, and gave prodigious sums of money to the clergy to pray for his soul, and rewarded them for their prayers with what he had by violence and extortion gotten of his subjects. It must be owned that his was a very busy reign, and full of many great and important actions, yet he managed his affairs so well, that he forced all his enemies to submit to his mercy, and was equally dreaded both abroad and at home. He lay for a long time before his death under very sharp and severe illnesses, which forced his physicians to make use of violent and painful applications, which though they were not so successful as to recover his health and save his life, yet, doubtless, they were very beneficial to his soul, and, perhaps, the chief means of saving it from eternal damnation, and fixing it in paradise, through His tender mercy who liveth and reigneth world without end.

Louis was indeed a great king and his virtues were appreciated by that sharp critic Francis Bacon (1561–1626) writing a century later.

Yet take him [Henry VII] with all his defects, if a man should compare him with the kings his concurrents in France and Spain, he shall find him more politic than Louis the Twelfth of France, and more entire and sincere than Ferdinando of Spain. But if you shall change Louis the Twelfth for Louis the Eleventh, who lived a little before, then the consort is more perfect. For that Louis the Eleventh, Ferdinando, and Henry, may be esteemed for the *tres magi* of kings of those ages.

Charles VIII

Charles VIII was born on 30 June, 1470 at the château of Amboise. He acceded on 30 August, 1483 and was crowned on 14 May, 1484.
He married, on 6 December, 1491, Anne of Brittany (1476–1514).
He reigned for fourteen years, and died, as a result of hitting his head, aged twenty-eight, at Amboise on 7 April, 1498. He was buried at St Denis.

Charles VIII was only thirteen when he ascended the throne and was cared for by his sister Anne of Beaujeu—Madame la Grande—and her husband Pierre who ruled as regents.
Comines has this to say of his education:

Upon the death of Louis XI who died on the 30th day of August, in the year 1483, his only son Charles VIII then dauphin of France, came to the crown. He was but thirteen years and two months old, when his father died; and therefore the solemnity of his coronation was deferred till the year following, that he might be full fourteen before he was crowned. The King his father had educated him at Amboise in such a private and solitary manner, that none but his domestics were ever permitted to have access to him; neither would His Majesty suffer him to learn any more Latin than this single sentence, '*Qui nescit dissimulare, nescit regnare*' [He who knows not how to dissimulate knows not how to reign]; not that he had any aversion to human learning, but only out of fondness and paternal care, he was afraid that too great an application to his studies might weaken and spoil the delicate and tender constitution of the prince. However, King Charles, after his coming to the crown, grew extremely desirous of learning, applied himself very closely to the reading of history and other books of humanity in the French language, and even endeavoured to make himself master of the Latin.

Brantôme bears Comines out:

I cannot do better than start with our little King Charles VIII. I say little because, during his lifetime and for some time afterwards, this is how he was described on account of his small stature and weak constitution, although in fact he was great in courage, spirit and honour. He was brought up by his father Louis XI at the château of Amboise in great seclusion and looked after by few people not at all in the style you would expect for a king's son. Who would have believed that a king so ill-fed could have developed such courage and ambition?

There is no need to labour the virtues of King Charles, of whom, according to my aunt, Madame de Dampierre, François I had said that he would always place this little King amongst the great Kings of France.

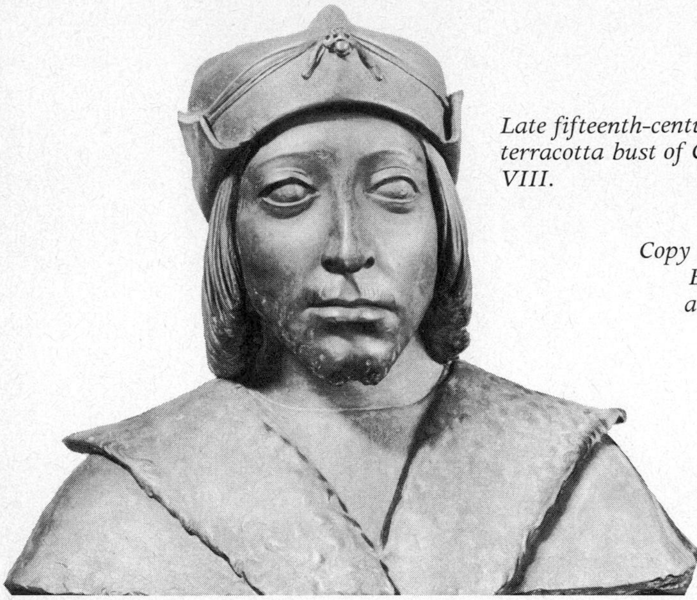

Late fifteenth-century Italian terracotta bust of Charles VIII.

Copy of a portrait of Anne of Brittany by an unknown artist. Sixteenth century, French school.

Queen Anne, his wife, was one of the most beautiful, honest and virtuous women in the world, with a pretty and radiant face.

The Venetian Senate required her ambassadors to make a full report on their embassy on their return from a tour of duty. This is fortunate for us for they were always well-informed, and frank.

The King is twenty-two, small and ill-shaped; he has an ugly face, with large white eyes—better formed for seeing evil than good. His hooked nose is larger and longer than it should be and his gross lips are always open. He has a nervous habit of twitching his hands which are far from beautiful, and his speech is slow. In my opinion, which may not be fair, I think that he is not worth much either in body or soul despite the fact that the whole of Paris praises him for his tennis playing, hunting and jousting—exercises to which, rightly or wrongly, he devotes a lot of his time. He is also praised for the fact that, unlike his earlier habits where he left the discussion of affairs of state to his secret council, he now wishes to be the one who makes the decisions, and he is reputed to do so well.

And of his wife, Anne of Brittany:

The Queen is seventeen; small, she too is thin and has an obvious limp despite wearing high heels. She has dark hair, a pretty face, and is, for her age, very wily. Once she has set her mind on something she will get it by any means, for she is jealous of and greedy for the King beyond reason, so much so that since becoming his wife there have been few nights that she has not slept with him—with such success that she is now eight months pregnant.

Two other Venetians on a later visit have this to say of Charles and Anne, whom they visited two days later:

We found His Majesty in a large room sitting on a daïs with a tapestry on the ground and a canopy of alexandrian velvet embroidered with gold fleurs-de-lys. There were two benches along the length of the room, the one on the right occupied by the princes of the blood, and that on the left by the resident prelates, both of whom constituted the King's privy council. At one end of the room was a bench for us and the King was most insistent that we should remain seated while we told him the purpose of our embassy. It was there that we presented our letters of credence to him.

She [the Queen] was in a room with Monsieur de Bourbon, Monsieur d'Orléans and a large number of ladies and gentlemen of the court. When we had greeted her and told her what Messer Francesco had told the King two days earlier, the vice-chancellor of Brittany replied on her behalf but neither I nor my colleagues could make out whether her reply was in French or Italian and you will forgive me if I do not transcribe the response since in truth I did not understand a word of it. We gave her the silks and cloths of gold which she graciously accepted.

Charles paid attention to the minor points of the good life:

Sir Treasurer,

Since I am to spend Christmas at Amboise I would like some good mustard made with non-fermented wine with which to regale my guests. To this end, will you please as soon as you receive this letter send me three dozen barrels of the best quality you can find with all speed, making sure there is nothing wrong with it.

When Charles came to maturity and had pacified Brittany by marrying the Duke's daughter, Anne, he felt the lure of Italy, as his predecessors had of the Holy Land, and he had dreams of glory. At first he was well received by the Italians and, going from victory to victory, he reached Naples. But the Neapolitans who had welcomed him with flowers at first, revolted against him. The rest of Europe did not care for such French aggrandizement and he was forced to retreat, although with a numerically smaller army he succeeded in winning the battle of Fornovo on his way home. But his behaviour in Italy was not altogether becoming.

The next day the King made his entrance into Florence, where Peter of Medici had prepared a noble apartment for him in his own palace; but as soon as His Majesty was informed of the flight of Peter of Medici, he fell a-rifling the palace, upon pretence that the bank at Lyons was in arrear to him for a considerable sum of money; and among other things he seized upon a whole unicorn's horn, valued at six or seven thousand ducats, besides two great pieces of another, and several other things; and other people followed his example.

Charles hit his head on a lintel post at Amboise, and Comines has plenty to say of his death and lying-in-state:

I shall give you an account of the death of Charles VIII, our King, who died suddenly at his castle of Amboise, where he began the most august and magnificent building that any prince had undertaken for a hundred years before, both in the town and the castle; and this appears by the remaining towers, to the top of which one may ride on horseback. As to his building in the town, the design was admirable, the model lofty, and would have required a great length of time. He had brought his artificers, as his carvers, painters, and such, from Italy, so that the whole fabric seemed the enterprise of a young prince, who thought nothing of dying so soon; for he collected whatever was commended to him, either in France, Italy or Flanders. Besides this great work, his mind was also bent upon another expedition into Italy, being sensible he had committed many great errors in his first; he spoke often of them, and resolved, if ever he recovered what he had lost in that country, he would keep it better than he had done.

The King had also resolved with himself to live a more strict and religious life than he had formerly done, to regulate the laws, to reform the church, and so to rectify his revenue that he would not raise above twelve millions of francs on his subjects by way of tax.

The King being in great glory in relation to this world, and in a good mind as to God, on the 7th of April 1498, being Palm Sunday eve, took his Queen, Anne of Brittany, by the hand, and led her out of her chamber to a place where she had never been before, to see them play at ball in the castle-ditch. They entered together into a gallery. It was the nastiest place about the castle, broken down at the entrance, and exposed to every nuisance; the King was not a tall man, yet he knocked his head as he went in. He spent some time in looking at the gamesters, and talked freely with everybody: I was not there myself, having retired to my country seat about a week before; but his confessor and the gentlemen of his bedchamber, who were then about him, told me what I write. The last expression he used while he was in health was, that he hoped never to commit a mortal sin again, nor a venial one if he could help it; and with those words in his mouth he fell down backwards, and lost his speech. It was about two in the afternoon when he fell, and he lay till eleven o'clock at night. Thrice he recovered his speech, but he quickly lost it again, as his confessor told me, who had confessed him twice that week, one of course, and the other upon occasion of his touching for the king's evil. Everyone went into the gallery that pleased. He was laid upon a course bed at first, and he never went off it till he died, which was nine hours after. The confessor told me, that every time he recovered his speech he called out upon God, the glorious Virgin Mary, St Claude, and St Blaise, to assist him. And thus died that great and powerful monarch, in a sordid and filthy place; although he had so many magnificent palaces of his own, and was building another more stately than any of them, yet he died in a chamber much unsuitable to himself.

The distemper of which the King died was an apoplexy, or a catarrh, which the physicians hoped would have fallen down into one of his arms, and though it might have taken away the use of that, they were in no fear of his death. His Majesty had four physicians about him, but his greatest confidence was in him that had the least knowledge and experience in physic; and by his directions he was so entirely governed, that the other three durst not give their judgments, though they saw the indications of death, and would have ordered him a purge three or four days before. All people addressed themselves to the Duke of Orléans immediately, as next heir to the crown; but the gentlemen of King Charles's bedchamber buried him in great pomp and solemnity. As soon as he was dead, service was begun for his soul. He lay eight days at Amboise, part of them in a chamber very richly furnished, and part in the church. In short, he lay in great state, and the whole solemnity was more costly than the obsequies of any of his predecessors had been. The gentlemen of his bedchamber, all that belonged to his person, and all the officers of his court, never stirred from his corpse, but waited constantly; and the service continued till his body was interred, which it was about a month after; and, as I have been told by some of the officers of his exchequer, this ceremony cost forty-five thousand francs. I came to Amboise two days after his death, went to pay my devotions upon his tomb, and stayed there five or six hours.

To speak impartially, I never saw so solemn a mourning for any prince, nor one that continued so long; and no wonder, for he had been more bountiful to his favourites, to the gentlemen of his bedchamber, and ten or twelve gentlemen of his privy chamber, and had treated them better, and given them greater estates than any king had ever done before; and indeed he gave some of them too much. Besides, he was the most affable and best natured prince in the world. I verily believe he never said that word to any man that could in reason displease him; so that he could never have died in a better hour to make himself memorable in history, and lamented by all that served him. I do really think I was the only person in the whole world he was unkind to; but, being sensible it was in his youth, and not at all his own doing, I could not resent it.

Louis XII

Louis XII was born on 27 June, 1462 at Blois. He acceded to the throne on 7 April, 1498 and was crowned on 27 May.
He married, on 8 September, 1476, Jeanne of France (1464–1505) whom he repudiated in 1498; on 8 January, 1499, Anne of Brittany (1476–1514); and on 9 October, 1514, Mary of England (1497–1534).
He reigned for sixteen years, and died, of gout, aged fifty-two, at the palace of Tournelles, Paris on 1 January, 1515. He was buried at St Denis.

Louis XII like other sons before him gave his father great trouble when he was the Duke of Orléans but endeared himself by not punishing his enemies when he came to the throne. 'The King of France,' he said, 'does not avenge the injuries of the Duke of Orléans.' He became one of France's great and best-loved kings, earning the title of Father of his People, despite what in his early years, the Venetian ambassador, Domenico di Trevisan, had to say of him:

The King is forty. He is tall and thin; he is abstemious in his diet, virtually living on boiled beef. He is mean, stingy and disliked; he greatly enjoys falconry which he practises from September to April.

and another Venetian tells of Louis's habits:

The King gave audience in an inn at Etampes.

You will say that a king should not hold court in an inn, but I would reply that in Etampes the best houses are the inns. There is a royal palace here where the Queen—wife of the late King—puts up but His Majesty wished to give audience in this pub, all draped in alexandrian velvet with gold fleurs-de-lys. The King looks very well and healthy. He is forty and seems very fit. Today he received the ambassadors in secret and they say that tomorrow he will confess, take communion and touch for the scrofula (it is said that the sufferers, once touched by the king, recover—a miracle). We are like gypsies here, like people with no fixed abode. Where are we going? I don't know. Some people say we shall return to Paris, some that we shall follow the King to Bourges. In sum, no one knows.

Whether Louis felt he had been forced to marry Jeanne, the daughter of Louis XI and sister of Charles VIII or not, he had been in love with Anne of Brittany for some time and on his accession he arranged for an annulment of his marriage. He promptly married

The portrait of Louis XII by Perréal which the King sent to Henry VIII of England in 1514.

OPPOSITE: *Painting of Jeanne of France as a saint in ecstasy before the sacred heart by Jean Boucher.*

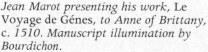

Jean Marot presenting his work, Le Voyage de Génes, *to Anne of Brittany, c. 1510. Manuscript illumination by Bourdichon.*

Charles's widow, thereby also retaining Brittany for the crown. Brantôme speaks of both Jeanne and Anne:

Jeanne of France, daughter of Louis XI, was religious but was so good-natured that after her death she was held to have been a saint and to have worked miracles on account of her noble behaviour after her husband, Louis XII, had repudiated her, when she lived at Bourges doing good works and never complaining of her separation. The King claimed that he had been forced to marry her fearing the wrath of her father and that he had never known [in the biblical sense] her nor touched her despite the fact that they had been married for a fair time and slept together. But Jeanne said that if her husband swore he had not known her she must be a virgin. One may doubt whether Louis, having slept with her so often during the reign of her father and Charles her brother, would have dared deny doing so during their lifetime but after their deaths he did.

Since I have to talk of ladies, I don't wish to bother with those of the past of whom the history books are full and it would be a waste of paper so I will deal principally with the French of my own times or those of whom I have hearsay knowledge.

I will begin with Anne of Brittany, the most worthy and honourable queen since Blanche of Castille, mother of St Louis.

Anne was the wealthy heiress to the duchy of Brittany, held to be one of the most beautiful women in Christianity and thus greatly sought after. Monsieur the Duke of Orléans, who became Louis XII, when young pursued her; then Maximilian, Duke of Austria, later Emperor, became engaged to her but Charles VIII, warned that it would not be good to have so powerful a sovereign with a foothold in his kingdom, broke his own engagement to Margaret of Flanders and married Anne himself.

However, even though she was sought after for her property she was worthy in herself. She was good-looking; with a good figure, of medium height. It is true that she had one leg very slightly shorter than the other but it did not spoil her appearance. Her moral virtues matched her physical beauty; she was virtuous, wise and straightforward; friendly, aimiable and gentle. She was charitable, though quick to take offence and not easily placated when aroused.

The King her husband went to Naples and while he was there she made a good governor of France with the counsellors the King had given her but she was very conscious of her station and kept her rank and privacy, despite her youth.

She was very sad at the death of Charles as much for the friendship she bore him as to see herself only half a queen as she had no children. I have it on good authority that her ladies commiserated with her at being the widow of so great a king and ill-suited to be considered of lower rank, for King Louis was married to Jeanne of France. She replied that she would rather remain his widow than lower herself with anyone else and that she did not despair of being the reigning queen again if she so wished. She was enabled to say this because she had hopes of revivifying Louis's love for her. And that is what happened for King Louis, having repudiated Jeanne his wife, remembered his early passion for Anne and took her in marriage.

But though Anne gave Louis children, one of whom was married to Louis's heir, the Count of Angoulême, Louis had no son, and on Anne's death in 1514 he was advised to remarry. Negotiations opened with Mary Tudor, the sister of Henry VIII of England. Louis wrote to Thomas Wolsey, then Archbishop of York:

Since it is a long time since I have had news of the King, my good brother and cousin, your master, nor of the Queen my wife, I send urgently by this my messenger court-crier of France to them and have instructed him to tell you and say to you at once and before all else, of his mission. Please believe what he will tell you: that on his return he should bring me, what I wish above all else, letters and news from them. Please also be good enough to present him to my wife and you will do me a great favour. I pray God, Monsieur de York, my good friend, keep you in His care.

and Mary replied to Louis in her own hand, the letter sealed with the arms of England and France:

Monseigneur, I humbly recommend me to your grace. I have received, from the Bishop

Detail from a portrait of Mary of England by Mabuse.

of Lincoln, the affectionate letters which it has pleased you to write. They have given me great joy and comfort and I assure you, monseigneur, that there is nothing I desire more than to see you, and the King my brother is hurrying to arrange for me to take sea passage, which I pray to God will be a short one. I beg you in the meanwhile, to console me, let me have your news often.

Mary and Louis were married in October 1514. Robert de la Marck, Seigneur de Fleurange, who was François, Count of Angoulême's boyhood friend, and had the delightful habit of referring to himself in his writings as the 'Adventurer', has this to say of the wedding celebrations:

The next morning the marriage was celebrated, not in church but in a fine large room draped in cloth of gold where all could witness it. The King and Queen were seated, and the Queen—with her hair flowing loose—had a hat on her head, the richest in Christianity and did not wear a crown because that is the custom unless she is crowned at St Denis.

After the ceremony the evening was spent at a great feast and at nightfall the King and Queen went to bed. Next morning the King reported that he had performed marvels. At least, that is what he said for he was not very virile. He was as kind a prince in war as in other things and in anything he set his mind to. It was a pity that he was troubled by gout for he was not an old man.

After the Queen had been crowned at St Denis she made her entry into Paris which was very splendid, for she was a fine lady and it was a long time since the English had seen the glories of France. So she went to her palace.

Monsieur d'Angoulême [later François I] then a young man, wished to show that he

Marble statues from the tomb of Louis XII and Anne of Brittany at St Denis from the workshop of the Juste family, 1517–31. The tomb was the first monumental tomb to be built in St Denis and was erected in 1531 by the orders of François I. The figures were sculpted under the direction of Jean Juste in about 1517–18 at Tours.

approved of this marriage despite the fact that if the Queen produced a son he would have been very put out. As it happened, two days after the wedding at Abbeville, he took the Adventurer aside on his way from the King's lodgings to his own and said, 'Adventurer, I am better pleased and more at ease than I have been for twenty years for I am certain—or have been lied to—that the King and Queen cannot have children which is to my advantage.' He must have heard this from his wife, Madame Claude, who didn't move from the room of the Queen and Madame d'Aumont who was her woman of honour and who slept in her room.

The King left his palace and went to lodge at Tournelles in Paris because it was a more salubrious spot and as he did not feel well. He wished to be a gentle companion to his wife but overspent himself for he was no longer man enough, having been ill for a long time and suffering from gout.

He had nearly died five or six years ago for he was given up for lost by the doctors and lived on a horrifying diet which he broke when he was with his wife and the doctors spoke truly when they said if he continued thus he would die.

The Parisian clerks said, 'the King of England has sent a mare to the King of France to take him quickly and gently to heaven or hell'.

He died on the first day of the year, on one of the worst days I have ever seen, and I swear on my faith that it was a pity, for he was a gentle prince who had done much good in his time.

After his death Monsieur d'Angoulême put on mourning, as the closest to the throne, and went to the palace and told everyone at court, and especially his mother. Strangely enough it was the first day of the year and he had been born on a New Year's day; his father had died on a New Year's day and he succeeded on New Year's day.

Brantôme has the final word:

Louis's enemies were unable to complain of anything about him or a single inch of his realm. For he died a peaceful and powerful king and entitled to be called the best and most honourable King of France, greatly loved by his people and called their Father, which gave rise to the belief that he was blessed and loved by God. His reputation was such that after his death when the people of France were groaning under the weight of taxes they would always hark back to the days of the good rule of Louis XII.

Even though he was as young as his predecessor when he came to the throne he achieved great deeds; for he was brave and worthy. When he engaged the Venetians in battle, he was told that the lodgings intended for him had been taken. 'So they are occupied, are they?' he said. 'Yes, sir.' 'O well,' he replied, 'we shall have to sleep on our bellies'—which he proceeded to do. Then he dislodged them, gave battle and beat them. And when the artillery fired he was told to keep back. 'Certainly not,' he said. 'I am not afraid; and if anyone is, let him get behind me and he will not suffer.'

He was handsome and good-looking as his portraits show.

He left two daughters, Claude, who became Queen of France, and Anne, who married the Duke of Ferrara. He had no children by his last wife Mary of England [Henry VII's daughter]. He didn't much care for her as I have said before. They didn't live together for long because this great beauty wore him out and the effort required of him was too much for his age so he died.

François I

François I was born on 12 September, 1494 at Cognac. He acceded to the throne on 1 January, 1515 and was crowned at Rheims on 25 January, 1515.
He married, on 18 May, 1514, Claude of France (1499–1524) and on 8 July, 1530, Eleanor of Austria (1498–1558).
He reigned for thirty-two years, and died, probably of syphilis, aged fifty-two, at Rambouillet on 31 March, 1547. He was buried at St Denis.

François I was handsome, gallant, noble in manner; the king of gentlemen and the gentleman king. He had a love of glory and grandeur and he wanted France to be foremost in both war and the arts. Fleurange, his friend, wrote:

The King, finding himself at peace on all his borders, young [21], rich, powerful and of good heart, and surrounded by people who did not discourage war— which is after all the most noble exercise for a prince or man of breeding if the cause be just—set about organising his army to travel to Italy.

He put together a fine army consisting of the flower of the French chivalry amongst whom shone the famous knight Bayard, he who was sans peur et sans reproche. *With great courage they crossed the mountains by almost inaccessible roads and they planned a surprise attack on Lombardy when they found their route barred by the Swiss. The Swiss, who had beaten Charles the Rash, were terrifying soldiers. The battle lasted the whole day and when night fell it wasn't clear who had won. Both armies slept on the battlefield and even the King bedded down on a gun-carriage. The fight started again at dawn but the Swiss gave in. The victory of Marignano (1515) was won, and François allowed himself to be knighted by Bayard. After this he made peace with the Swiss and the French have never been at war with them since.*

Shortly afterwards the Emperor of Germany died. Emperors of Germany did not succeed each other from father to son as did the French; they were elected, as deputies are today. The conqueror of Marignano was himself a candidate since he hoped to keep the imperial crown from a prince he had reason to fear. Charles V was a grandson of Charles the Rash, and was already in possession of much territory in Europe and in America, which Christopher Columbus had just discovered. However Charles V was elected and became Emperor. He was a redoubtable enemy for France and the battle with him lasted many years.

François I had seen the danger. His first worry was whether Henry VIII of England would take Charles's side against him. So to win his friendship he gave a great feast known as 'the Field of the Cloth of Gold' because of the rich materials, cavalcades and parties given at it. But Henry, fearful that François should show himself more magnificent and generous than he, was jealous and favoured the Emperor.

Thus it was that one of the most terrible attacks on France began. The front extended along the whole of France's borders. Bayard performed prodigies of valour, but he was killed in battle and wished to breathe his last with his face turned towards the enemy. François I himself paid with his own body. When Charles's imperial soldiers invaded Provence he marched against them, forced them back and followed them into Italy. There at the battle of Pavia (1525) it seemed at first as if the French were winning, but François thought the victory was too quickly won and continued to thrust into the fight so impetuously that the French guns had to cease firing lest they hit him. Soon, isolated and with his best knights fallen by his side, he had to give in. On the night of Pavia he wrote to his mother, Louise of Savoy: 'All is lost save honour.'

The King of France, as in the time of Jean the Good, was a prisoner again. Charles kept him for a long while and only released him when he promised to cede Burgundy to him. But the Burgundians wanted to stay French and an assembly decided that since the promise was extracted by force it was void, and in any case no province of the realm could be ceded to a foreign power.

François wrote to Charles from his prison in Madrid:

Monsieur, my brother. I have heard from the Archbishop of Ambrun and my first president of Paris the resolution they have heard about my release and it displeases me that what is asked is not in my power, for you know that I wish to be and remain your friend. But knowing that you cannot with honesty say to me that you wish to keep me prisoner forever, which would be to ask the impossible, for my part I am willing to take imprisonment in my stride, since I am sure that God who knows that I do not deserve a long one, being taken in war, will give me the strength to bear it patiently. I have no regrets save only that your good words which you sent during my illness had no effect. Being by blood and by marriage your brother and friend, François.

When François returned to France he made up for lost time, not only with women but in building fine palaces and encouraging the arts, so that he may truly be called a prince of the Renaissance. Brantôme is blunt but fair:

François had too many affairs; when young and free, he made love indiscriminately and would go a-whoring anywhere. It was from this that he caught the syphilis which shortened his life for he died at no great age.

When he saw the difficulties his illness caused him and was told that if he continued in this promiscuous way he would get worse, and that he must be more careful about whom he made love to, he set up a court, to which beautiful and virtuous princesses, great ladies and young women of quality flocked. Its purpose was to keep him on a straighter, narrower and healthier path.

When he returned from his imprisonment he took as his mistress Mademoiselle

Portrait of François I between 1525 and 1530 by Jean Clouet.

d'Helly who was pretty and suited. Later he created her Duchess of Etampes, married her to Monsieur de Poinctièvre and gave her many lavish gifts. But he did not reform to the point where he had no other mistresses; it was just that she was the most important, and indeed she was not faithful to him either. Unfaithfulness is not surprising in women who have made a career out of love and who have enjoyed its fruits but she was a worthy and straightforward lady and did not abuse her position.

But, in spite of all his love affairs, the King did not neglect the country nor the affairs of state or anything connected with its well-being or honour. He did not become enslaved by his women nor did he allow himself to be led by the nose by them nor preyed upon as so many previous kings and princes have done. He loved them in moderation and with discretion, and when he needed them he took them without much ado. He gave them generous presents and was open-handed with them for what woman, of whatever station, does not like gifts? Moreover it is right to believe that one good deed deserves another; what is wrong is to lose one's substance over them; and in this respect the King, like his son Henri II, is blameless.

Not only did this King keep a magnificent table, but what magnificent buildings did he erect! At Fontainebleau, which was a wilderness, he has built the most beautiful house in Christendom. I call it a wilderness for before this King that is what his predecessors called it and treasury records show letters signed 'from our desert at Fontainebleau'. François has created a château that is large and spacious with room for a small world, with beautiful gardens, boskets, fountains and all manner of pleasing arrangements for leisure activities. He was very open-handed and derived great pleasure from his generosity.

He gave generously to the gentlemen and captains who served him well during his wars but not as liberally as his grandson does. He never forgot their names but, even more praiseworthy, knew and acknowledged the greater part of the nobility, was cognisant of their family history and took pity on those who had become impoverished, helping them by saying nothing in the world was worse than to be poor having been rich. Everyone wondered how he could sustain the huge expenses of the wars and at the same time be so open-handed, especially to women, for he gave them a great deal, and he gave many parties and erected expensive buildings. His furniture cost a great deal too.

Benvenuto Cellini, who enjoyed François's patronage, tells as much about himself as he does about the King in his Memoirs:

So when I brought my Jupiter into this same gallery, and saw the grand display, all arranged with such art, I said to myself, 'This is being under a very hot fire. Now God be my aid!' So I set up my statue, placing it to the very best advantage possible; and then I waited till the great King came in. In his right hand my Jupiter grasped his thunderbolt, as if about to hurl it; in his left he held the world. Among the flames of the bolt I had skilfully inserted a white waxen torch. Now Madame d'Etampes kept the King away till night came on, seeking to harm me, either by preventing him from coming at all, or at least till darkness should hinder my work being seen to advantage. But God protects those who have faith in Him; and so just the contrary happened. For as soon as I saw the night falling, I lit the torch in the hand of the Jupiter, and as it was somewhat raised above the head of the statue, the light fell from above and made it seem much more beautiful than it had appeared by daylight.

Well, the King appeared at last, with Madame d'Etampes, the dauphin, his son (now the King), the dauphiness, his brother-in-law, the King of Navarre, and Madame Marguerite, his daughter, besides several lords of the court, who had been schooled by Madame d'Etampes to speak against me. When I saw His Majesty come in, I made my lad Ascanio push the statue gently forward; and as my contrivance was arranged with some skill, this movement gave to the striking figure an additional appearance of life. The antiques were now left standing somewhat behind; and mine was the first to catch the eyes of the spectators. The King exclaimed on the instant, 'This is by far the finest thing which has ever been seen; and much as I delight in works of art and understand them, I could never have imagined the hundredth part of the wonder of this one.' Even the lords, whose part it was to speak against me, seemed as if they could not praise my work enough.

Claude of France surrounded by her daughters and daughters-in-law. From a miniature in Catherine of Medici's Book of Hours. Early sixteenth century.

Drawing of Madame d'Etampes, French school, sixteenth century.

But Madame d'Etampes said boldly, 'Surely you have no eyes! Do you not see the fine bronze antiques over there? In them is displayed the real power of a sculptor's art; not in this modern rubbish.' Then the King came forward—the others following him—and glanced at the casts; but as the light was below them, they did not show up well, and he cried, 'Whoever wished to harm this man has done him a great benefit; for this statue of his is now proved to surpass these wonderful figures with which it is compared. So Benvenuto cannot be made too much of; for not only do his works hold their own with the antiques, but they surpass them.' Thereupon Madame d'Etampes said, if they were to see the work by day, it would not seem a thousandth part as fine as now it did by night; besides they had to consider that I had put a veil over the figure to cover up its faults. Now this was a very thin veil, which I had gracefully hung over the Jupiter, to enhance its majesty. At her words I removed it, lifting it from below, and disclosing the fine genital members. Then, giving vent to my anger, I tore it to pieces. She thought I had uncovered these parts to shame her; but the wise King, seeing her anger, and perceiving, too, that I was overcome by passion, and was about to speak my mind, said, uttering the words deliberately in his own tongue, 'Benvenuto, not a word. Keep silence, and you shall have a thousandfold more money than you can wish for.'

When he came to my house, I led him to certain large apartments on the ground floor, in

Portrait of Eleanor of Austria, c. 1530. Spanish school.

which I had put together the whole of my large door. When he came upon it, the King was wonderstruck, so that he could not find utterance for the abuse he had promised Madame d'Etampes he would hurl at me. Still he did not want to fail altogether to find an opportunity of reproving me according to his promise. So he began thus: 'There is a most important thing, Benvenuto, that men like you, full of talent though you are, should ever keep in mind. It is this: that with all your great abilities you can do nothing by yourselves. You can only show your greatness through the opportunities we put in your way. I counsel you, therefore, to appear more docile—less proud, less headstrong. I remember that I expressly ordered you to make me twelve silver statues; and I did not ask for anything else. You have undertaken to make a salt-cellar, and vases, and heads, and doors, and ever so many other things; so that I am quite overwhelmed, seeing all my particular wishes set aside, while you are bent on carrying out your own. So if you think you can go on like this, I'll soon let you see what I am wont to do, when I wish things done in my own way. Therefore I say to you: take care to obey the orders given you; for if you are obstinate in pursuing your own fancies, you'll be running your head against a wall.'

François, having learned his lesson with the Emperor Charles V, thought only of keeping France out of the way of so redoubtable an enemy, and tried not to provoke him again. He even invited him to visit him and gave him as splendid a reception as he had Henry VIII on the Field of the Cloth of Gold. Nevertheless François made life difficult for him and in order to protect France he was prepared to ally himself with both the infidel Turks and Protestant princes of Germany. Protestantism, which was to cause so much bloodshed in France, had already gained ground with many Germans.

Sanguine drawing of François I in his last years, taken from the life. School of Clouet.

With these alliances, France was able to resist new attacks by Charles V and despite their efforts the imperial forces failed to reach Paris. Charles, discouraged, signed peace and when the gentleman king died, he was able to say that he left France intact and that, despite his power, the Emperor had failed to beat him.

Marino Cavalli, the Venetian ambassador, has left us a very clear portrait of the King at the end of his life:

The King is now fifty-four [actually 52]. He has a wholly regal appearance and if one had seen neither his face nor his portrait, one would, simply by looking at him, say 'This is the King'. His whole appearance is so noble and majestic that no other prince can equal him. His constitution is magnificent and he has great staying power else he would never have been able to endure the excessive fatigues of the past and those of the present encountered on his many expeditions and journeys. There are few men who have had to put up with so much. And now nature has found a means by which once a year he may be rid of the ills which beset him daily in such a way that will enable him to live for a long time. He eats and drinks a lot, sleeps well, and most important of all, dreams only of leading a happy and satisfactory life. He is fond of dressing well, and likes trimmings and richly embroidered ornaments on his clothes. His doublets are worked in gold thread and he likes his fine shirts to show beneath them in the French style—all of which conduces to the pleasure of his life and the good of his health.

His judgment is good, his knowledge wide; there is no subject in which he cannot argue and on which he cannot give a considered verdict. Not only does he know about war in all its aspects—logistics, the conduct of an army, how to mount an exercise, how to conduct it, how to fight it, the art of assault or defence of a city and affairs at sea; but he also knows about hunting, painting, all forms of literature, languages and all forms of bodily exercise suitable to a gentleman. It is true that despite such wisdom and knowledge his exploits in warfare were dogged by ill fortune. It could be said of him that he 'never said a foolish thing and never did a wise one'. But the truth is that the adversities he has suffered, in my view, are the results of a paucity of capable servants and because he himself did not wish to be bothered with detail or any administrative work. Thinking that to be in charge was good enough, he left the rest to subordinates.

One would have liked more care and patience though one could not fault him on experience or knowledge. He is quick to pardon offences, and forgives quickly and easily. He is also generous although hard times have tempered his largesse.

Henri II

Henri II was born on 31 March, 1519, at St Germain-en-Laye. He acceded to the throne on 31 March, 1547 and was crowned at Rheims on 26 July, 1547.
He married, on 28 October, 1533, Catherine of Medici (1519–1589).
He reigned for twelve years, and died, as a result of an accident, aged forty, at the palace of Tournelles, Paris on 10 July, 1559. He was buried at St Denis.

A Venetian ambassador has left this description of Henri II as dauphin:

The dauphin is twenty-three, well set up, large, neither fat nor thin, with powerful sinewy limbs, indefatigable as a hunter and at swordplay at which he is as good as if not better than any courtier in France. I have seen him play exceedingly well for long stretches at a time, with both strength and dexterity not only with the sword, but also at bowls. His temperament is melancholic and saturnine. He rarely smiles, and indeed there were some at court who averred that they had never seen him smile. His hair is black, his complexion pale, and he is a bit spiteful although he is a good companion. I once saw him joke with and make fools of his brothers as if they were friends rather than brothers. He spends his income freely and with regularity and pays his staff on time.

On his accession, Henri II did not take long to see that the Emperor still wanted to dismember France. However, Henri had as counsellor the wise Duke of Guise, a prince of Lorraine, who said to him, 'Sire, do not waste your time and effort in Italy. If you want to preserve your country, enlarge its borders beyond the Rhine. There are towns there which are French in heart and will welcome you with joy.'

The Duke of Guise spoke truly. When French troops appeared, Metz, Toul and Verdun opened their gates to them, for these three cities had only been separated from France by chance when the heirs of Charlemagne divided his empire in 843 with the treaty of Verdun which gave France west of the Rhône and Saône to Charles the Bald, Austrasia, Bavaria, Swabia and Saxony to Louis the German and 'Lorraine' to Lothaire.

Charles V was furious when he saw the King of France watering his horses in the Rhine. He swore to recapture Metz but the Duke of Guise resolved to defend the town to death. In vain did the Emperor fire fourteen thousand cannonades, in vain did he lance his best troops on the assault. Metz resisted heroically saying that it did not wish to be governed by a gouty old fellow like him. Charles V had to raise the siege. This time he finally abandoned his intention of bringing France to her knees. He abdicated, retired to a small house near a monastery and, as if he were already dead, had a mass said for himself, and assisted at his own funeral service.

His son Philip II was no luckier than he and in his turn was again repulsed when he attacked Henri II. France had escaped from her most dangerous enemy. And then the

Duke of Guise performed a bold stroke. He had already saved Metz. He decided to take Calais which had remained in English hands since the Hundred Years War. In eight days it was his. In London Queen Mary died of grief. 'When they open my heart,' she said, 'they will see the word "Calais" on it.'

The same Venetian was sent back to the French court on the death of François I and found Henri much changed in the intervening six years:

His Majesty is twenty-nine, and although I told you once that he was pallid and melancholic and rarely known to smile, he is now gay, with a good colour and in perfect health. He has very little beard, although he shaves it. His eyes are large but he keeps them lowered. His face between his jaw and forehead is small, and he has a small head. His body is well-proportioned, on the large side. He is full of courage and most enterprising. He likes playing tennis so much that he never misses a day unless it rains for he plays on an open court, and sometimes even after the most rigorous hunt. Sometimes in addition he will even practise for two or three hours sword play, a sport in which he excels. Since my first embassy I have watched these jousts and I must say that they are not without danger. Running against the barriers without seeing them clearly one day, father and son tumbled over each other and one gave the other such a blow on the head that he broke the skin. The King is also a valiant soldier as well as a good leader. And I have been told by someone whom one can trust that when the King found himself in a dangerous situation he would not run away from it but deal with it squarely.

His Majesty is devout; he does not ride on Sundays at least not in the morning. Madame la Sénéschale [Diane of Poitiers], his favourite, told one of her ladies of honour, who told me, that noticing the depth of religious emotion he displayed when he received the crown and having asked him later why he had prayed so fervently to God, the King replied that his only reason was as follows: if the crown he was about to receive signified good government and would assure the health of his people, God should leave it with him for a long time, and if not, He should remove it quickly.

Brantôme has a lot to say about Henri's activities:

The King greatly enjoyed horses as much for amusement as for war, which gave him pleasure for he found it a satisfying pastime. He particularly delighted in hunting the stag and he had two breeds of hunting dogs—one was grey and had been bred by his father, the other was white and a strain invented by him. It was more wiry than the grey but not as assured or as obedient. If he was not hunting stag, he went to the nets, to falconry, and if he was not on horseback, he played tennis, at which he was very good. He liked it when the Queen and her ladies came to watch him play and give their opinion from the windows above the court. He also played at various ball games, or at pallmall. If it was very cold or there was frost he liked skating, especially at Fontainebleau or if there was heavy snow, he had snow fights. He was never idle and always anxious that

Portrait of Henri II by François Clouet, 1559.

everyone should join in; he knew the names of all his courtiers, praising them if they excelled. Such were his outdoor exercises. If it rained and he had to stay indoors he played with the ladies and gentlemen of the court. He spent the mornings and the evenings, when he rose and went to bed, dealing with his business—at least three hours in the morning and more or less at night depending on the amount of work. He was very devout and went to mass regularly. After he had dined he went with his court to the rooms of the Queen whom he greatly loved, and found there a troupe of human goddesses, one more beautiful than the other. After supper there were frequent balls.

Henri's queen was Catherine of Medici, a forceful Italian, from the great Florentine banking family. Brantôme said of her:

She was a fine figure of a woman, and of great splendour. Sweet-tempered when it was necessary, elegant and of good appearance, with an agreeable and handsome face, full-chested and white-skinned. Her skin and her body were spotlessly clean; she was full-figured, with good legs and thighs, and she took especial pleasure in being well-shod. She had the most beautiful hands I have ever seen and her son Henri III inherited his from her. She was always magnificently dressed, in the height of fashion and her innate beauty made her lovable. She was good company and withal gay, loving exercise such as dancing, at which she excelled. She also loved hunting.

Chateaubriand, writing at the beginning of the nineteenth century, was less adulatory:

Catherine was an Italian, the daughter of a merchant and brought up in the leadership of a republic; she was accustomed to popular storms, factions, intrigues, poison and dagger thrusts; she had none and could have none of the attitudes of the French aristocracy and monarchy, that haughtiness towards the great and contempt for the little, those pretensions to divine right and love of absolute power as if it were their monopoly; she was unacquainted with our laws, and had little respect for them; for she attempted to place the crown of France upon the head of her daughter. Like the Italians of her time, she was superstitious and unbelieving; had no real aversion to the Protestants, but destroyed them for political reasons. In fact, if we follow all her actions, we see that she looked upon this vast kingdom, of which she was the sovereign, as an enlarged Florence; and considered the riots of her little republic, the quarrels of the Pozzi and the Medici, as the struggles of the Guise and the Châtillon.

Catherine, who was not really the beauty that Brantôme painted her, produced no children for the first ten years of her marriage and was then almost permanently pregnant, giving Henri ten children. Henri had, however, fallen in love with a real beauty, Diane of Poitiers (1499–1566) and his love affair with her lasted for twenty-three years until her death, although she was twenty years older than him.

Drawing of Diane of Poitiers, French school, sixteenth century.

A Venetian ambassador, writing ten years after the start of the affair was a little naïve:

This prince has a robust constitution and a slightly melancholic disposition. He is an accomplished swordsman, and though not very quick-witted, he holds clear and concise opinions, of which he is very tenacious. His intelligence is not very rapid either but men of this sort often succeed best just as autumn fruits ripen last but, for this reason, are better and last longer than those of spring or summer. He wishes to keep a foot in Italy and never thought Piedmont should have been ceded and to this end entertains Italians who are dissatisfied at home. He spends his money both wisely and well. He is not addicted to women, his wife satisfies him; for conversation he seeks Madame la Sénéschale [Diane of Poitiers] who is forty-eight. He is devoted to her but he is not thought to be in love with her; it is rather the relationship between mother and son. It is said that this lady has undertaken to teach, correct and help him and to steer him on a suitable course. She seems to suit him admirably. From being vain and scornful, and careless of his wife, he has become another man, having eradicated various other youthful faults.

Henri wrote Diane impassioned letters:

Mamie, I beg you to send me news of your health, because of the distress with which I have heard of your illness, and so that I may govern my movements in accordance with your condition. For, if your illness continues, I should not wish to fail to come and see you, to endeavour to be of service to you, and also because it would be impossible for me to live so long without seeing you. And, since I did not fear, in time past, to lose the good graces of the late King, in order to remain near you, I should scarcely complain of the trouble that I might have in rendering you any service, and I assure you that I shall not be at my ease until the bearer of this returns. Wherefore, I entreat you to send me a true account of the state of your health and to inform me when you will be able to start. I believe that you can understand the little pleasure that I experience at Fontainebleau without seeing you, for, being far from her upon whom all my welfare depends, it is very hard for me to be happy. With which I will conclude this letter, from fear that it will be too long, and will weary you to read it, and will present my humble recommendation to your good graces, as to that which I desire ever to retain.

And, after receiving the anxiously-awaited letter:

Madame mamie, I thank you very humbly for taking the trouble to send me news of yourself, which is the thing most pleasing to me on earth, and entreat you to keep your promise to me, for I cannot live without you, and if you knew the little enjoyment that I find here, you would pity me. I shall not write you a longer letter, save to assure you that you cannot come as soon as is the wish of him who remains for ever your very humble servant.

A more sophisticated Venetian makes their relationship quite clear:

The person whom without doubt the King loves above all others is Madame de Valentinois. She is a woman of fifty-two; he has loved her much, he loves her still, and still enjoys her, old though she is. And though she has never made use of rouge as is the custom in France and perhaps because of the care she takes of herself, she is far from appearing as old as she is. She is a woman of intelligence, who has inspired the King since his days as dauphin and has even assisted him with her purse, a help which he is conscious of and obliged to her for. At the beginning of his reign he created her Duchess of Valentinois, and gives her what she wants and does everything that she wishes. She does not interfere in matters of state unless secretly; however she is informed of everything and each day, as a rule, without fail, the King goes to see her after dinner, and remains an hour and a half to discuss matters with her; and tells her everything that happens.

Brantôme too thought that Diane even at an advanced age was a great beauty:

I saw Madame de Valentinois at the age of seventy, as beautiful, as youthful-looking and as fresh as she had been thirty years earlier. Six months before her death a heart of stone would have been melted by her beauty, even though she had broken a leg by falling from her horse on the cobbles at Orléans.

Henri II was yet another king who at his death left France larger than when he inherited

Henri II mortally wounded by Montgomery, 30 June, 1559.
Engraving by Tortorel and Périssin.

it. Unfortunately he enjoyed jousting and tournaments of the kind practised in the days of chivalry.

As bad luck would have it, the accident happened in the evening when the tournament was practically over and he [Henri II] wanted to break one more lance. He sent for the Count of Montgomery and ordered him into the lists. Montgomery refused point blank and made every excuse but the King would not take no for an answer and gave him a direct command. The Queen sent for him twice and begged him, for love of her, not to go on, and that enough was enough. Nothing doing; he replied he was only playing for love of her. She begged Monsieur de Savoie to dissuade him, saying that it would please her if he would stop, and that he had done so well already he could not do better, and that he should join the ladies. Still no luck.

And so, Montgomery having entered the lists, the King rode against him. Either public ill-will or his own fate impelled him, for in the counter-attack part of the lance entered his head through his eye, and he fell against the lists and was instantly picked up by his grooms. Monsieur de Montmorency who was acting as a marshal, went to him and found him badly wounded. The King remained unflurried and did not lose heart; he said it was nothing and instantly forgave the Count of Montgomery.

It is pointless to ask if the court and the Queen were worried. After they tried their hardest to save him, imploring the aid of God and men, the King died a few days later, as fine a Christian and catholic king as any of his predecessors. His death was regretted not only by his own people but by all Christendom, for he was good and nothing pleased him more than to give pleasure.

Tomb effigy of Henri II by Pilon, 1563–70, at St Denis.

On Henri's death, Catherine of Medici's first act was to send Madame de Valentinois packing. She found herself in a position of great power with her eldest son only fifteen. Her mourning impressed the Venetian who saw it:

She was in a room entirely hung in black; not only were the walls draped but the floor was too. The only light came from two candles on an altar covered in black cloth, as was the Queen's bed. Her Majesty was dressed with the utmost severity; a black dress with a train and its only decoration was one row of ermine round the neck. The Queen of Scotland [Mary Stuart] was in the same room, dressed from head to toe in white; the late King's sister, Madame Marguerite, wife of the Duke of Savoy, the daughters of France, the Queen of Spain, the Duchess of Lorraine and their young sister Marguerite all in white were there and had to keep their mourning for forty days. The Queen Mother replied for her entire entourage but she did so in so feeble and emotional a tone of voice that no one could hear what she said however hard one tried. For in addition to her feebleness of voice she was wearing a black veil which entirely covered her and hid even her face.

Medal of Catherine of Medici in mourning by Pilon.

François II

François II was born on 19 January, 1544 at Fontainebleau. He acceded to the throne on 10 July, 1559 and was crowned at Rheims on 8 September.
He married, on 24 April, 1558, Mary Stuart (1542–1587).
He reigned for seventeen months, and died of meningitis, aged sixteen, at Orléans, on 5 December, 1560. He was buried at St Denis.

François II was the eldest of Henri's sons and had little time, coming to the throne at fifteen and reigning only for seventeen months, to make his mark. One of the Venetian ambassadors had this to say of him as a boy:

By this Queen His Majesty [Henri II] has three sons. The first, called the dauphin, is ten, and he has a fine face and a well-shaped body, but he is miserable by nature and not a great lover of books which displeases His Majesty somewhat because he has been put in charge of the best tutors, whose principal task is to deny him nothing that he asks, with the result that with long and great habit he accustoms himself to liberality and royal majesty, but withal it appears that they succeed ill.

He has been given the Queen of Scotland as wife; she is a great beauty with exceedingly good manners and appears marvellous to all who consider her qualities. The dauphin is happy with her and takes great pleasure in talking to her and being in her company.

Although Mary Stuart, Queen of Scots, belongs so closely to Scotch and English history, her beauty and her fate moved French writers too for she had been brought up at the court of France.

Widowed, she set sail for her native Scotland on her eighteenth birthday, and spent five hours leaning against the poop of the vessel, sighing 'Farewell, dear France, I will never see you again.' Brantôme, her contemporary, writes:

People wishing to write about this illustrious Queen of Scots have two vast subjects—the one her life, the other her death—in both of which she was ill-served by fortune.

As she grew up and reached fifteen her great beauty became apparent, she was so beautiful that she eclipsed the light of the sun. Her spirit too was rare. She was learned in Latin, understanding and speaking it well. Her French was fluent and as long as she was

Drawing of François II, about 1557. French school.

in France she spent two hours a day reading and studying, being particularly fond of poetry and poets, among them Ronsard and du Bellay. She composed verses herself and I have seen some of them which certainly do not resemble those attributed to her about her love for Bothwell. They are far too vulgar to have come from her as Ronsard, with whom I discussed them, agreed. She wrote elegant prose and well-composed letters.

See what graces and virtues allied to such beauty she possessed that even when dressed in the barbaric costume of her native land she appeared a veritable goddess. She looked exceedingly well in her white mourning [worn for Henri II's death] for the whiteness of her skin accorded well with the whiteness of her veil. She had a gentle and fine voice; she sang well, to the accompaniment of the lute which she played with her own fair hands.

Renauld de la Beaulne preached a sermon in Notre Dame in Paris at the requiem mass held for her on 12 March, 1587. She had been executed by her cousin Elizabeth of England at Fotheringay after nearly nineteen years of imprisonment:

Many of us saw this Queen in the place where we are now assembled to mourn her, on the day of her wedding, arrayed in her regal garments, so covered in jewels that the sun shone not more brightly, as beautiful and as charming as any woman has been. These walls were covered with cloth of gold and precious tapestries and every space was filled with thrones and benches, occupied by princes and princesses, who came from every part to share in the rejoicing. The palace was full of magnificence, splendid fêtes and masques; the streets with jousts and tourneys. In short it seemed as if our century had succeeded that day in surpassing the pomp of all past centuries combined and the glories of ancient Greece and Rome. A short time has passed as if it were a cloud. And we have seen captive she who appeared then so triumphant, a prisoner who had restored prisoners to liberty, a beggar who had been so liberal, disdained by those on whom she had conferred honours, and finally, in the hand of a base executioner, she who was doubly a Queen. Her body which had honoured the nuptial bed of a great King of France, fell dishonoured on a scaffold, and that beauty (which had been one of the wonders of the world) faded in a harsh prison, and at last effaced by a piteous death. Today we mourn her tragic end; we offer up for her our wishes and prayers for the repose of her soul, which we believe happy in God's presence, having died in His service. This place, where she was surrounded with splendour, is now hung with black for her. Instead of nuptial torches we have funeral tapers; in the place of songs of happiness, we have sighs and groans; for clarions and hautboys, the tolling of the sad and funeral bell. Oh God, what a change!

Portrait of Mary Stuart by François Clouet. Probably painted in 1559 when Mary wore white mourning on the death of her father-in-law.

Charles IX

Charles IX was born on 27 June, 1550 at St Germain-en-Laye. He acceded to the throne on 5 December, 1560 and was crowned at Rheims on 15 May, 1561.
He married, on 26 November, 1570, Elisabeth of Austria (1554–1592).
He reigned for thirteen years and died of tuberculosis, aged twenty-three, at the château of Vincennes on 30 May, 1574. He was buried at St Denis.

Until now there had only been one religion in France. It was a great novelty when Frenchmen became Protestants as followers of Calvin. At first no one took much notice of them. But soon, bitter quarrels ending in violence broke out between Catholics and Protestants—or Huguenots, as they were called—and France was involved in civil war of a particularly bloodthirsty kind.

The Catholics were led by the Duke of Guise, the hero of Metz and deliverer of Calais [*see page 146*]. *Admiral Coligny, who had defended St Quentin against the imperial army, was the Protestant leader.*

Henri II's three sons who reigned one after another in quick succession were powerless by comparison with these two men, each of whom had practically half France behind him. The brother of François II who succeeded him was called Charles IX. As he was only ten, his mother, Catherine of Medici, became regent; she tried as best she could to hold the balance between the Catholics and the Protestants. But the two groups were too angry with each other and each complained bitterly if the other was accommodated; soon they started fighting without it being clear who started it.

One of the Venetian ambassadors saw Charles IX shortly after his accession:

I will speak of Charles IX, child though he is of eleven years, though perforce my information is based on hearsay. He is good-looking, with fine eyes like his father's and in all his actions is as gracious and loving as anyone of his age. It is true that he is unhealthy and weak. He eats and drinks little. He has to be careful about exercise which he enjoys, he tires easily and needs a lot of rest, finding breathing difficult. Book work does not please him though he works rather unwillingly to please his mother.

Another Venetian ambassador wrote more fully but in much the same vein eight years later:

His Majesty [aged 19] is quite tall but feeble, because his spindly legs do not support his height. He does not walk altogether straight, and his pallor betrays his unhealthiness. However, he works willingly, and takes exercise, more successfully on horseback than

Portrait of Charles IX. French school, sixteenth century.

on foot, and greatly enjoys hunting, especially deer, after which he chases boldly. He does not much care for business, although he listens patiently and is available from three to four to deal with the affairs presented to him. He refers all decisions to his mother, who may rightly claim that he is a most obedient son with whom she runs no risks. It is true that the excessive respect he has for her (which may be due to fear) does not increase his reputation although of course it does hers. For the rest, he is a polite prince, humane and pleasant to all, and will be, in my judgment, easy to direct.

Catherine of Medici had good advice to give on royal deportment even if her political advice was not always wise.

I am anxious, my dear son, that you should arrange a time for your *levée* and to give pleasure to your nobility, do as did the King your father. As he took his shirt and as his clothing arrived, princes, lords, knights, gentlemen of the bedchamber and other servants entered at the same time and he spoke to them and they saw him which gave them pleasure. That done, he went about his business with only the people he needed, and four secretaries. If you do the same everyone will be well pleased as they are used to it from your father and your grandfather. Then devote an hour or two to the despatches and matters which require your presence.

At ten go to mass as did your father and your grandfather and take the whole court with you, not just your archers as you do at present. Then dine, if it is late, or if not, take a walk for your health. Do not dine later than eleven. After you have eaten, give an audience at least twice a week which will please your subjects. Then you may retire and visit me or the Queen [when he should be married]. After half an hour or an hour of showing yourself you may retire to your study or be private as suits you. At three take a walk or ride to show yourself and to observe the nobility and to spend your time in worthy exercise with the young, if not every day at least twice or three times a week. Then sup with your family, and after supper, twice a week show yourself in the ballroom for I have heard it said to your grandfather that you need two days to live in peace with the French and so that they should love their king keep them happy and occupied.

On reaching his majority, Charles IX found himself in something of a spot. He had no antipathy towards Protestants for his wet nurse had been a Huguenot. He rather fancied them and there were a large number of them at his court. This irritated the Catholics who

OPPOSITE: *Portrait of Henri II in armour (which is at present in the Musée de l'Armée, Paris) attributed to Primaticcio.*

OVERLEAF: *Henri III and Louise of Lorraine; detail from 'Fontainebleau' in the series of Valois tapestries. These were woven in Flanders almost certainly by Lucas de Heere who worked for a time at Fontainebleau and who used drawings by the French court artist, Antoine Caron, as source material. The tapestries were taken to Florence by Catherine of Medici's grand-daughter, Christina of Lorraine, when she went there in 1589 to marry the Grand Duke Ferdinand I.*

were led by Henri of Guise, the 'Scarred One', son of the one who had been assassinated. Charles clearly found 'this religion a horrible thing' as he writes to his ambassador at the court of his Catholic Majesty the King of Spain.

Monsieur de Fourquevaux, I am sending you this despatch to warn you that three days ago an unbelievable and unheard of conspiracy was discovered—directed against me and mine even as far as the person of the Queen, my mother, my brothers and myself—if the information which I have from countless places is true—and that it became the more apparent to me yesterday whilst returning from Meaux, accompanied in this town by a band of Swiss who have troubled my realm before, having already taken over some towns of my realm two days ago. They brought in a large number of cavalry with which they came to meet me and tried to fight me and attack my person. But God so willed that all they carried away was shame, and so they revealed their intention which can no longer be concealed under a cloak of religion for up to now no restrictions have been made on the enjoyment of the edicts which I made before this—and this religion is such a horrible thing that I am sure that it must be found just as alien by all the princes of the world, that it would be unfortunate to follow its example and run to meet the evil that can ensue from it for everyone; and I wish you to warn the Catholic King my good brother and as God has brought me back to this town where I am well escorted I hope that He will give me grace to provide for everything and since I have other such good subjects and that they will not abandon me in such an urgent affair, especially as I have such a strong natural affection towards all my subjects and the desire I had to maintain my realm and all those who stay there.

For which I state that Our Lord will not forsake me. Neither do I want to forget that his ambassador came to me yesterday to offer all that is in the power of his master to help and assist me.

Brantôme does his best for a king who was a typical Valois and who after all had authorised the Massacre of St Bartholomew. The Catholics took advantage of the presence of a large number of Protestants in Paris attending the wedding of Charles's sister Marguerite to Henri Bourbon. During the night of St Bartholomew (18 August, 1572), more than two thousand Protestants were murdered, their houses having been marked out with a white cross. Coligny was one of the first to be killed. His body was thrown out of the window, landing at the feet of the Duke of Guise.

I must now finish this book, and as I started with that great Emperor Charles V, so I must finish with a great king of France, Charles IX—not that his achievements were as notable as those of the Emperor but he was courageous and willing to undertake dashing enterprises which might have succeeded if he had not had the setback of civil wars, which often occur with young kings, and if he had lived. For he died young at an age when the Emperor had started to take up arms and leave Spain.

When this young King came to the throne several astrologers, amongst them Nostradamus, anxious to predict his future, saw that one day he would be a great, valiant and lucky prince and would rival his ancestor Charlemagne in all his qualities. Even our French poets, flatterers by nature, but normally wishing to contradict the astrologers, wrote and published eulogies of him.

Charles IX was so brave, ebullient and rash that if his mother, to whom he was devoted and whom he feared, had not at an early age prevented him when the civil war broke out against him he would have taken up arms himself and made himself a general. I remember that at the start the Huguenots everywhere believed that they were not waging war against the King nor that he was fighting them but that it was against the King of Navarre and the Triumvirate [the Duke of Guise, the constable of Montmorency and the marshal of St André].

Elisabeth, wife of Charles IX, was by all accounts one of the best, most gentle, wisest and most virtuous queens known to France. She was good-looking with as fair and delicate a complexion as any lady at court, and quite charming. She had a good figure although she was on the small side. She was wise, and pious, and never gave offence by the least word to anyone. She spoke little, and that in Spanish. She was extremely devout, though not bigoted, and fulfilled her duties openly but without excess of zeal.

She was fond of the King even though she knew of his amorous disposition and his mistresses whether for show or for pleasure but she never complained of them and bore her jealousy in patience. She behaved very well towards him and was suited to him; it was like fire and water mixed—he was fast, agitated, bubbling, while she was cool and collected.

I was told that during her widowhood, one of her women (and there is always one tactless one amongst them), thinking to please her said, 'At least, madam, if God had given you a son instead of a daughter you would have been Queen Mother now.' 'Ah,' replied the Queen, 'As if France has not enough troubles that I should have burdened her with another. If I had had a son, imagine the arguments and quarrels that would have taken place during his minority—there would have been even more wars than usual.'

This shows her goodness. And she knew nothing about the Massacre of St Bartholomew. She went to bed in the usual way and when she woke in the morning was told what had happened. 'Oh dear,' she asked, 'did my husband know of it?' 'Yes indeed; it was he who ordered it.' 'My God,' she replied, 'who can have given him that advice? I pray you will forgive him, because if you do not take pity on him, I fear this great sin will not be pardoned.'

Charles, worried about the succession and order in France, wrote to the Count of Matignon the day before he died. It was said that he died racked by remorse.

You have already heard of my indisposition which has become so much worse since yesterday that today I am waiting for God, to do what He will with me, and am ready to

Painting of Elisabeth of Austria by François Clouet.

accede to His wishes, in whose hands we all are.

In the meantime I have begged the Queen my mother, in view of my illness, to watch over my affairs and those of state with even greater care than usual, since she has acquitted herself so well to date, and I require that she should be obeyed in all she asks as long as I am ill or until it pleases God to take me until my brother, the King of Poland, who is my legitimate heir, returns.

I know that you, Monsieur de Matignon, will continue to do your duty and keep everything in good order in the government, and ask you to make known to my subjects the authority of my mother and to ensure their loyalty to my brother, bringing to the notice of the nobles and other estates in your charge the loyalty and faithfulness the French people have always rendered to those legitimately in power, and recognised by all the nations of the world so that no ill may follow. I have told my brothers, the Duke of Alençon and the King of Navarre, of my wishes and they have promised to obey my mother with the love and affection they have given me and to ensure the tranquillity of the nation.

Brantôme was in at his death:

He died on Easter Day 1574 at three o'clock at a time when the doctors and surgeons and everyone at court believed him to be better, for the day before he had seemed so well we believed him cured. He asserted the power and authority of the Salic Law in connection with a daughter of his marriage [Marie-Elisabeth, born 27 October, 1572, died 2 April, 1578]; declared his brother, the King of Poland, his heir and successor, and the Queen his mother regent until his brother's return. His will was speedily taken to the *Parlement* of Paris, which, having heard it, approved it and gave probate although some said, and still say, that kings cannot testify and their wills are void.

He begged his brother to maintain order and not to conspire against the state saying that kingdoms are acquired by virtue or succession and that those who do otherwise come to a bad end.

After some fine words and acts of Christian charity, he died, only twenty-eight days short of twenty-four years of age, having succeeded to the throne aged [nearly] eleven. The next day his body was opened in the presence of the magistrate but nothing suspicious was found, clearing any suggestion of poison. Monsieur d'Estrosse and I asked his chief surgeon Monsieur Ambroise Paré for an account of it. He opined that he had died from sounding his horn too often during the hunt which had exhausted his febrile body and said no more.

Some said he was poisoned when his brother left for Poland, and that it was achieved by means of powdered horn from a sea unicorn, which works slowly and eventually snuffs one out like a candle.

Pierre de l'Estoile (1546–1610) kept a daily journal of life in Paris and quotes for June 1574 an epitaph for Charles, written, he supposes, by a Huguenot:

More cruel than Nero, craftier than Tiberius;
Hated by his subjects, scorned abroad;
Brave when hidden from danger:
Malign to his sister, at daggers drawn with his mother;
Envious of his brother Henri's valorous deeds;
An enemy since his early youth; changeable;
He broke his word and was faithless; eager for revenge;
A rotten judge and an adulterer in public;
He sold church lands first
And spent their revenues on himself.
He packed the chivalric orders with villains
And France with ignorant prelates and advisers;
His entire reign was a blood bath
And he died shut up like a mad dog.

Henri III

Henri III was born on 19 September, 1551 at Fontainebleau. He acceded to the throne on 30 May, 1574 and was crowned at Rheims on 13 February, 1575.
He married, on 15 February, 1575, Louise of Lorraine (1553–1601).
He reigned for fifteen years, and died, aged nearly thirty-eight, assassinated at St Cloud, on 2 August, 1589. He was buried at St Denis.

Henri III was Henri II's third son but did not care to be a younger son, and accepted the elective throne of Poland. Two Venetians wrote of him when he was twenty-one:

He aspires to a high station because he sees that if he stays in France and if his brother has children, as one supposes he will, there will come a time when he will be of no more account than any prince of the blood. As I wrote to you when you heard of the victory at Lepanto he grumbled to his friends that he had not been allowed the opportunity to acquire glory at the battle.

At the present all his warlike instincts and ambitious schemes have completely vanished. He has become idle, letting voluptuousness dominate his life. He never takes exercise, which astonishes everyone. He spends most of his time with the ladies covered with scent, crimping his hair, wearing earrings and jewellery of various kinds. One has no idea of the amount of money he spends on the beauty and elegance of his clothes. He greatly endears himself to the ladies, in particular by the expensive presents he lavishes on them. He is the apple of the Queen Mother's eye. She never leaves him—even on their journeys—and she frequently eats with him. All her hopes now rest with him. She had wanted a foreign crown for him, rightly, wishing to avoid the kind of rivalry that is likely to exist between brothers. It was for this that negotiations for an English marriage [to Queen Elizabeth] were undertaken and affairs were so advanced that had he not expressed doubts it would have taken place. Proceedings are now going forward to have him elected as King of Poland.

Pierre de l'Estoile takes up Henri's story on his return from Poland to become King of France after Charles IX's death, and recounts his manner of life from 1575–7:

On Friday 11 February the King arrived at Rheims and was crowned on the Sunday.

When the crown was about to be placed on his head he said in a loud tone that he blessed it and it slipped twice as if it were going to fall—an ill omen.

On the 14th the King was affianced to Louise of Lorraine and he married her on the 15th. Many people, amongst them the most noble in France and abroad found the marriage deeply unsuitable and rushed, as if it were brought about for diplomatic reasons. But it was said that the King, on his way to Poland the previous year, had seen her in Lorraine and found her handsome and charming, well-spoken of and well-behaved and maintained this opinion on his return and was supported in it by the Queen Mother and hoped that from such a well-set up girl he might breed healthy stock. Be that as it may, what really interested the Queen was that she was a gentle and devout princess who would prefer a life of devotion to interfering in politics—as indeed happened.

On Sunday 19 June Monsieur de Lorraine and Monsieur de Vaudemont, the Queen's father, came to Paris to celebrate the marriage of the Marquis of Loménie, his eldest son, and Mademoiselle de Martiques. During one of the celebrations attendant on the marriage the Queen Mother ate so much that she thought she would die, and was further troubled by diarrhoea. They said it was due to eating too many artichoke hearts and cockscombs of which she was very fond.

At the beginning of November the King went round the churches of Paris, giving alms and going daily to pray, wearing a shirt with the collar turned down in the Italian style instead of one with tassels to which he had previously been so attached. He went by coach with the Queen through the streets of Paris collecting small dogs who went willingly to them both. It seemed that they also went to convents on the outskirts of Paris doing the same with the dogs to the great regret and displeasure of the ladies to whom they belonged. He read grammar and learned his declensions.

The word *mignon* began at this time to be used by the populace to whom it was odious, for the *mignons* were disliked as much for their bantering and haughty ways as for their effeminate and indecent dress but they were hated too because the King gave them such lavish and expensive gifts that the populace thought their poverty was due to them.

The King gave a series of entertainments on Sunday 24 February at which he appeared dressed as a woman, with his blouse open displaying his chest, wearing a pearl necklace and three ruffs as did the women at court.

On 15 May the King gave a fête for his brother at which the women who were dressed in men's clothing did all the waiting. The Queen Mother gave a banquet at Chenonceau which cost they say nearly a hundred thousand francs and at which served the most beautiful and honest ladies at court who were half naked with their hair dishevelled.

The Venetian ambassador Morosini bears out Pierre de l'Estoile:

He [the King] has a noble enough bearing, a gracious presence, and the most beautiful

Drawing by an unknown artist of Henri III, c. 1580.

hands of all men and women in France. His manners are serious although from affability he abandons a modicum of solemnity and the grave demeanour natural to him. He is full of contradictions; his habits, his manner of dressing, his love of personal adornment all tend to make him seem delicate. In addition to his lavish costumes, decorated with gold, jewels and pearls, he wears the most luxurious shirts and hats, and he wears a double gold and amber circlet round his neck which gives off a subtle aroma. But what to my mind detracts from his seriousness most, is to have had his ears pierced like women. He is not content to wear a pair of ear-rings, but needs must wear two on each ear, with hanging pendants enriched with semi-precious stones and small pearls.

And another, Michiel, has this to say of Henri's queen, Louise of Lorraine:

[The Queen] is nineteen or twenty, and really pretty. She is largish, of medium rather than small height, and does not need high heels. She is a good shape but rather thin. She has a fine profile and an honest dignified face not without charm and happiness. Her eyes, although white (which pleases the French) are lively, and she has a wonderful complexion. Her hair is fair, which gives the King great pleasure since it is rare in a country where most people's is dark but she uses no artificial colouring. She is good-humoured and deals gently with all who come into contact with her. They say she does good works and is generous with what she has; high-spirited and quick-witted. She is devout in her religious duties and above all obedient to the King, so much in love with him that no one could conceive of a happier union.

Priuli, another Venetian ambassador had much the same to say of Henri six years later:

I will not describe his external appearance because all of you have already told about it. I will only say that Henri III was born on 19 September, 1551 so that this September he will complete his thirty-first year. For a prince he has always been delicate and far from strong. He has also had illnesses of some severity from one of which he lost the hearing in his right ear, and suffered from headaches to such an extent that he went about with his head shaven. So he always kept it covered, even when receiving the sacrament. He also suffered from having been, as the young will, intemperate in his youth and frequenting too many women. Two years ago, he found himself in dire straits and underwent a most solemn purge, and now is having another one though this time it is less severe. But His Majesty has improved greatly in eight months so I leave him in a better state than he has been for many years. Even with all these indispositions the King used to take a lot of exercise, not with extreme energy, but with agility and dexterity and he used to dance a good deal. In the evening after supper he would dance for two or three hours. The doctors did not predict a long life for him and the astrologers said that His Majesty would not survive his thirty-seventh year. He lives soberly enough but still indulges the flesh.

He is passionately addicted to beauty and good manners, and fine clothes both for himself and for his servants and is generous in this respect. He is very loving to his intimates and when once he takes to someone he is lavish in his affection so that he wishes to share his crown with them. He is fond of the arts and science and delights in poetry and recitals which he performs miraculously well. He is melancholic, keeping away from the affairs of state and finding negotiations tiring and difficult. His doctors, partly on account of his health and partly sycophantically have always advised him to avoid work and he has gladly followed their advice. He lives away from the court for most of the year with a few of his cronies.

His Queen is a daughter of Monsieur de Vaudemont of the house of Lorraine. He chose her on account of her beauty and her virtue.

He has not had a son by her and has little hope of so doing on account of the thinness of the Queen, who also has the white flux. Nevertheless prayers have been ordered throughout the realm to beg that God will grant them male issue. Many people have been sent on pilgrimages to this end especially as the King would have to be succeeded by a brother he does not care for.

Henri's life was not all primping. He had no child, and the religious problems of his brother's reign had by no means been solved, but to whom would the throne pass?

To a distant cousin, descended from St Louis; Henri of Bourbon, King of Navarre. But he was a Protestant. At the thought of a Protestant king, the Catholics revolted and formed a League led by the Duke of Guise. It was not disbanded until Henri IV became a Catholic.

In the meanwhile Henri III, adhering firmly to the Salic Law, made it quite clear that Henri of Navarre was to be his heir. So civil war broke out again—the Catholic League against the King of France—and Henri was chased out of Paris by Guise. Henri decided that Guise must be done away with but Guise thought himself above the law and that Henri would never dare be rid of him. He fell, at Blois, stabbed to death on the King's orders. The King of France had killed the 'King of Paris'. 'It is not enough to cut out,' said Henri's mother, Catherine, 'you must also sew.'

Henri's last remaining brother died in 1584. Having finally decided to retake Paris from the Catholics with the help of Henri of Navarre he was assassinated on the eve of the siege by a monk called Jacques Clément. Henri was the last of the Valois, and Francis Bacon had little sympathy for him:

Shepherds of people had need know the calendars of tempests in state, which are commonly greatest when things grow to equality; as natural tempests are greatest about the equinoctia, and as there are certain hollow blasts of wind and secret swellings of seas before a tempest, so are there in states.

Also, as Machiavel noteth well, when princes, that ought to be common parents, make themselves as a party, and lean to a side; it is, as a boat that is overthrown by uneven weight on the one side; as was well seen in the time of Henri the Third of France; for first himself entered league for the extirpation of the Protestants, and presently after the same league was turned upon himself: for when the authority of princes is made but an accessary to a cause, and that there be other bands that tie faster than the band of sovereignty, kings begin to be put almost out of possession.

Henri's dying words to his heir were:

I die happy at seeing you by my side. The crown is yours . . . I order all officers to recognise you as their King after me . . . you will suffer many a rebuff if you do not make up your mind to accept another faith. I exhort you to do it . . .

Marble tomb effigy of Catherine of Medici by Pilon, 1563–70, at St Denis.

A view of the Louvre, c. 1630. Etching by Callot.

The Bourbons

THE BOURBONS

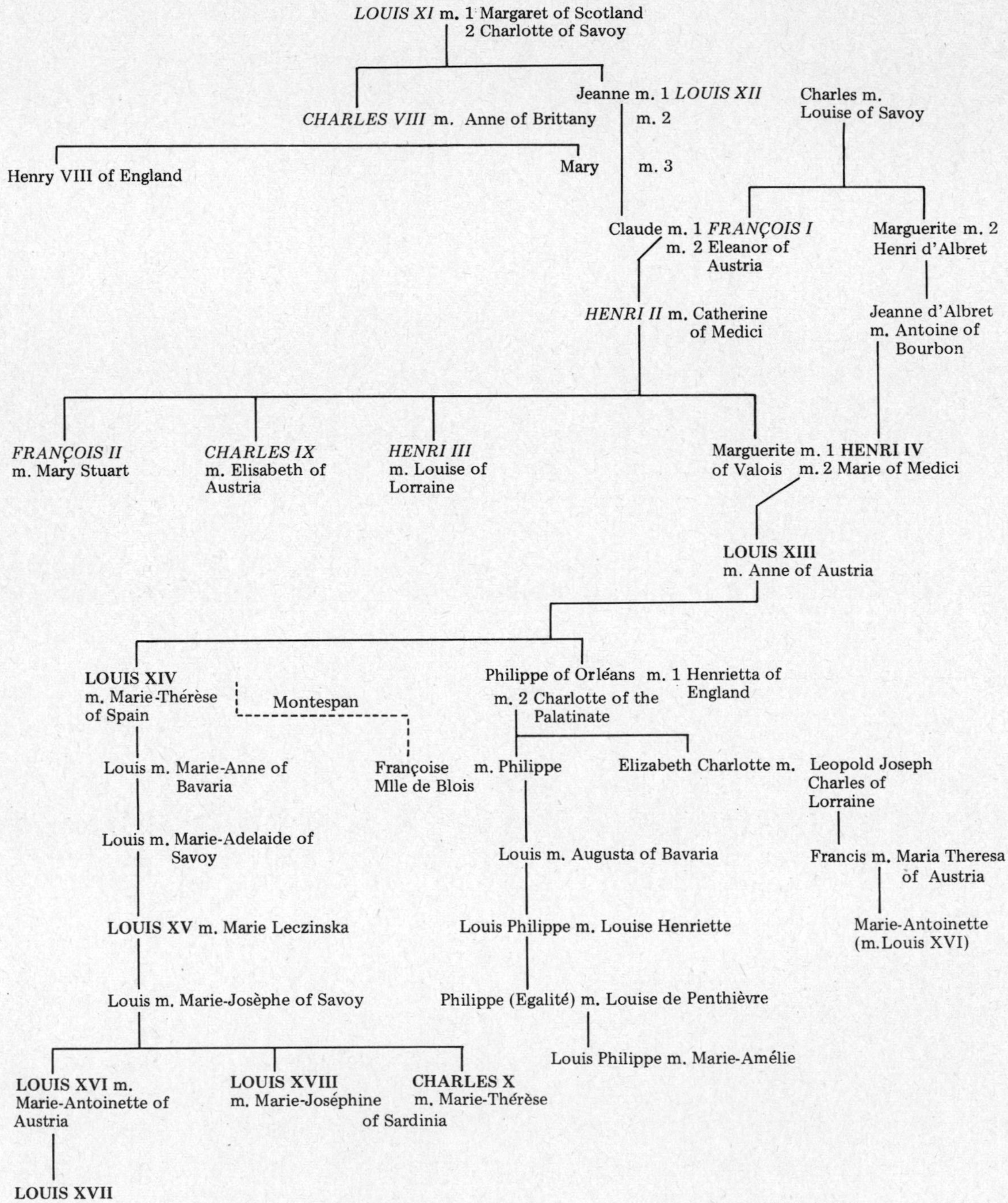
LOUIS XI m. 1 Margaret of Scotland
2 Charlotte of Savoy
CHARLES VIII m. Anne of Brittany
Jeanne m. 1 *LOUIS XII*
m. 2
m. 3
Charles m.
Louise of Savoy
Henry VIII of England
Mary
Claude m. 1 *FRANÇOIS I*
m. 2 Eleanor of
Austria
Marguerite m. 2
Henri d'Albret
HENRI II m. Catherine
of Medici
Jeanne d'Albret
m. Antoine of
Bourbon
FRANÇOIS II
m. Mary Stuart
CHARLES IX
m. Elisabeth of
Austria
HENRI III
m. Louise of
Lorraine
Marguerite m. 1 HENRI IV
of Valois m. 2 Marie of Medici
LOUIS XIII
m. Anne of Austria
LOUIS XIV
m. Marie-Thérèse
of Spain
Montespan
Philippe of Orléans m. 1 Henrietta of
England
m. 2 Charlotte of the
Palatinate
Louis m. Marie-Anne of
Bavaria
Françoise
Mlle de Blois
m. Philippe
Elizabeth Charlotte m.
Leopold Joseph
Charles of
Lorraine
Louis m. Marie-Adelaide of
Savoy
Louis m. Augusta of Bavaria
Francis m. Maria Theresa
of Austria
LOUIS XV m. Marie Leczinska
Louis Philippe m. Louise Henriette
Marie-Antoinette
(m.Louis XVI)
Louis m. Marie-Josèphe of Savoy
Philippe (Egalité) m. Louise de Penthièvre
Louis Philippe m. Marie-Amélie
LOUIS XVI m.
Marie-Antoinette of
Austria
LOUIS XVIII
m. Marie-Joséphine
of Sardinia
CHARLES X
m. Marie-Thérèse
LOUIS XVII

Henri IV

Henri IV was born on 13 December, 1553 at Pau. He acceded to the throne on 2 August, 1589 and was crowned at Chartres on 27 February, 1594 (the Archbishop of Rheims being a prisoner of the Guises).
He married, on 18 August, 1572, Marguerite of Valois (1553–1615), and, on 17 December, 1600, Marie of Medici (1573–1642).
He reigned for twenty years, and died, aged fifty-six, assassinated in Paris on 14 May, 1610. He was buried at St Denis.

On the death of Henri III with no heirs, Henri of Navarre was the obvious legitimate successor and was moreover married to Henri III's sister. But he did not succeed to the throne of a France torn by religious strife with ease. He had to fight the Catholic League on one hand, and renounce Protestantism on the other in order to gain Paris—worth a mass, he is reported as saying.

The first Bourbon king, the vert galant, *who wanted every family in his country to be able to afford a chicken for lunch on Sundays, was an astute and determined man who tempered his absolutism with a geniality and benevolence which was apparent at a very young age. Henri made this impression on a Bordeaux magistrate, when he was only thirteen:*

He behaves towards everyone with such a relaxed air that people crowd round him, and his every action is so noble that one can see he is a prince. His conversation is that of a straightforward man; it is always to the point, and if it turns on court matters, one discovers that he is well-informed, and he never speaks out of line. I shall always hate the new religion for having claimed so worthy a man.

He insinuates himself with all hearts with incredible skill. If men honour and esteem him, women do so no less. They do not find his flaming beard unattractive. His face is well-made, the nose neither too big nor too small; he has gentle eyes, a ruddy complexion and soft skin; his vivacity is so extraordinary that he is certain to succeed with the ladies.

He likes gaming, and good living. When he is short of money he finds means to acquire it, means quite new and as useful for others as for himself. For he sends to those of either sex whom he believes to be his friends a promise in his own hand bearing his own signature, and begs that they will send him back the note or the money. You can imagine that there are not many houses which refuse him. It is held to be a great honour to have one of this prince's notes, and they are received with pleasure, for there are two astrologers here who say that either their art is a fake or that this prince will one day be one of the greatest kings in Europe.

There was much to be done in the realm. The country was impoverished and the King himself complained that his doublets were frayed at the elbows.

Religious toleration of a sort was granted to the Huguenots by the Edict of Nantes in 1598 and although neither side was wholly satisfied. the fighting stopped.

Henri, like his grandson Louis XIV, was a good chooser of men and was fortunate in having as superintendent of his finances Sully, with whom he set about putting the country in order once religious peace had been restored.

Maximilien de Béthune, Baron of Rosny and later Duke of Sully, who said that ploughing and pasturing were the twin breasts of France, had this to say of his master:

However that may be, such was the tragical end of a prince, on whom nature, with a lavish profusion, had bestowed all her advantages, except that of a death such as he merited. I have already observed that his stature was so happy, and his limbs formed with such proportion, as constitutes not only what is called a well-made man, but indicates strength, vigour and activity; his complexion was animated; all the lineaments of his face had that agreeable liveliness which forms a sweet and happy physiognomy, and perfectly suited to that engaging easiness of manners which, though sometimes mixed with majesty, never lost the graceful affability and easy gaiety so natural to that great prince. With regard to the qualities of his heart and mind, I shall tell the reader nothing new, by saying that he was candid, sincere, grateful, compassionate, generous, wise, penetrating; in a word, endowed with all those great and amiable qualities which in these memoirs he has so often had occasion of admiring in him.

He loved all his subjects as a father, and the whole state as the head of a family: and it was this disposition that recalled him even from the midst of his pleasures to the care of rendering his people happy and his kingdom flourishing: hence proceeded his readiness in conceiving, and his industry in perfecting, a great number of useful regulations; many I have already specified: and I shall sum up all by saying, that there were no conditions, employments, or professions, to which his reflections did not extend: and that with such clearness and penetration, that the changes he projected could not be overthrown by the death of their author, as it but too often happened in this monarchy. It was his desire, he said, that glory might influence his last years, and make them at once useful to the world and acceptable to God: his was a mind in which the ideas of what is great, uncommon, and beautiful, seemed to rise of themselves: hence it was that he looked upon adversity as a mere transitory evil, and prosperity as his natural state.

I should destroy all I have now said of this great prince if, after having praised him for an infinite number of qualities well worthy to be praised, I did not acknowledge that they were balanced by faults, and those, indeed, very great. I have not concealed, or even palliated his passion for women; his excess in gaming, his gentleness often carried to weakness; nor his propensity to every kind of pleasure: I have neither disguised the faults they made him commit, the foolish expenses they led him into, nor the time they

Painting of Henri IV by an unknown artist.

made him waste: but I have likewise observed (to do justice on both sides) that his enemies have greatly exaggerated all these errors. If he was, as they say, a slave to women, yet they never regulated his choice of ministers, decided the destinies of his servants, or influenced the deliberations of his council. As much may be said in extenuation of all his other faults. And to sum up all, in a word, what he has done is sufficient to show that the good and bad in his character had no proportion to each other; and that since honour and fame have always had power enough to tear him from pleasure, we ought to acknowledge these to have been his great and real passions.

Sully quotes Henri as having said this of himself:

Some blame me for being too fond of buildings and great works; others for liking hunting, dogs, and birds; one says that I have a passion for cards, dice, and other kinds of gaming; another condemns me for my attachment to women, to the pleasures of the table, to assemblies, plays, balls, running at the ring, and other amusements of that kind; where, say they, I appear as gay and lively with my grey beard, and am as proud of having gained the goal, and received a ring from some fair lady, as I could have been in my youth, or as the vainest young fellow of the court. I do not deny but there is some truth in all this; but if I am guilty of no excesses in these pleasures, my conduct deserves more praise than blame; and, indeed, some little indulgences I ought to have in amusements which bring no inconvenience upon my people, in consideration of the labours I have endured from my infancy to fifty years old.

In addition to putting the house of France in order, Henri devoted much of his life to love affairs despite his own good intentions:

I pray to God every day for three things: first that He would be pleased to pardon my enemies; second to grant me victory over my passions, and especially sensuality; and third, that I may make a right use of the authority He has given me and never abuse it.

Henri was greatly loved, and many anecdotes were told of him:

The King, going to the Louvre one day, and meeting a poor woman driving a cow, stopped her, and asked the price of the cow; the woman having told him the price, '*Ventre-saint-gris*!' says the King, 'she is not worth that; I will give you so much.' 'I see,' replied the woman, 'you are not a dealer in cows.' 'What makes you think so?', says the King, who had many noblemen with him. 'Don't you see all these calves are following me?'

Painting of Louis XV, 1745, by Nattier. The King commissioned the painting in 1742 but it was not delivered until 1745. Two copies were made and Louis gave one to the Duchess of Châteauroux, and the other to one of her sisters, Madame de Lauraguais.

Portrait of Henri IV aged fifteen by an unknown artist, c. 1569. This is perhaps the portrait sent by Henri's mother, Jeanne d'Albret, to the Protestants in Geneva.

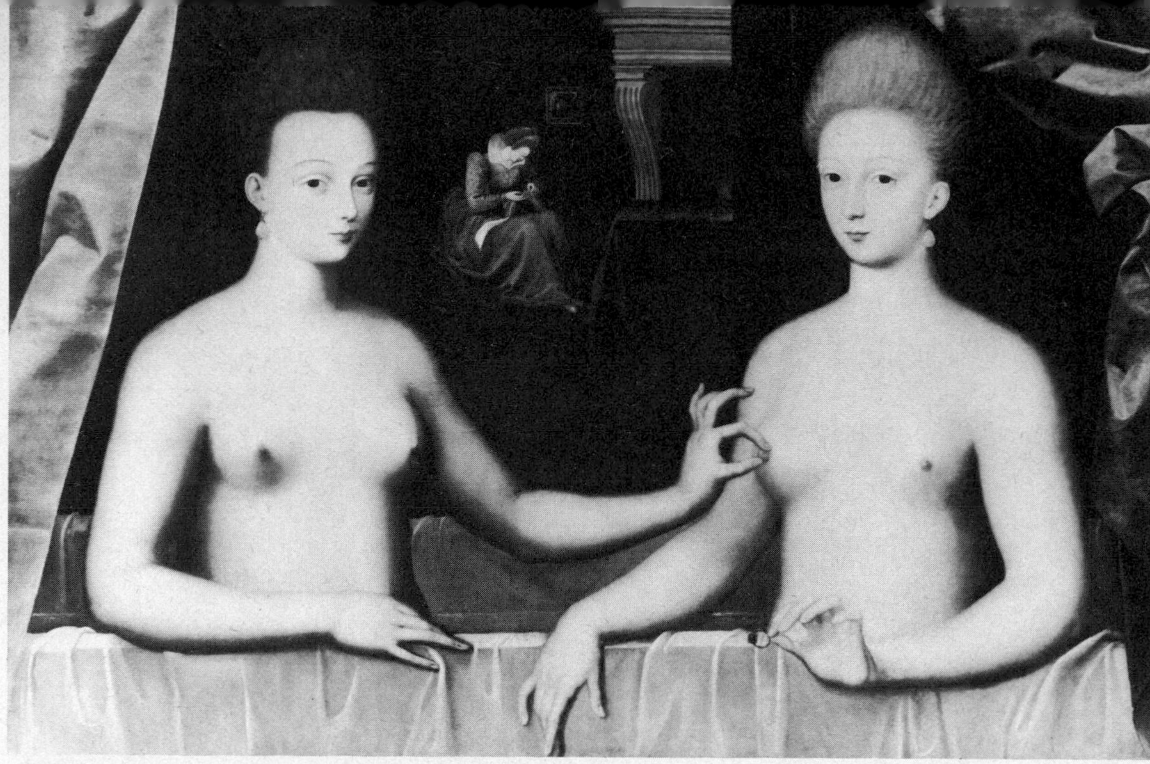

Gabrielle d'Estrées and her sister, the Marquise de Villars.
Painting by the school of Fontainebleau, about 1594.

Henri is reputed to have had fifty-six mistresses and a very great number of bastards, all of whom he was very fond of and took with him on his travels.

He wrote many love letters: to 'la Belle Corisande', Diane of Andouins, the Countess of Gramont, to 'la Belle Fosseuse', Mademoiselle de Montmorency-Fosseux, and notably to Gabrielle of Estrées. She had been sold by her mother to Henri III, then to Zamet, a famous financier, and to various others including the Cardinal of Guise. She became the mistress of the Duke of Longueville and was with the Duke of Bellegarde when Henri IV first saw her on 10 November, 1590 at the château of Coeuvres.

His letters to her were frequent and impassioned:

My beautiful angel, if I was allowed at all hours to weary you with the memory of your subject, I think that the end of one letter would be the beginning of the next. I am dressed only in black, and indeed I am a widower of all that can give me any joy and happiness. No one has lived with so pure a faithfulness as I have for you. Glory in it.

I do not know what charm you have used, but I did not bear previous absences so impatiently as I do this one. It seems to me that a century has passed since I left you. You have only to wish for my return. I have neither artery nor muscle that does not at every moment bring the thought of seeing you before me and make me feel distressed at your absence. Believe me, my dear sovereign, never did love do me such violence as it does now.

Not a single day have I failed to send you a messenger. My love makes me as exacting in my duty as in demanding your favour, which is my only treasure. Believe me, my lovely angel, that I esteem the possession of it as highly as the honour of winning ten battles. Be glorious in the fact that you have vanquished me, who was never entirely vanquished except by you, whose feet I kiss a million times.

To spend the month of April apart from one's mistress is not to live.

I had hoped to send Bidet back to you but I find that as Loménie and all my trusties have gone I cannot even find a piece of paper. That is the truth, my love, and not an excuse. I shall bring you a group of fairly good violin-players to divert both you and your subject, who will greatly cherish you. I had a pleasant surprise in church. An old woman of about eighty took my head and kissed me. I was not the first to laugh. But tomorrow you shall disinfect my mouth.

No woman is like you, and no man equals me in knowing how to love. My passion remains the same as when I first began to love you, my desire to see you again is more violent than it was then. In short, I cherish, love and honour you miraculously.

My love, two hours after the arrival of this messenger, you will see a cavalier of whom you are fond—he who is called King of France and of Navarre, certainly an honourable title though a burdensome one, that of your subject is much more attractive. The three together don't make a bad combination no matter how you mix them.

I write to you, *mes chères amours,* from the feet of your portrait, which I worship only because it was done for you, not that it resembles you. I can be no competent judge of it, for I have painted you all perfection to my soul, my heart and my eyes.

Gabrielle of Estrées wrote less extravagantly impassioned letters than the King, but her concern for him was genuine. When he was ill, she wrote:

I am dying of fear; reassure me, I beg you, by telling me how the finest man in the world is. I fear his illness is serious since no other reason could deprive me of his presence today. My cavalier, tell me your news, because you know your least worry cuts me to the quick. Even though I have heard twice today of your condition, I shall not be able to sleep without sending you a thousand goodnights for I am not gifted with a shabby constance. I am the Princess Constance—sensitive to all that touches you, insensible to everything else, good or evil, in the world.

Although neither Henri nor Gabrielle were faithful to each other, and despite opposition from Sully and the court, Henri wished to rid himself of his queen, Marguerite of Valois, sister of François II, Charles IX and Henri III, and marry Gabrielle. But the negotiations were long drawn out, and to Henri's genuine regret, Gabrielle died suddenly on 14 April, 1599. His sister, Catherine, married to the Duke of Bar, wrote to console him. He replied:

I am greatly consoled by your letter. I need it badly because my loss is as great as was she who caused it. Regrets and misery will accompany me to the tomb. In the meantime, since

Painting of Marguerite of Valois aged seventeen by François Clouet.

Henriette de Balzac d'Entragues, Duchess of Verneuil. Sixteenth-century engraving by Leu.

God caused me to be born for the good of my kingdom and not my own, all my abilities and all my energies will be employed to the advancement and conservation of my realm. The root of my love is dead, and will never more reject me but that of my friendship will remain green forever, my dear sister, I embrace you a thousand times.

In the meantime, however, Henri became embroiled with Henriette of Entragues whom he created Marquise of Verneuil in 1599 and to whose father he wrote:

We, Henri fourth, by the grace of God, King of France and of Navarre, promise and swear before God on our faith and word as King, to Messire François de Balzac, Lord of Entragues, a Knight of our Orders, that giving us as companion Demoiselle Henriette-Catherine de Balzac, his daughter, if in the event of, in six months, beginning on the first day of this present one, she should become pregnant, and should give birth to a son, then and at that moment we will take her to be our wife and legitimate spouse, whose marriage we will solemnize publicly and in the presence of our Holy Church according to the required and customary rites. For greater confirmation of the present promise, we promise and swear as herein stated to ratify and renew it under our seals, immediately after we have obtained from our Holy Father the Pope the dissolution of our marriage with the Lady Marguerite of France, with the permission to marry again as may seem fit to us.

Sully meanwhile was negotiating a more suitable match and Marguerite consented to a

Painting of Marie of Medici, 1683, by Rubens.

divorce when she knew that Henri's intended bride was to be Marie of Medici, with a handsome dowry.

Henriette had told Henri that the promise of marriage was only to satisfy her father but when she found herself pregnant, Henri free to marry her and negotiations with Tuscany well advanced, she complained of Henri's deceit and he replied:

Mademoiselle, the love, honour and benefits which you have received from me would have checked the most lighthearted of souls had it not been accompanied by such an ill nature as yours. I will not scold you further, although I could and ought to do so, as you well know. I beg you to send me back the promise you know of, and not to give me the trouble of recovering it by other means. Also send me back the ring which I returned you the other day. Such is the subject of this letter, to which I require an answer by tonight.

In 1600 Henri married Marie—a jealous and difficult woman. His marriage to her was fruitful but not happy and he continued his affair with Henriette. The two women lived with him in separate establishments in the Louvre, giving birth to children at the same time. Henri still wrote to Henriette:

My dearest love, I have just received the letter you have sent. I have arrived here [Fontainebleau] safe and sound, except for love sickness which I gladly suffer and it is so agreeable to me that if I had to choose a method of death, that would be it. My heart, it seems a century since I left you [echoes of similar letters?] goodnight, my all, love me dearly and believe in my inviolable faithfulness for you, I kiss you a million times.

Four days later he wrote again:

My darling heart, an hour after I had written to you, Lafont came to talk to me of your affairs, with which I will deal tomorrow if God pleases. I am about to go hunting and if I catch anything I will send it to you. Meanwhile go on loving me and take care of your belly. Remember to go and see the pancakes being made; it will give you pleasure. Goodnight, my all, I kiss you a million times. Monsieur d'Entragues has been to see my son—he thinks he is very handsome.

But all was not rosy in their relationship and Henriette had to do as she was told. At one time she became too tiresome and was replaced as maîtresse-en-titre *by Mademoiselle de Beuil; it cost Henri 85,504* livres *to have the lady married to the Count of Sesy, on condition that he left her free for him. Henri told Sully to pay the sum but he couldn't keep away from Henriette despite having to write sharply to her in 1604:*

If your deeds bore out your words, I would not be as dissatisfied with you as I am. Your letters speak affectionately; your behaviour towards me smacks of ingratitude. It is five years and more since you have lived in this way, which everyone finds extraordinary. Think how it affects me of all people. It is useful to you that people think I love you and shameful to me that they should see me suffer because I do. That is why you write to me and why I reply with silence. If you treat me as you should, I will be more yours than ever. If not, keep this letter as the last that you will ever receive from me, who kisses your hand a million times.

He was now trapped between the quarrels of his wife and two mistresses. He was a jealous husband and lover, but a good, if prolific, father. All his children, legitimate and illegitimate, lived together at St Germain, under the rule of their governess, Madame de Montglat. He found his wife boring, as he writes to Sully:

I receive neither society, amusement, nor content from my wife; her conversation is unpleasing, her temper harsh, she never accommodates herself to my humour, nor shares in any of my cares; when I enter her apartment, and offer to approach her in tenderness, or begin to talk familiarly with her, she receives me with so cold and forbidding an air, that I quit her in disgust, and am obliged to seek consolation elsewhere.

James I's ambassador to the French court, Sir George Carew, did not find Marie so unattractive:

The Queen is a lady adorned with much beauty and comeliness of body, and with much beauty and virtue of mind; very observant in all exercises of her religion; and very charitable in performing towards the poor works of mercy; governing the young women and ladies about her with gravity, and causing them to spend their time in works of their needle, and thereby containing them from those disorders, which commonly follow idleness and vanity. Her main and sole opposition is against the Marquise of Verneuil, who being of an excellent, pleasant and witty entertainment, maintaineth still a strong hold in the King's affections; and the Queen by her eagerness doth work herself some disadvantage.

At the end of his life, a contemporary printer Jean Richer, described him thus:

This great king was of medium size; he had hair grey with age and work, a gentle and venerable face, an aquiline nose, wide open eyes, a big forehead and a good colour for an elderly man.

Bishop Péréfixe agrees:

Henri was of medium height, active and agile, hardened by work and cares. His body was well-shaped, his temperament strong and robust; and he had stupendous health, despite the fact that by the time he was fifty, he had had several attacks of gout which passed off quickly and left him unscathed. He had a deep forehead, lively and commanding eyes, a long nose and a ruddy colour—in all a noble and calm face, which nevertheless betrayed the warrior. His hair was thick and brown, he wore a large beard but kept his hair short. He started to go grey at the age of thirty-five.

On his way one fateful day to visit Sully:

On Friday the 14th May, 1610 at four in the afternoon the King was in his coach, without any guards, only Messieurs d'Epernon, Montbazon and four or five others with him, passing St Innocent to go to the Arsenal. His coach was held up because a pig and a handcart were blocking the way and he had to stop at the corner of the rue de la Ferronerie in front of notary Poutrain's house. He was there killed and assassinated by a wicked and desperate good-for-nothing named François de Ravaillac, a native of Angoulême, who used the opportunity he had come specially to Paris for (having planned it for a long time and about which he had even warned the King who had taken no heed of the warning).

While the King was listening to a letter which Monsieur d'Epernon was reading, Ravaillac threw himself upon him in a rage with a knife in his hand and gave him two thrusts in the breast, of which the second penetrated to the heart, cutting an artery, which stifled the King's breath and life so that he could not even speak. Monsieur d'Epernon, seeing blood pouring from all sides, covered the King with a coat and having seen, with the others, that he was dead, tried to reassure the assembled mob as best he could, shattered as they were by the accident. He said that the King was only slightly wounded and they were reassured. They turned the coach back towards the Louvre, from which the King, swimming in blood, was only removed dead.

On the same day the King's body was opened and all his members were found to be healthy and in a good state (except for his lungs which were slightly injured) and the doctors said that in the course of nature he could have lived another twenty years. His heart was small but fat and compact and in good shape. It went to the Jesuits as they wished.

The tortures Ravaillac underwent defy repetition even today. Some however were inflicted not by official torturers but by the people of Paris, for whom—as for the rest of France—Henri of Navarre, the first Bourbon, the vert galant, *had become a great king.*

Henri IV's death mask taken from his corpse at St Denis when the tomb was desecrated in October 1793.

Louis XIII

Louis XIII was born on 27 September, 1601 at Fontainebleau. He acceded to the throne on 14 May, 1610 and was crowned at Rheims on 17 October.
He married, on 24 November, 1615, Anne of Austria (1601–1666).
He reigned for thirty-three years and died, of tuberculosis, aged forty-one, at St Germain-en-Laye on 14 May, 1643 and was buried at St Denis.

Louis was only nine years old at the time of his father's assassination. We are fortunate in knowing a great deal about his infancy and childhood for Jean Héroard had for thirty years been physician to Charles IX, Henri III and Henri IV when, at the age of about fifty, he was chosen by Henri IV to attend to his heir from birth. Héroard stayed with Louis XIII and kept a daily journal for just over twenty-six years.

Louis, brought up with the children his father had by his mistresses, was an obstreperous boy with a speech defect. His language as a child was foul and his father's example and behaviour with him was not altogether regal, or perhaps seemly:

He [Louis—aged five] gave some of his bread to his small dog. Madame de Montglat said, 'You should not give bread to dogs; you should give it to the poor.' 'Are dogs rich?' At half past nine, undressed and peed. 'This is how Papa pees,' he said displaying his wholly belly.

At half past nine he [Louis—aged nine] undressed, went to bed, slept with the King with whom he capered about all night, putting his feet on his chest and under his chin. The King kept on tickling him and eventually withdrew without waking him.

When Louis was told of his father's death he was very upset but was man enough to say, 'Had I been present with my sword I would have killed him'. His mother, Marie of Medici became regent. Until he was eight Louis remained in the hands of women and on 9 January, 1609 the Marquis of Souvré became his governor. One of his first tasks was to clean up the boy's language.

The boy King continued with his childish occupations:

He [Louis—aged 13] went to Villiers-la-Garenne, to Mademoiselle Brisset, where he ate. Then he went into the kitchen, placing Monsieur the Count of Rocheguyon at the door as usher and set himself to carry the eggs, having been to the poultry woman to fetch them himself. He gave two *écus* to a woman who brought him six, and a chicken, set about cooking plain poached eggs and poached eggs with black butter, and hard-boiled eggs chopped up with bacon to a recipe of his own invention. Monsieur de Frontenas made an omelette; the King told the little Humières to take the stave and officiate as *maître d'hôtel*, the others to carry the dishes and himself took the last one, and thus they marched in to

Detail of a painting of Louis XIII, 1616, by Pourbus.

the room where Monsieur de Souvré was waiting to be served on his instructions. He made him taste the dish he was carrying, sat down, ate the omelette, some black grapes and a lot of bread though he drank nothing. He came back at five o'clock and played billiards.

Louis's tutors were not very learned or skilful and he did not care much for his lessons:

Studied; found the lesson dragged on. Asked Monsieur de Fleurence [his tutor—in orders], 'If I give you a bishopric, will you shorten my lessons?' 'No, Sire.' The King did not reply.

Shortly after his birth Louis had had an operation on his tongue for the frenulum had had to be cut, and his stammering gave cause for constant worry, and talk about further operations. The child worried a good deal about the fear of having his tongue cut, which may have contributed psychologically to his sexual difficulties. For reasons of state his mother affianced him to Anne of Austria, daughter of Philip III of Spain, who was his own age. Queen Marie told the boy of her intentions:

In the evening the Queen said while he was playing after supper, 'My son, I wish you to be married; will that suit you?' 'Yes indeed, madam.' 'But you do not know how to make children.' 'Excuse me.' 'And how do you know?' 'Monsieur de Souvré has taught me.'

Héroard tells of the marriage day and night:

Louis went in a carriage to see the Queen incognito and arrived at Castres, five leagues from Bordeaux. There he saw her through a window as she was getting into her carriage. She set off, and a little later, two leagues from the town on a good road, he stopped his carriage alongside hers and walking slowly had a good look at her. Shortly afterwards turned to her laughingly pointing his finger saying, 'I am incognito, I am incognito, touch me, coachman, touch me.' A league further on he mounted on horseback and reached Bordeaux at seven o'clock. The Queen Infanta arrived at eight. He went into an antechamber and went up on to a high raised platform. There were six or seven steps up and three chairs at the top. The Queen Mother led the Queen Infanta to the King who went down two steps to greet her, and take her and his mother back to sit down in the middle of them. They stayed there for a quarter of an hour and at nine o'clock he and the Queen Mother took her to her rooms and he went back to his.

At one o'clock he went to the Queen who was dressing and presented Monsieur de Souvré and me. She wanted a red feather to put with a white one. The King gave her his hat in which there were two, telling her to take the one she preferred. She took one, gave him back his hat, at which point he suddenly said, 'You must give me one of your bows', which were red. She, laughingly, gave him one, and he attached it like a badge to his feathers.

At four o'clock he went to St André, went round the church, heard mass and performed the usual ceremony with the Queen. They heard mass together. He came back at half past five, and took the Queen to her room. He was tired; he went to his, went to bed and supped there at a quarter to seven. Monsieur de Gramont and several young courtiers told him coarse stories to build up his courage. He was ashamed and very frightened but took his dressing-gown and went to the Queen his wife's room at eight accompanied by his mother. At a quarter past ten he came back, having slept for about an hour and having performed, according to him, twice; he appeared, with a red *g* . . .

The Queen Mother, also for reasons of state, was anxious that the world should believe that the marriage had been consummated and did her best to bring it about, according to another contemporary document:

After the ceremony, about seven in the evening, Their Majesties having spent some time chatting together, the King and the little Queen returned with as much order as the hour allowed and took the shortest route from the Archbishop's palace while the Queen Mother also went back by the small door and being there gave the order for the blessing of the nuptial bed to be given with no other ceremony than by one of the almoners or chaplains.

As soon as the King had eaten he went to bed in his own room and in his own bed as usual whereupon the Queen his mother, who until then had stayed in the room of the little Queen whom she had put to bed in the first room, went to find him about eight o'clock, crossing a room from which she had sent out the guards and everyone else, and finding the King in his bed said these words:

'My son, it is not all to be married, you must come and see the Queen your wife who is waiting for you.'

The King replied:

'Madam, I was only waiting for your command. I will go at once with you if it please you.'

At the same time he was put into his dressing-gown and his furry slippers and thus he went with the Queen his mother across the said room to the room of the little Queen, into which there went in with Their Majesties the two nurses, Monsieur de Souvré, his governor, Héroard, his chief doctor, the Marquis of Rambouillet, his wardrobe master, carrying his sword, and Belinguant, his chief valet, carrying a candle. The Queen Mother greeted the little Queen: 'My daughter, I bring you your husband; take him to you and love him well, I beg you.'

She replied in Spanish saying that her only wish was to please both of them, and then the King got into bed on the door side while she got in on the other side. The Queen Mother, seeing them there together, said something to them so quietly that no one heard it and then left saying, 'Let us all go'. She told the two nurses to remain and to leave the young couple together for an hour and a half, or two hours at most.

So they were left and thus the marriage was consummated, twice according to the King himself and the two nurses, and after they had slept a little the King woke up of his own accord and went back to his own room. The little Queen got up at the same time and went into her little room and her own little bed she had brought from Spain.

But in fact there is much doubt that the marriage was consummated then and there is no evidence that Louis had any further sexual relations with her at least until several years later, when the Duke of Luynes was instrumental in getting him back to Anne's bed.

Although Héroard, usually so explicit, gives no hint of a homosexual relationship, his recounting of one of Louis's dreams at his own insistence, may well be relevant:

He said that he had dreamed that the Duke of Luynes, a gentleman of whom he was fond, was dressed as a Swiss guard, with yellow slashed breeches, a large green cod-piece and a huge ruff like those worn by women, and that he was playing a fife. Also that his mistress was also dressed as a Swiss guard and was playing the tambourine, which she was good at striking but not so good at making hum (which he said unwittingly) [There is a Freudian pun here in French]. He told everyone of his dream and instructed me to write it down.

However, on 26 January, 1619—that is four years later, confirming reports that flew across Europe the next day, Héroard has this to say, although Anne's first child was not born until twenty-three years after the marriage:

Painting of Louis XIII, after 1628, by Champaigne. 'Louis XIII through the whole of his reign exercised no will of his own; he resigned it entirely to Richelieu.'

Went to bed, said his prayers. At about eleven, without expecting him, Monsieur de Luynes arrived to persuade him to sleep with the Queen. He stoutly resisted even to the point of tears but was carried there and put to bed; performed twice, it is said—to my certain knowledge.

At two o'clock he came back; undressed; went to bed and slept until nine in the morning.

Louis's appearance is described in a contemporary letter:

As far as the outer man is concerned, that is to say his body, he has a most pleasant face and in particular that part which some have called the mirror and others the seat of the soul. For he casts looks of such acuteness and grace on all who surround him even in the greatest crowds that it is a byword in the Louvre that he governs the court with his eye. He is well-shaped from head to foot and has such a strong and vigorous constitution that there is not a soldier in the guards who can support better all sorts of fatigue and drudgery. When he is out hunting, which is his favourite recreation, there is no one who can keep up with him, for to cross even five or six leagues on foot is nothing to him.

He bears hunger and thirst with incredible fortitude. He normally eats little and drinks less. The last time that I had the honour of dining in the gallery he did not empty his glass, a far from rare occurrence. And the little that he does eat and drink he does with so little ceremony and such lack of delicacy that all those who attended his meals were disgusted.

It is the same with the accessories of his clothes. He abjures all sorts of affectation and mincing get-up so that one sees that the real marks of royalty do not lie in the magnificence and sumptuousness of clothing. He has not worn either decorations or embroidery since his last sumptuary edict of which he requires such strict observance that a little while ago a prince had to remove the gloves he had on. There has never been any means of persuading him to curl or powder his hair; he objects to all such vanities and scorns the young sprigs of fashion who waste half their lives perfuming and prinking themselves.

He is always moving, like the sun, and if one discounts the time spent in the sweet necessity of sleep, of which he has little, and the time required for undressing, there is no time of the day when his active and ready humour does not prompt him to some laudable exercise. He is brilliant at everything, in particular riding which as soon as he took up one would have sworn he had done for ten years. From whence comes this word from the Sieur de Pluvinel: the King on foot is King of his subjects, but the King mounted is King of Kings. He was also unparalleled in the use of firearms—he performed small miracles in this field as I myself saw.

His memory was so good that there was no prayer at divine service that he did not know by heart, and he always paid extreme attention to his devotions. He heard mass every morning with as much reverence as attention, and even on the days when he was purged which happened from time to time, and when taking his bath, he had mass said in his room.

He certainly had a vivid imagination and there is much evidence to prove it. To speak only of hunting, he invented contrivances which no one else had thought of and he had marvellous manual dexterity. He often spent time in the foundry casting and forging arms. I cannot personally vouch for his painting but it is certain that had he been one half as talented as he was the apprentices of Apelles [portrait painter to Philip and Alexander of Macedon] would not have laughed at him. Moreover he had a great natural inclination for music and his aptitude for it was so marked that without having studied the rules he sang with the masters hardly ever getting a wrong note.

As for his judgment this could be seen every day in all his actions and in particular at his council deliberating over important affairs of state. His understanding was instantaneous, his comment wise, and his decision just. Moreover, he tempered the severity of his justice with a sweet clemency. He let natural justice run its course believing that the best cement for the law was the blood of those who defaulted. But he himself had a kindly and benign nature.

He spoke few words but those he uttered were of import. He never undertook anything which he did not bring to fruition, and he tempered his royal authority to the public good to such an extent that he was rightly surnamed the Just. He was generous to the poor and each month distributed eight hundred *écus* out of the thousand he allowed himself for court entertainment, thinking it a better pastime to alleviate the sufferings of the afflicted.

Louis's youth and the regency gave once again an opportunity for the nobles to revolt against the crown, for although Henri IV and Sully had worked miracles, the country was not unwilling to take advantage of a queen regent with a small son. The nobles objected to increased centralisation of power and the Protestants complained that the Edict of Nantes did not give them enough. But like his father, Louis was lucky in finding a minister who could deal with the situation. Cardinal Richelieu decided that the Huguenots must be brought to heel and he starved La Rochelle into submission. He dealt equally severely with the nobility, beheading them as necessary and going so far as to put to death two young men who persisted in duelling despite it having been banned.

France needed internal stability for as usual the German emperor showed signs of increasing power and France had to go to war to protect herself. In doing so, she managed to enlarge her territories yet again and when Louis died, six months after Richelieu, between them they left France almost the size of ancient Gaul.

Louis died leaving his widow regent and an heir of five. A court lady writes of Anne when Queen Mother, at the age of fifty-eight:

Endowed by nature with generous sentiments, all her feelings are noble; she is a gentle but determined soul, and, although it is not my intention in speaking to exaggerate her qualities I can say in general that in some respects she is the equal of the greatest queens of antiquity.

She is tall and well-proportioned, with a sweet and majestic air which never fails to inspire love and respect in all who see her. She was one of the great beauties of the century and today enough traces of her former beauty remain to enable her to outshine the young who claim to be attractive. Her eyes are very beautiful and combine gentleness with seriousness. Their power was fatal to many famous people and entire nations have suffered to their cost from the power they had over men. Her mouth, though most innocent, supplemented the devastation caused by her eyes. She is small and rosy and nature has been liberal in endowing her with enough gifts to render her perfect. With but one smile she can conquer a thousand hearts; even her enemies cannot resist her charm. I have often seen people who ambition has rendered senseless swear that the Queen was more loved by them, even when they sought to avoid their duty.

Her hair, a clear chestnut, is fine and she has a great deal of it. Nothing is more agreeable than to watch her comb it. Her hands, which are renowned from all over Europe, are made to please the eye, to carry a sceptre and to be admired and they combine dexterity with extreme whiteness. So that one can say that it is a pleasing spectacle to watch this great Queen whether at her toilette or at meals.

Her bosom is beautiful and well-shaped and those to whom it gives pleasure to see beauty have reason to complain of the care which the Queen takes to hide it. Her whole skin is of a pure whiteness and of a delicacy which it would be hard to over-praise. Her complexion is of another line—it is not so beautiful because she neglects it and takes no steps to preserve it. Since she practically never puts on a mask she does nothing to improve it. Her nose is not as perfect as her other facial features; it is large although its size does not accord badly with her large eyes and, it seems to me, if it diminishes her beauty at least it contributes to render her expression more serious. Her entire person is worthy of the greatest praise but I would offend her modesty and mine if I said more about it. So I will only add that she has pretty feet too, small and well-formed.

She is not a slave to fashion although she dresses well. She is neat and tidy. One could say that she loves beautiful things and has no strange affectations. Many Parisian women spend more than the Queen does. She is governed by habit, not vanity. She is fond of simple decoration because it is natural for her to be well turned out whether she is on her own or at court.

It is fair to start discussing her moral virtues with her piety which seems to be one of the principal merits of this august princess. She certainly has great respect for the law of God, is charitable and likes to help the poor. She is indefatigable in the exercise of her devotions and she has extraordinary confidence in God. She is exact in her observance of fast days, has great religious zeal and greatly respects the Pope.

Her merits lie in her reliability and unassuming manners. Her modesty is not affected by innocent fun and her purity serves as an example to all other women. She finds it easy to believe in good and not relish evil. Tale-bearers and gossips do not impress her and when she once decides to believe in someone she does not change her mind easily. She is courtesy itself. She strongly disapproves of the rude and uncivil manners of the present time and if the young people of this century followed her maxims people would be better behaved and politer than they are.

She is gentle, affable and friendly with all who come near and who have the honour to serve her. Her goodness allows her to suffer the small as the great and although she does not lack discernment she is willing to enter in conversations with many people of a lower social order.

Her gentle temperament does not detract from her air of regal dignity and does not prevent her from distinguishing those who are dutiful and those who are lacking in respect due to ignorance or the current habit of casualness.

She has a pretty, natural wit, speaks well and carries on pleasant conversations. She enjoys a friendly argument and never takes anything the wrong way. Her views on serious matters are always dictated by reason and good sense and in business matters her judgment is always conducted with equity and justice. But she is lazy and she never reads anything. This does not bother her because her intimate relationship with the great men of our day, her great knowledge of the world and her long experience of the affairs and intrigues of a court, where she always played a great part, make up for any deficiency in book knowledge and if she is ignorant of the history of Pharamond [the legendary founder of the French monarchy] and of Charlemagne, on the other hand she knows that of her own time well.

She only takes pleasure in going to the theatre in order to please the King who because of his love for her, likes to have her with him; and for this the whole of France must be grateful. She likes gaming and spends several hours a day at play. It is said by her fellow

Bronze statue of Anne of Austria by Guillain, who was one of the twelve founding members of the Academy in 1648.

players that her game is rational and that she has no desire for gain.

The Queen is indifferent to her position and has no wish to appear superior. She cares for few people but those to whom she gives her confidence may count themselves fortunate in her love. Having found herself, by the death of her husband, regent and with power to wield she was forced to accord her friendship to a person whose ability could sustain her and on whom she could count for faithful advice. The love she had been unable to give her husband she devotes to her children—especially her son, the King [Louis XIV]. She detests her enemies with the same passion that she gave to her early friends. By nature she is revengeful and she is capable of sustaining her revenge, although reason and her conscience prevent her from excesses. She rarely loses her temper, remaining always in control of herself. To my knowledge only the interests of the crown, the state and her son move her.

She is open-handed and capable of great generosity but as she is sparing with herself she forgets to distribute gifts. Her most striking characteristic is her strength of purpose. She is fearless at all times and neither death nor bad luck worry her. She sticks to her own opinion come what may once she thinks she is in the right, and finds in her innocence and rectitude her refuge and her consolation. She has come to terms with herself and lives free from worries. She finds neither in the past nor in the future any memory or fear which might threaten her peace. She thinks only of following the advice of the Evangelist and that of the philosophers of passing her time, tasting with gentleness the good which she finds without complaining of the ill she encounters. The thought of death in no way bothers her and she foresees its coming without grumbling about its fatal power.

Louis XIV

Louis XIV was born on 5 September, 1638 at St Germain-en-Laye. He acceded to the throne on 14 May, 1643 and was crowned at Rheims on 7 June, 1654.
He married, on 9 June, 1660, Marie-Thérèse of Spain (1638–1683).
He reigned for seventy-one years and died, of gangrene, aged nearly seventy-seven, at Versailles on 1 September, 1715. He was buried at St Denis.

Once again France had a child king. Louis's mother, Anne of Austria, had become regent and she was guided by Mazarin, the Italian cardinal bequeathed to her by Richelieu. France was still fighting the Emperor but with the help of two of her ablest generals, Condé and Turenne, became, by the Peace of Westphalia in 1648, 'the arbiter of Europe'. Mazarin, despite this great triumph, was unpopular within the country and his financial policy and the desire of the Paris Parlement *to achieve greater power led to a series of uprisings known as the Fronde. One day when still very young, Louis XIV returned to Paris after the Fronde, and appeared in his hunting costume, whip in hand, at one of the sittings of* Parlement. *He told the magistrates that he intended to be obeyed and if he did not actually ever say, 'the state is me', he certainly thought it. It was clear who was to be master. Louis had succeeded in defeating the Frondeurs and had learned the lesson of allowing one minister too great a power. He took the reins of government into his own hands and was never to let them go. The era of the Sun King had begun.*

Louis saw himself as the embodiment of power. His contemporaries throughout his very long life tended to write glowingly of him. Madame de Motteville, one of his mother's ladies-in-waiting, saw his regal appearance as early as 1653:

Since the peace and his glorious return to Paris, [after the Fronde] he has grown in all

Marble bust of Louis XIV by Bernini. When Bernini went to see the King with his drawings for his project at the Louvre in June 1665, Louis said he would be pleased if Bernini, before leaving France, would do a bust of him. The King gave Bernini twenty sittings during one of which Louis said he would prefer to sit, and Bernini replied that he had to remain standing.

things. His fine figure and good looks provoke admiration, and he carries in his eyes and in his whole bearing that air of majesty which by virtue of his crown is innate in him.

As soon as peace allowed the re-establishment of the pleasures of court, the prince attached himself not to the most beautiful of Cardinal Mazarin's nieces but to Mademoiselle de Mancini, sister to Madame de Mercœur. Confirming the view I took when she arrived from Italy, it seems as if all the efforts of nature and youth are not able to beautify her. She has fiery eyes and despite her facial faults, the virtue of being eighteen years of age has its effect. Anyhow she attracted the King and he saw a great deal of her.

The Grande Mademoiselle, Louis's first cousin, who hoped to marry him, wrote in her Mémoires:

The King was in a much better temper since he had fallen in love with Mademoiselle Mancini. He was gay and talked to everyone. I think she had told him to read novels and poetry, for he had a large number of them and collections of verse and comedies and seemed to derive pleasure from them and when he spoke of them he did so with the authority of a man who has read a good deal and has a fair knowledge of them. I have never seen a man with such natural good judgment who spoke so sensibly; and I am glad to see that I was not wrong in this opinion, which is now universally shared.

Mademoiselle collected together a gallery of portraits, in which the King of course figured. In it Madame de Brégis, another lady-in-waiting to Anne of Austria, wrote of the King under the guise of the shepherd 'Tircis' in about 1658:

Although he ranks as a god, let us dress 'Tircis' in a shepherd's clothes so that I may have the temerity to attempt to draw a portrait of him. He is a shepherd who can as well carry a sceptre as a crook, he has a conqueror's heart; with those of his own sex he is a hero, with those of ours he is the most gallant and honest man in the world. He is better made than other men; tall and of such an excellent build that he need not grow any more to achieve perfection. [He was twenty.] His locks are the colour of cedar; they are so beautiful and plentiful that they seem to be a crown and enable him to rule even where sceptres are not necessarily obeyed. His features are not beautiful but since beauty is that which pleases, one can say that the shepherd Tircis is the most handsome man alive. His legs and arms and feet are so perfectly made that no one should worry that they are there to walk over us. He has an ease and skill for all exercise and dances better than anyone. His elegant and fashionable clothes combined with his healthy appearance single him out as a king amongst the shepherds. He is prudent, attentive to the ladies, discreet and always answers in a most judicious and aimiable manner. His temperament is a little reserved and haughty but generous and good-natured.

A rather more far-fetched piece of adulation, this time by a man, was also included in Mademoiselle's gallery. Monsieur Martinet, who may have been one of the court officials to officiate at ceremonies, writes:

His figure is tall, straight, free, full, strong, with wide chest and shoulders, large arms, legs in proportion and shapely; a proud but sweet-natured face not otherwise remarkable. When he wishes to go about incognito he fails because he is instantly recognised as the master for he has the air, the bearing and all the marks by which one distinguishes those whom one used to say had gods' blood in their veins. His hair has recently been sacrificed to his health, during an illness when he was despaired of. His eyes shine as brightly as those of Augustus and are as piercing but not so bold, and their shading lids and clement air are to be likened to the rays of the sun, which when seen through a light haze diffuse the brilliance which would otherwise be insupportable. His face is lightly pocked [the King had measles in 1647] but his illness has not lessened the vivacity of his colouring and has served only to strengthen those features which were perhaps too delicate for so virile a man and to give a hero's beauty to a king who rules people who have never wept for the death of Adonis. His pallor has remained to contrast with the beautiful coral of his mouth by comparison with which roses pale and from which oracles and graces pour. The chin which terminates this perfect oval begins to ornament itself with the last example of youthfulness, with that rich fluff the shaving of which was the opening of a career to illustrious persons in other times [Roman]. But to know the grace and majesty of this entirely royal and august body, one must see him mounted, or in a ballet, where the advantages of nature and habit are so obvious.

Louis was married in 1660 to another Spanish princess, Marie-Thérèse, a dull woman who bored him and of whom he said that her death was the only trouble she ever caused him. A contemporary Italian writes of their life together:

Marie-Thérèse and the dauphin by Mignard.

The King treats her with all the honour due to her position. He eats and sleeps with her, and fulfils his family duty. His mistresses are never mentioned in his conversation with her. For her own amusement, she has half a dozen little fools whom she addresses as 'my heart', 'poor boy' or 'my son'; she also has a number of small dogs who get better treatment than the buffoons. They have their own carriages and servants to take them out, and are fed at table. Someone once told me that they cost 400 *écus* a year, while the buffoons are lucky if they get a penny.

After eight o'clock the Queen plays cards until ten when the King comes to fetch her to eat. She likes playing *ombre* best but she is so simple that she always loses.

The famous 'Mazarinettes', Cardinal Mazarin's nieces. Marie-Anne, Duchess of Bouillon (right); Olympe of Soissons (centre) and Marie (left), who said to Louis XIV, 'You are the King; you love me and yet you send me away.' French school, seventeenth century.

Louis did not suffer from his father's affliction as far as women were concerned and his fondness for them started early as he worked his way round Cardinal Mazarin's nieces, the Mancini girls. He had a string of mistresses of whom Louise de la Vallière and Athénaïs de Montespan lasted longest. Voltaire writes:

Louis gave to his court, as to his reign, so much verve and brilliance that the most trivial details of his life have fascinated posterity just as they were objects of curiosity to his contemporaries and the other courts of Europe. The splendour of his government shone over his smallest actions. People, especially in France, were thirstier for knowledge about the details of life at his court than for news of revolutions in other countries; so great was his reputation.

That is why there is no lack of historians to recount his early tastes for the Baroness of Beauvais, Mademoiselle d'Argincourt, the niece of Cardinal Mazarin . . .

Madame de Montespan, the King's most long-standing mistress, has a catty little piece about the Queen in her Memoirs:

French cookery, by common consent, is held to be well-nigh perfect in its excellence; yet the Infanta could never get used to our dishes. The Señora Molina, well furnished with silver kitchen utensils, has a sort of private kitchen or scullery reserved for her own use, and there it is that the manufacture takes place of clove-scented chocolate, brown soups and gravies, stews redolent with garlic, capsicums and nutmeg, and all that nauseous

Louise de la Vallière, about 1663, by Nocret. 'She had an elegant figure with a very slight limp, brunette, thin with a gracious face and eyes the gentleness of which ravished you when she looked at you.'

Madame de Montespan, after Mignard.

RIGHT*: Madame de Maintenon, about 1687, by Elle.*

pastry in which the young Infanta revels.

I am not unjust, and I admit that a husband's public attachments are not exactly calculated to fill his legitimate consort with joy. But, fortunately for the Infanta, the King abounds in rectitude and good-nature. This very good-nature it is which prompts him to use all the consideration of which a noble soul is capable, and the more his amours give the Queen just cause for anxiety, the more does he redouble his kindness and consideration towards her. Of this she is sensible. Thus, she acquiesces, and, as much through tenderness as social tact, she never reproaches or upbraids him with anything. Nor does the King scruple to admit that, to secure so complacent a partner, it was well worth the trouble of going to fetch her from the other end of the world.

Louise left court aged thirty and lived on in a convent for another thirty-six years; Louis's passion for Athénaïs waxed and waned from her establishment as maîtresse-en-titre *in 1667 and nine babies later until about 1678; there was a succession of women, but after the Queen's death in 1683 and Louis's increasing religious zeal he married, secretly, Madame de Maintenon, who had come to court originally to look after Athénaïs's babies by the King. Voltaire gives his explanation for her hold—from the age of forty-eight—on the King:*

When men are no longer in their first youth [Louis was forty-five] they generally require the society of an accommodating woman: it is above all the pressure of business affairs that urges them to seek this consolation. The new favourite, Madame de Maintenon, who saw the secret power she commanded over him grow day by day, behaved with that art so natural to women and far from displeasing to men.

Louis wanted his reign to be the most brilliant that had ever been seen and he succeeded, for one still thinks of his epoch as France's apogee. He himself had very clear ideas about his position as Sun King, and the symbolism of his choice of the sun as a device, as well as the nature of kingship, as he wrote in his own Mémoires:

Then I began to use as a symbol the one I have used ever since, and which you see everywhere. I thought that it would represent in some way the duties of a prince and would be a constant reminder to me to fulfil them. The choice was the sun—the most noble of all and which, by virtue of its unique quality, the brilliance which surrounds it, the light it gives to the other stars which behave as a court to it, the equal and fair division of this light it spreads throughout the whole world, the good it achieves everywhere, creating joy and life on all sides the whole time by its perpetual motion even though it appears at rest, the constant and invariable course from which it never moves or deviates, is without doubt the most vivid and beautiful image for a great king.

Kings are often compelled to do things against their inclination and which go against their nature. They must take delight in giving pleasure and they must often punish and therefore lose the support of persons to whom they naturally wish well. The interest of the state must come first. One must overcome one's own wishes and not find oneself in the situation where one can reproach oneself over something important that could have been done better but which some private interest prevented and which deflects one from the greatness, good and power of the state.

Once one has decided on a course of action which one believes to be for the best, one must proceed with it. Often this is what has led me to success. The faults which have given me infinite sorrow that I have committed were due to complacency or to listening too readily to the advice of others. Nothing is more dangerous than feebleness, of any kind whatsoever. To rule other people one must raise oneself above them and having heard what everyone has to say, one must make decisions using one's own unprejudiced judgment. One must never give commands which might be lacking in dignity or which do not redound to the greatness of the state. The calling of king is great, noble and delightful when one holds oneself to be worthy of fulfilling all that is required of one. But he is not exempt from grief, fatigue or uncertainties. Uncertainty sometimes produces despair but when one has spent a reasonable time examining a problem one must decide the best course of action and despatch it. When one has the state in mind one is working for oneself. The good of one produces the glory of the other.

Each profession in its own way supports the monarchy. The labourer by his work supplies the food to sustain the great body of the state. The artisan by his industry creates objects for the convenience of the public while the merchant collects from a thousand different places everything that is useful or pleasant in the whole world and supplies it as and when it is required. The financiers, who collect the public money, contribute to the maintenance of the state; the judges, who apply the laws, keep law and order; the clergy, who give religious instruction, assure the benediction of heaven and peace on earth.

So you see, far from despising any of these occupations or giving preferential treatment to one rather than another, we must provide ideal conditions in which they may all flourish and convince ourselves that we do not reward unjustly those whom we hold higher in our esteem than others who may rightly object.

His principles were exemplified in his life. He wanted to have a palace of his own to show off his grandeur. He left the Louvre, which his ancestors had lived in, and set about the construction of the château of Versailles. Colbert, his first minister who was careful about money, often grumbled about the huge expense. He was the son of a wool merchant in Rheims, and a bourgeois like many of the monarch's ministers. While the King was putting order into the country he was putting order into the country's finances, which is why he sighed so greatly over Versailles. The King let him sigh.

Visconti, an Italian, who was at the court of Louis, gives a picture of the King's daily routine there:

The King does everything in his power to show that he is not dominated by his ministers, and never was a king less governed. He wants to be kept informed on all matters; affairs of state from his ministers, events in the *parlements* from their presidents, the most trivial facts from his judges, and affairs of the heart from his mistresses. In short, not a day passes without him knowing what is going on and there are few people about whose name and activities he does not know.

In general his own daily activities are well regulated. He always rises at eight, works in his study from ten until half past twelve when he goes to mass with the Queen. At one o'clock he visits his mistress, until two, when he dines, in public, with the Queen. Then he hunts or goes for a walk, or, more often than not, works. From nightfall until ten o'clock he talks to the ladies of the court, plays cards, watches a play or attends the dancing. After supper, at eleven he goes again to his mistress's rooms. He always sleeps with the Queen. He has so divided the hours of the day and the night between business and pleasure, religious observance and his duty that his courtiers know exactly what he is doing and his whereabouts at any given moment.

The King requires constant hard work from everyone in his service whatever their profession; never had idleness a more formidable enemy. He is himself always occupied, whether in reviewing his troops, moving them about, building fortifications, shifting earth; he encourages navigation and keeps both his friends and enemies throughout Europe in a continual state of turmoil as a result of his demands. He has a hearty constitution and enjoys good health, so that his healthiness and good luck combined result in his ability to keep people on their toes in emulation of him.

It is a fine sight to see him leave the château with his entourage; it reminds one of a queen bee.

The Duke of St Simon, the greatest memorialist of his, or very nearly any other, day, was at court during the last twenty years of Louis's life. Louis frequently told him to hold his tongue but suffered him because he liked Madame de St Simon. The waspish little Duke did not like the King much either but was not unfair in his assessment:

He was a prince in whom no one would deny good and even great qualities, but he had many others that were petty or downright bad, and of these it was impossible to determine which were natural and which acquired. Nothing is harder to find than a well-informed writer, none rarer than those who knew him personally, yet are sufficiently unbiased to speak of him without hatred or flattery, and to set down the bare truth for good or ill.

This is not the place to tell of his early childhood. He was king almost from birth, but was deliberately repressed by a mother who loved to govern, and still more so by a wicked and self-interested minister, who risked the state a thousand times for his own aggrandizement. So long as that minister lived the King was held down, and that portion of his life should be subtracted from his reign. Nevertheless, he throve beneath that yoke, for he learned to know love, and discovered that idleness is the enemy of glory. He made feeble excursions in both directions. After Mazarin's death, he had enough intelligence to realize his deliverance, but not enough vigour to release himself. Indeed, that event was one of the finest moments of his life, for it taught him an unshakable principle namely, to banish all prime ministers and ecclesiastics from his councils. Another ideal, adopted at that time, he could never sustain because in the practice it constantly eluded him. This was to govern alone. It was the quality upon which he most prided himself and for which he received most praise and flattery. In fact, it was what he was least able to do.

Born with an intelligence rather below the average, his mind was very capable of development with training and education, for he could learn easily from others and not parrot-wise. He profited immensely from having always lived among people of the highest quality with the widest knowledge of life, men and women of vastly different ages and characters, but all of them personalities.

Let me repeat. The King's intelligence was below the average, but was very capable of improvement. He loved glory; he desired peace and good government. He was born prudent, temperate, secretive, master of his emotions and his tongue—can it be believed?—he was born good and just. God endowed him with all the makings of a good and perhaps even of a fairly great king. All the evil in him came from without. His early training was so dissolute that no one dared to go near his apartments, and he would sometimes speak bitterly of those days and tell how they found him one night fallen into the fountain at the Palais Royal. He became very dependent on others, for they had scarcely taught him to read and write and he remained so ignorant that he learned nothing of historical events nor the facts about fortunes, careers, rank, or laws. This lack caused

Louis XIV in armour, 1695, by Rigaud. 'You have been raised to heaven . . . because you have impoverished France in order to bring incurable monstrous extravagance to court . . . Your name has grown odious, and the whole French nation has been made intolerable to our neighbours . . . But the whole of France is only one great poorhouse, desolate and without sustenance. Even the people who have so loved you are beginning to lose their friendship and their confidence, and even their respect.'

him sometimes, even in public, to make many gross blunders.

His ministers, generals, mistresses, and courtiers learned soon after he became their master that glory, to him, was a foible rather than an ambition. They therefore flattered him to the top of his bent, and in so doing, spoiled him. Praise, or better, adulation, pleased him so much that the most fulsome was welcome and the most servile even more delectable. They were the only road to his favour and those whom he liked owed his friendship to choosing their moments well and never ceasing in their attentions. This is what gave his ministers so much power, for they had endless opportunities of flattering his vanity, especially by suggesting that he was the source of all their ideas and had taught them all that they knew. Falseness, servility, admiring glances, combined with a dependent and cringing attitude, above all, an appearance of being nothing without him, were the only means of pleasing him.

The poison gradually spread until it reached a degree almost unbelievable in a prince who was not unintelligent or without experience of the world. For example, although he had no voice nor ear for music, he could often be heard in his private rooms singing the verses written in his praise in the prologues of the plays and operas. You could see that he revelled in them, and sometimes even at state suppers he hummed the words under his breath when the orchestra played these tunes.

It was chiefly with talk of campaigns and soldiers that he entertained his mistresses and sometimes his courtiers. He talked well and much to the point; no man of fashion could tell a tale or set a scene better than he, yet his most casual speeches were never lacking in natural and conscious majesty.

He had a natural bent towards details and delighted in busying himself with such petty matters as the uniforms, equipment drill, and discipline of his troops. He concerned himself no less with his buildings, the conduct of his household, and his living expenses, for he always imagined that he had something to teach the experts, and they received instruction from him as though they were novices in arts which they already knew by heart. To the King, such waste of time appeared to deserve his constant attention, which enchanted his ministers, for with a little tact and experience they learned to sway him, making their own desires seem his, and managing great affairs of state in their own way and, all too often, in their own interests, whilst they congratulated themselves and watched him drowning amidst trivialities.

Pride and vanity, which tend always to increase, and with which he was fed continually without even his perceiving it, even from preachers in the pulpits in his presence, were the foundations on which his ministers raised themselves above all other ranks.

Private audiences in his study were rarely if ever granted, even when the matter concerned state affairs. Never, for example, to envoys returning or going abroad, never to generals, unless in extraordinary circumstances, and private letters written to the King always passed through the hands of some minister, except on one or two most rare and special occasions.

Nevertheless, in spite of the fact that the King had been so spoiled with false notions of majesty and power, that every other thought was stifled in him, there was much to be gained from a private audience, if it might be obtained, and if one knew how to conduct oneself with all the respect due to his dignity and habits.

Once in his study, however prejudiced he might be, however much displeased, he would listen patiently, good-naturedly, and with a real desire to be informed. You could see that he had a sense of justice and a will to get at the truth, even though he might feel vexed with you, and that quality he retained all through his life. In private audience you could say anything to him, provided, as I have already remarked, that you said it respectfully, with submissiveness and proper deference, for without that you would have been in a worse plight. With the proper manner, however, you could interrupt him when it was your turn to speak, and bluntly deny his accusations, you could even raise your voice above his without vexing him, and he would congratulate himself on the audience and praise the person he interviewed for ridding him of prejudices and the lies he had been told; moreover, he would prove his sincerity by his subsequent attitude.

It is therefore enough to make one weep to think of the wickedness of an education designed solely to suppress the virtue and intelligence of that prince, and the insidious poison of barefaced flattery which made him a kind of god in the very heart of Christendom. His ministers with their cruel politics hemmed him in and made him drunk with power until he was utterly corrupted. If they did not manage entirely to smother such kindness, justice, and love of truth as God had given him, they blunted and obstructed those virtues to the lasting injury of himself and his kingdom.

From such alien and pernicious sources he acquired a pride so colossal that, truly, had not God implanted in his heart the fear of the devil, even in his worst excesses, he would literally have allowed himself to be worshipped. From this false pride stemmed all that ruined him. We have already seen some of its ill-effects; others are yet to come.

The frequent entertainments, the private drives to Versailles, and the royal journeys, provided the King with a means of distinguishing or mortifying his courtiers by naming those who were or were not to accompany him, and thus keeping everyone eager and anxious to please him. He fully realized that the substantial gifts which he had to offer were too few to have any continuous effect, and he substituted imaginary favours that appealed to men's jealous natures, small distinctions which he was able, with extraordinary ingenuity, to grant or withhold every day and almost every hour. The hopes that courtiers built upon such flimsy favours and the importance which they attached to them were really unbelievable, and no one was ever more artful than the King in devising fresh occasions for them. In later days, he made great use of the Marly excursions for that purpose, and Trianon, too, for although every man had the right to go there to pay his court, only the ladies ate with him, and they were specially selected for every meal. Another of his contrivances was the ceremony of the candlestick, which he allowed some courtier to hold every evening at his *couchée*. He always chose from among the most distinguished persons present and called his name aloud as he went out from prayers.

Louis XIV took enormous pains to be well-informed about all that went on in public places, in private houses, society, family business, or the progress of love-affairs. He had spies and reporters everywhere and of all descriptions. Many of them never realized that their reports reached the King, others wrote directly to him, sending their letters by secret channels of his own devising. Their letters were seen by him alone and he always read them before proceeding to other business. There were even some who spoke privately with him in his study, entering by the back way. Through such secret informants, an immense number of people of all ranks were broken, often most unjustly, and without their ever discovering the reason, for the King, once suspicious, never trusted again, or so rarely that it made no matter.

He loved the open air and exercise so long as strength was given to him. In his youth, he had excelled in dancing, at pall-mall, and at the *jeu de paume*, and all his life he was a superb horseman. He liked men to acquit themselves well in such pastimes; gracefulness or clumsiness in them he regarded as a virtue or discredit, for he used to say that such pursuits were unnecessary and it were better not to do them at all than do them badly. Shooting he loved and was better than the average. He liked beautiful setter bitches and always had seven or eight in his rooms and fed them with his own hands so that they learned to know him. He also loved stag-hunting, but after he broke his arm he rode in a carriage. He drove himself in a small open carriage, drawn by four ponies with five or six relays, and went alone, going full tilt with a skill that few professionals could equal and all the elegance which he habitually displayed. His postillions were children between nine and fifteen years of age, whom he trained himself.

In everything he loved magnificently lavish abundance. He made it a principle from motives of policy and encouraged the court to imitate him; indeed, one way to win favour was to spend extravagantly on the table, clothes, carriages, building, and gambling. For magnificence in such things he would speak to people. The truth is that he used this means deliberately and successfully to impoverish everyone, for he made luxury meritorious in all men, and in some a necessity, so that gradually the entire court became dependent upon his favours for their very subsistence. What is more, he fed his own pride by surrounding himself with an entourage so universally magnificent that confusion reigned and all natural distinctions were obliterated.

But Louis had a private as well as a public face as both Voltaire and Madame Campan recognised:

It seemed that nature herself then took delight in producing in France men of the first rank in every art, and in bringing together at the court the most handsome and well-favoured men and women. Louis stood out above all his courtiers by the nobility of his bearing and the majestic beauty of his countenance. The sound of his voice, both noble and endearing, won the hearts of those whom his presence intimidated. His bearing was appropriate only to him and one of his rank and would have been ridiculous in anyone else. The embarrassment which he inspired in those to whom he spoke secretly flattered the complacency with which he viewed his superiority. A veteran officer who became flustered and who stammered in asking for a favour, when, unable to produce his request, he said, 'Sire, I do not tremble thus in front of your enemies', had no difficulty in having it granted.

Madame Campan:

Louis XIV was very good to his body-servants but the moment he put on his garb as sovereign, people quite used to seeing him in the most intimate moments of his life became as frightened as if they were ushered into his presence for the first time.

Members of his household who wished to put their case to him over a dispute chose two of his body-servants, called Bazire and Soulaigre, to represent them. When the King's *levée* was over he called them in; they entered confidently. The King looked at them and took up his official stance. Bazire should have spoken but Louis-the-Great had his eye on him. He no longer saw the prince on whom he waited; he was frightened and bereft of words. He pulled himself together and started; 'Sire,' he blurted out and was then overcome again and completely forgot what he had to say. He could only repeat 'Sire', until he stammered out 'Sire, here is Soulaigre'. Soulaigre was cross with Bazire, and thinking he could do better, picked up the word 'Sire', but found that like his comrade, all he could do was repeat it until in his turn he said, 'Sire, this is Bazire'. The King smiled and said, 'Gentlemen, I know why you are come. I will deal with your problem. I am pleased with the way you have fulfilled your mission.'

But time took its toll of even the most glorious monarch. Voltaire quotes a letter from Madame de Maintenon to Madame de la Maisonfort at St Cyr which he claims he had seen in manuscript although it does not appear in later more scholarly editions of her letters. It would seem that she thought life with the ageing Louis was not all pleasure:

O that I could tell you of my trials! That I could reveal to you the boredom which assails the great, and the difficulty they have in finding something to occupy their time! Do you not see that I am dying of *ennui* in the midst of wealth such as you would find it difficult to imagine? I was once young and pretty: I tasted all the pleasures, was the centre of attraction. When I grew older I enjoyed for many years the conversation of a brilliant and witty society. I came to favour, and I protest to you, my dear girl, that all conditions of life make one sensible of a frightful emptiness.

As the reign progressed so Louis's fortunes foundered. His desire to establish what he called the natural frontiers of France led to wars which impoverished the country and his revocation of the Edict of Nantes—apart from being a foolish act of intolerance—was a further economic blow, for many of his most productive workmen were Huguenots. He was no longer served by men of the calibre of Colbert and his ablest generals were dead. An act of national heroism such as that of the Dutch, who flooded their land rather than let French troops capture it, military defeats by Marlborough, some of the worst winters France had known and personal tragedy in the death of first his brother (1701), his son (1711), then in 1712 his grandson, the Duke of Burgundy, and bitterest blow of all, Marie-Adelaide, Duchess of Burgundy, who had brought such pleasure into his life, left him sad and depressed. Life at Versailles was no longer the gay fun it had been. Voltaire:

Louis XIV concealed his sorrows in public; he made himself behave in his usual way, but in private the pain of so many misfortunes grieved him, and he was prostrate. He suffered all these family losses at the end of an unsuccessful war, before he was certain of peace, and at a time when his whole kingdom was in a miserable condition. He was not seen for a single instant to give in to his afflictions. The rest of his life was sad. The disorder of the finances, which he could not put right, alienated much affection from him; his whole-hearted confidence in the Jesuit, Père Tellier, a violent man, moved people to revolt. It is a remarkable thing that the public, who forgave him his mistresses, could not forgive him this confessor. He forfeited, in the last three years of his life, in the estimation of the majority of his subjects everything great and memorable he had done. Deprived of nearly all his children, his love for the Duke of Maine and the Count of Toulouse, whom he had legitimised, made him declare them heirs to the throne thereby tempering the severity of received laws by natural law.

Towards the middle of August 1715 on his return from Marly Louis was overcome by the illness which was to end his days. He approached his end with a greatness of spirit. To Madame de Maintenon he said, 'I thought it would be more difficult to die', and to his servants, 'Why do you cry; did you think I was immortal?' He calmly continued to give his orders, even on the subject of his own funeral service. The presence of many witnesses makes the act of dying easier to bear. Despite the glory of Louis's life and death his passing did not occasion the regret that was due to him. A love of novelty, an approaching minority during which everyone would jockey for position and the quarrel over the constitution which embittered men, all led to the fact that the news of his death was received with feelings beyond even indifference. We see these same people, who in 1686 prayed to heaven with tears in their eyes for the recovery of their sick king, follow his hearse with very different emotions. They say that the Queen his mother said in his early youth, 'My son, be like your grandfather and not your father.' And on being asked why by the King, she replied, 'they cried on Henri IV's death but laughed at that of Louis XIII'.

Although one may reproach him for his minor defects, the harshness of his zeal against the Jansenists, excessive arrogance with foreigners when he was victorious, a weakness for women, too great a strictness over personal matters, wars lightly undertaken, the conflagration of the Palatinate, persecution against the Reformed Church, nevertheless his great qualities and deeds when put into the balance at the end outweigh these faults. Time, which ripens men's views, has put the seal on his reputation, and in spite of everything written against him, his name is not mentioned without respect nor without bringing to mind the idea of a century which will live forever. If one contemplates this prince in his private life, one sees him, in truth, too full of his own importance, but affable; not allowing his mother any part in government but never failing towards her in his duty as a son, and behaving to his wife with an outward propriety, a good father, a good master, always correct in public, hard-working in his study, scrupulous in business, right-thinking, speaking well, and with a kindly dignity.

The King's death was protracted and painful. St Simon gives his account of the last days:

The King's health had been failing for more than a year. The personal valets were the first to notice it, and observed every symptom without daring to speak. Fagon [Louis's chief physician], now weak in body and mind, was the only one of that great household who noticed nothing. Maréchal, the chief surgeon, spoke to him several times but was harshly rebuffed.

Because he had once been afflicted with long attacks of gout, Fagon had taken to swaddling him [the King], as it were, every night, in a great heap of feather pillows, with the result that he had to be changed and rubbed down each morning.

During the last years he became increasingly constipated, and Fagon used to make him begin his meals with iced fruit, such as mulberries, melons, and figs, often half-rotten with over-ripeness, and he ate still more for dessert, with an astonishing number of sweetmeats. All the year round, he consumed an immense amount of salad at his supper. His soups were strong meat juices, exceedingly rich, and all that was served to him was very highly spiced, at least as much as is normal, and very hot.

In the end, the fruit taken after soup flooded his stomach and took away his appetite, which never before had failed in the whole course of his life. So much water, so much fruit, unrelieved by any alcohol, turned his blood gangrenous by lowering his vital spirits, and weakened his digestion by nightly sweatings.

On Wednesday 14 August he was carried to mass for the last time. On Thursday, the feast of the Assumption, he heard mass in bed. He had been restless and thirsty during the night. He dined in his bed before the entire court, rose at five o'clock, and had himself carried to Madame de Maintenon's, where there was the small orchestra. He supped and retired to bed as on the previous day. There was the same routine every day afterwards, as long as he was able to leave his bed.

On Friday 16 August his night was no better; he suffered much from thirst and drank a great deal.

On Saturday 17 August, the night was as before. That was the first night on which Fagon slept in his room.

Sunday 18 August was like the other days. Fagon still denied that he had a fever.

On the night of Monday 19 August the King was just as restless; on Tuesday 20 August, the night was like the previous ones. He supped in his armchair, wearing his dressing-gown. He never again left his apartments or put on his clothes.

On Wednesday 21 August, four doctors saw the King; but all they did was to praise Fagon, who prescribed senna. For some days past they had noticed a difficulty when he swallowed meat, or even bread, of which he ate sparingly throughout his life, and for a long time past nothing but the crumb because he had no teeth. He took rather more soup than usual, and some very light mince, with eggs to supplement it; but he ate extremely little.

By Thursday 22 August, the King's health had deteriorated. He saw four other doctors, but like the four who had preceded them, they only applauded the admirable learning and treatments of Fagon, who prescribed quinine and water for that evening, and asses' milk for the night.

The night of Friday 23 August, was much as usual and the morning also. He dined standing in his dressing-gown, and saw the courtiers; he did the same for supper.

The night of Saturday the 24th was only a little worse than usual, for all had been bad; but his leg was considerably worse, and gave him more pain. Mass was as usual; dinner in his bed; he supped standing in his dressing-gown in the presence of the courtiers, for the last time. I noticed that he swallowed only liquids, and that it distressed him to be looked at. He could not finish, and asked the courtiers to move along, that is to say, to leave him. He made them put him back into bed, and they examined his leg, on which black spots had begun to appear. He sent for Père Tellier, and confessed. Panic set in among the doctors. They had been trying milk and quinine with water; now both were cancelled and no one knew what to try next.

Sunday 25 August was the feast of St Louis; the night was far worse. They made no mystery now of the danger, and suddenly it was seen to be serious and imminent. [Later in the day] Madame de Maintenon sent for the ladies of his circle and the orchestra arrived at seven in the evening. Yet the King fell asleep while the ladies conversed. He woke up in confusion, which caused them some alarm, and made them send for the doctors. They found his pulse so weak that they did not hesitate to recommend the King, whose senses had returned, to delay no longer in receiving the sacraments. [They were administered.] The Cardinal [de Rohan] spoke briefly of this great, final act, during which the King appeared perfectly collected, but deeply moved. He sent also for Monsieur the Duke of Orléans, with whom he talked alone for a somewhat longer period.

As soon as he was gone, the Duke of Maine, who had been waiting in the study, was sent for. The King spoke with him for longer than a quarter of an hour, and then asked for the Count of Toulouse, who spent a further quarter of an hour alone with the King and Monsieur du Maine. Only very few of the most necessary valets remained in the bedroom with Madame de Maintenon. She had not approached while the King was speaking to Monsieur the Duke of Orléans. All this time, the King's three bastard daughters, two of Madame la Duchesse's sons, and the Prince of Conti had been arriving in the study. When the King was finished with the Duke of Maine and the Count of Toulouse, he called for the princes of the blood, whom he had noticed standing in the study doorway, and spoke a few words to them altogether, but nothing private nor in a whisper. The doctors came to dress his leg; the princes withdrew; only those persons who were absolutely essential remained, and Madame de Maintenon. After the dressing, the King was told that the princesses were in the council chamber; he called for them, said a couple of words to them out loud, and made their tears an excuse to beg them to leave him, as he wished to rest. They left with those few who had entered; the bed-curtains were drawn, and Madame de Maintenon went into the outer studies.

The day and the night of Monday 26 August were no better. His leg was dressed and he heard mass. The King dined in bed in the presence of those who had the *entrée*. He made them gather round him when the meal was being removed, and uttered these words, which were recorded at that very time. 'Gentlemen, I ask your pardon for having set you a bad example. I have much to thank you for in the manner in which you have served me, and for your constant devotion and faithfulness. It saddens me to think that I have not done for you all that I could have wished. The bad times were the cause. I pray you, show my great-grandson the same devotion and fidelity that you have shown to me. He is a child who may have many troubles to bear. Set an example for all my other subjects. Obey the orders which my nephew will give you; he will rule the kingdom; I hope he will rule well. I hope also that you will all remain united, and that if one should stray, the rest will help to bring him back. I feel moved to tears, and I think that I am moving you, too. I beg your pardon. Gentlemen, farewell, I trust that you will sometimes think of me.'

Later on, he sent orders to the Duchess of Ventadour, telling her to bring the dauphin. He called the child to him and said these words, in the presence of Madame de Maintenon and a few of the more intimate of his friends and valets, who wrote them down: 'My child, you will soon be a great king. Do not imitate me in my love of building, or my liking for war; try to live at peace with your neighbours. Render to God that which you owe Him; remember your duty to Him; see that your subjects fear Him. Always follow good counsel; try to lighten your people's burdens, as I, alas! could never do. Never forget your debt of gratitude to Madame de Ventadour.' 'Madame,' said he, turning to her, 'let me embrace him', and, so doing, he added, 'Dear child, I bless you right gladly.' As they lifted the little prince off the bed, the King asked for him again, and again embraced him, raising his eyes and hands to heaven. It was indeed a touching sight.

On Tuesday 27 August no one entered the King's room, save for Père Tellier, Madame de Maintenon, and for his mass only, the Cardinal of Rohan, and the two almoners on duty. At two o'clock, exactly, he sent for the chancellor and, alone with him and Madame de Maintenon, made him open two boxes full of papers, making him burn many of them, and giving him orders for the disposal of the rest. At six o'clock in the evening, he asked again for the chancellor. Madame de Maintenon did not leave his room the whole of that day, and no one else entered it except the valets and, from time to time, those who were essential for his service. During the evening, he sent for Père Tellier and, almost immediately after, for Pontchartrain, commanding him to have his heart taken to the professed house of the Jesuits in Paris, as soon as he was dead, and to have it placed opposite to the heart of the King his father, and after the same manner. Later on, when he had given these orders, he said to Madame de Maintenon that he had heard tell of the difficulty of resigning oneself to death; but that as he approached the awful moment, he did not find it too hard to submit. She replied that it must be very painful if one were attached to people, or hated them in one's heart, or had restitutions to make. 'Oh!' said the King, 'as for restitutions I owe nothing to any individual; and for what I owe to the kingdom, I trust in the mercy of God.' The following night was terribly agitated. He could be seen pressing his hands together, and they heard him reciting prayers which he had been wont to say when well, and beating his breast at the *Confiteor*.

On the morning of 28 August, he gave a word of comfort to Madame de Maintenon, which she so little relished that she did not answer. He said that the thought which consoled him in parting from her was the hope that, considering her age [she was eighty] they would soon be reunited. At seven that morning he had sent for Père Tellier and, as they spoke of God, he had seen reflected in the mirror above the chimney-piece two of his pages in tears, sitting at the foot of his bed. He said to them, 'Why are you crying? Did you think I was immortal? I myself have never thought so, and considering my age, you should have been prepared to lose me.'

On Thursday 29 August, the previous day and night having been so very bad, the absence of the dispensers, who had done all that they could, left more room in the King's bedchamber for the high officials who until then had been excluded. On the Thursday morning he seemed somewhat stronger, and even a shade better, although this was so greatly exaggerated that the news spread in all directions. The King was even able to eat two biscuits in a little Alicante wine, and appeared to enjoy them.

The late evening did not fulfil the much vaunted promise of that morning, at which time the curé of Versailles had taken advantage of the emptier room to tell the King that people were praying for his life. The King had replied that it was not now a question of that, but of his salvation, for which prayers were badly needed. When he had given his orders that morning, he had let slip the words, 'the young King', when speaking of the dauphin. He observed the sudden movement among the onlookers, and said, 'Well, what of it? That does not trouble me at all.' At eight o'clock he took some more of the elixir of that man from Provence. His head appeared to be confused, and he said himself that he felt very bad. At eleven, they examined his leg. Gangrene had spread all over his foot and knee, and his thigh was much swollen. He fainted during the examination. He was distressed to notice the absence of Madame de Maintenon. He sent to fetch her from St Cyr; she returned in the evening.

Friday 30 August was as distressing as the night before had been; a deep coma set in and in the intervals his mind wandered. From time to time he swallowed a little jelly in plain water, for he could no longer take wine.

The day and the night of Saturday 31 August were horrible indeed. There were only brief and rare moments of consciousness. The gangrene had reached his knee and spread over his entire thigh. Towards eleven in the evening, they thought him so ill that prayers for the dying were said over him. The bustle brought him to his senses. He recited the prayers in a voice so strongly that it could be heard above those of the many priests, and above those of all the people who had entered with them. When the prayers ended he recognised the Cardinal of Rohan and said to him: 'Those are the last blessings of the church.' That was the last person to whom he spoke. He several times repeated '*nunc et in hora mortis*', then said, 'O God, help me. Haste Thou to succour me.' Those were his last words. He lay unconscious throughout the night. His long agony ended at a quarter past eight, on the morning of Sunday 1 September, 1715, three days before his seventy-seventh birthday, in the seventy-second year of his reign.

Engraving of Louis XIV lying in state.

Louis XV

Louis XV was born on 15 February, 1710 at Versailles. He acceded to the throne on 1 September, 1715 and was crowned at Rheims on 25 October, 1722.
He married, on 5 September, 1725, Marie Leczinska (1703–1768).
He reigned for fifty-eight years, and died, from smallpox, aged sixty-four, at Versailles on 10 May, 1774. He was buried at St Denis.

The Duke of Orléans became regent during the King's minority, but he inherited a France sorely weakened financially. Young Louis had few cares of state in his early days. Madame, the Duke of Orléans's mother, had some innocent fun with him:

I don't get on too badly with the King. I played a prank on his governors yesterday which rather amused me. The King had colic the day before yesterday, and yesterday I gravely went up to him and put a little piece of paper into his hand. Maréchal de Villeroy asked me in a pompous voice, 'What note are you giving the King?' I answered, equally seriously, 'A remedy for the colic'. The Maréchal: 'Only the King's physician may prescribe for the King.' I answered, 'As to that, I am sure that Monsieur Dodart would approve. It is even in verse and to be sung.' The King grew embarrassed, read it secretly and began to laugh. The Maréchal said, 'May one see it?' I said, 'Yes, it is not secret,' and he found the following words:

You with your collywobbles
With your rumbling winds
They are dangerous
And to rid yourself of them
Fart
Fart, you can do no better than to
Fart

Happy, happy to be rid of them
Oh poor unfortunates, to set them free
Fart
Fart, you can do no better than to
Fart
Happy
To be rid of them

Everyone laughed so hard that I was almost sorry to have played the joke. The Maréchal de Villeroy was quite put out of countenance.

Louis was known in his early days as 'the Well-beloved'. A Persian ambassador found him as handsome as young kings should be:

At the age of sixteen to seventeen Louis XV was like Adonis reborn, of noble bearing, of a splendid height, his limbs ideally proportioned, from his almond-shaped eyes a gentle look would captivate all those who approached him, his delicate health added to all this languid grace. His education had been neglected for fear of tiring him, but encircled by the culture of France he imbibed in time a certain knowledge of intellectual matters which atoned for much which he had never been taught.

The Duke of Luynes, who knew Louis well, spent the years between 1735 and his death in 1758 writing his memoirs. He kept a careful record of the activities and gossip of the court:

During the King's last visit to Rambouillet things went a little differently from previous visits. Since that Saturday in the diocese of Chartres was a fast day, the King, arriving from hunting, remembered that he had eaten eggs that morning and consequently did not wish to sup. So he went to sleep on the spot and rose at 10.30, played cavagnole [a kind of lotto then very much in fashion] until midnight, ate meat for dinner which lasted till 3, played again until 5, went to the first mass in the parish, went back to bed at 6 until 12.30, played cavagnole again until 3 or 4 and then went to table as usual with those of his suite who had the honour to accompany him. This meal was what was called at Rambouillet the 'royal pot', that is to say a sort of luncheon on the gaming tables set together. His Majesty was at table until 7, then played again and arrived at Versailles by midnight to go to bed. I heard of all this from Monsieur the baillie of Froulay who was there.

We talked of the pleasure the late King had for Trianon and the care he devoted to its original undertaking. There were an enormous number of flowers, all in stone pots which were sunk in flower beds so that they could be changed, not only daily if one wished, but even twice a day. I was told that there were as many as 1,900,000 pots in existence either in the flower beds or in store.

A brand new outfit was brought for the Queen today. It is the third since she has been married. The one she is parting with today which is silver brocade with gold embroidery has lasted her five years and is very worn. This new one is blue velvet embroidered in a great deal of applied gold. The pattern, by the designer Lajoue is splendid and striking. This outfit cost about 17,000 *livres* in total. The old one went to Madame de Luynes.

The Queen went to perform her devotions at the chapel today, which gave rise to a difficulty. Normally when the King sleeps with the Queen, the French and Swiss guard go into the *cour des ministres* without fear of waking them and the guard marches in to present arms while the Queen passes in her chair to go to the chapel. Today with the King sleeping in his room and not awake by 8 o'clock, which is when the Queen goes to chapel, caused embarrassment for fear of waking the King. Madame de Luynes, at the request of the French guard, asked the Queen yesterday if she would give the order that they should not present arms when she passed, on account of the King. The Queen replied that she would gladly. As the gentlemen of the guard did not wish to have to enter the courtyard since they had been ordered not to present arms, Madame de Luynes was asked by them to ask the Queen if it was necessary for the guard to enter. The Queen said they should follow their normal practice. As yesterday the Queen was shut up in her rooms all day without seeing anyone, it was difficult to get new orders from her so that Monsieur de Gramont had to send several messengers to Madame de Luynes saying that if the guard had to enter the courtyard, they would have to present arms but that the Queen could well give the order either that they need not enter at all, or if they did enter they need not present arms when she passed by; but they could not enter without presenting arms unless the order was given by the King.

Monsieur the Duke of Gramont cited the occasion of what happened to my father in the time of the late King. He claimed that when the King was suffering from his last illness the guard entered without presenting arms for fear of making a noise and that the King had been angry with Monsieur the Duke of Gramont because of this lapse.

So today the guard entered presenting arms although the King was not awake and did not do so when the Queen went past.

On the night of Sunday to Monday the King started sleeping with the Queen again for the first time since her confinement. His Majesty was due to make his devotions today and touch for the king's evil according to tradition. The necessary orders were given and we should have been on duty with him at a quarter to eight. However, he had found himself incommoded with the Queen, he rose at six and took something to relieve him. Consequently he had to take a drink in order to swallow the remedy, so that he was prevented from making his devotions and he did not touch for the king's evil. He went neither to first matins nor vespers and it is not certain that he will go to mass at midnight.

Louis had been affianced to the Spanish infanta ten years younger than him but at the age of fifteen it had been clear he was ready for marriage at once. He married Marie Leczinska, the daughter of the exiled King of Poland living at Lunéville, seven years his senior. By the time the King was twenty-seven they had had ten children.

Madame du Deffand (1697–1780) amused herself by describing her as 'Themira' in a letter to Horace Walpole:

Themira was witty, with a susceptible heart, a gentle humour and a striking appearance. Her upbringing had implanted in her a piety so strong that it became the centre of her being and ruled all other feelings. Themira loved God first and pleasure thereafter. She knew how to reconcile the substance and the shadow, sometimes occupying herself with the one or the other and sometimes achieving both simultaneously. One might say that her virtues were the seed and the mainspring of her being.

To moral rectitude she brought extreme sensibility, to modesty a desire to please which in itself achieved its object. Her perspicacity was such that she understood human frailty and saw through the pretentious so that she could accept them with patience and rarely laughed at them. She was so concerned with pleasure that she often overlooked quite serious faults. She respected people of virtue and liked the friendly and it was this weakness, if it be one, that was responsible for her charm. If one had the good fortune to know Themira one would do anything for her in the hope of giving her pleasure. The

Marie Leczinska by Nattier. The Queen has her Bible to hand. 'Nothing the Queen did was by chance; her days were ordered and occupied so that although she spent a large part of them by herself she was always short of time. The mornings were spent in prayer, reading worthy books, a visit to the King and then some small relaxation. Usually it was painting. She had never learned to paint although one could not tell from seeing her works.'

respect she commanded was due more to her virtues than to her position; neither spirit nor senses were repelled. Her wit was such that one shared it with her and her understanding so universal that one could discuss any subject with her without the explanations one might have supposed due to her rank. In her presence one forgot that anything except sentiment existed.

Perhaps the best, if most cruel, summing-up of the King's character comes from the Marquis of Argenson:

Brought up by the Cardinal [Fleury], whom he must have admired to have been so obsequious to him for so long, he had developed a number of petty faults, for the Cardinal was pettiness itself and if the King had had greater spirit he would not have served the Cardinal for so long. Some of these petty aspects of character could have been useful to good government; a grave demeanour, a love of mystification and a measure of order in imitation of the late King. Louis was wittier than the Cardinal and had a loftier outlook. But he was timid and kept people about him out of habit and for no other reason than that he feared making new acquaintances. He only liked decent people because he was lazy and because untrustworthy people give trouble and it is too much like work to be on one's guard against them, although because of his perspicacity he was a better judge of men than the late Cardinal.

The King conducts himself in his work and with his ministers with such distaste and annoyance as hardly seems natural. Seeing and knowing His Majesty as I do it is inconceivable that he should have become so indifferent to such capital matters of honour and interest.

Louis XV was blessed by providence. Chosen in preference to his elders to reign, his life preserved, his health going from strength to strength, he avoided many dangers in childhood and from his early youth his anointing preserved him as the finger of God. Believers comment that these miracles are enough to convert the most dubious whereas philosophers opine that he should therefore render greater love to God and his people than ordinary mortals.

It is the innate goodness of princes which makes them great; and from this comes justice. If not there is only violence which induces fear. Their reign is transitory, for there is only a moment of need and illusion. But if one examines how kings have prevailed in the world one finds that the founders of monarchies have attracted confidence by esteem and good deeds and that their successors have only survived one might say on the reputation of their ancestors, that power is destroyed by tyranny and is only re-established under happy reigns.

Do you want details of this character? One will find he has all those French characteristics so well-known to foreigners—contrast everywhere, the results of too light and too controlled an imagination, talents lost to sight, an erratic good taste, exactitude in small things, inconstancy and lack of foresight in big; a master-planner without political or military application. He has a talent for drawing and a taste for architecture, but only for small enterprises; a combination of luck and imprudence in affairs, a wit and a fire, a good memory without hindsight; a man of habit and inconstancy, of mystery and indiscretion with a need for novelty, but bored and weary, with a total apathy about what is to follow him. He despairs at the thought of losing a mistress, but is unfaithful; he has favourites whom he does not love, and gives his esteem without confidence; in sum a good master but inhuman.

When his queen originally arrived at Versailles, Louis had fallen in love with her but after her children were born her dowdiness and lack of sparkle began to bore Louis, and he started the series of affairs with both noblewomen and those of humbler birth that were to characterise the rest of his reign, and eventually bring him into disfavour with his people.

Like his grandfather with the Mancini girls, he worked his way round the Nesle sisters; first Madame de Mailly, then her sister Madame de Vintimille, who died in childbirth, and then Madame de Châteauroux. In 1744 he went to join his army fighting on the eastern front and took Madame de Châteauroux with him, and yet another sister, Madame de Lauraguais. There he fell severely ill and the psychological effects of this 'Metz incident', as it came to be known, remained with him all his life.

When his life was despaired of, his mistresses were sent packing so that he could receive the last sacraments, and the clergy made the fatal mistake of publishing diatribes against adultery. The Duke of Luynes:

On Saturday 8 August the King fell ill. He woke at five in the morning with a temperature and a bit of a headache. He had several enemas with good results but his headache, although his temperature did not rise, required him to be bled, from the arm, at about two o'clock. His temperature was not preceded by any shivering. On Friday the King had gone on horseback to see the fortifications; he had a poor colour and looked sad.

As the first sign of his convalescence the King was shaved today, 26 August. He ate a little bread with some clear soup and he saw one or two people. I wanted to know what La Peyroniece thought about this illness. He told me that the King in his normal state of health was in the habit of going to the loo twice a day and copiously, that several days before his illness eating the same as usual he only went rarely and passed very little, causing a considerable build up which affected his blood. In addition he thought he had a touch of sunstroke which seemed to explain the violent pain in the side of his head, which he had throughout his illness and which rightly caused his doctors worry. As soon as he saw the Queen on the Monday evening he begged her pardon for the scandals he had caused and the pain he had given her.

At the beginning when the Queen arrived here it was hoped that the King's well-known indifference for her might change. Not only had he asked her forgiveness but he seemed to offer her friendship. However, since the stay at Metz things seem quite different—his coldness is even greater than usual. Either the too frequent and too animated conversations she has with the dauphin in his presence have displeased him, or the effect of the sentiments he has had for her for a long time which one had hoped to sustain and augment, or it may be that his rotten temper was the only cause. Perhaps it was all these reasons.

Since the beginning of this campaign the King has got into the habit of no longer praying on his knees, neither in the evening nor in the morning, contrary to the practice of a lifetime. One must suppose that he says his prayers in his bed, but the public is no longer a witness. One would have thought that the present moment would have been a good one to start thanking God on his knees again; however, things are as they were at the start of the campaign and one can only hope that it is feebleness which prevents him from kneeling.

On his return to Versailles, Louis took up again with Madame de Châteauroux but she died shortly afterwards of pneumonia caused, it is said, by having a bath after rushing from a feverish sick bed in her haste to join him. Madame Campan, writing later of gossip she had heard, laughs at the Queen's superstitiousness at this point:

Marie Leczinska was not pretty; but she was intelligent, had a lively countenance and a simplicity of manners, heightened by the grace of a Polish lady. She loved the King and found his early infidelities painful to bear. Nevertheless the death of Madame de

Châteauroux, whom she had known since her youth, and who had even been honoured by her kindness, made a painful impression on her. The good Queen was affected by superstitious education; she was afraid of ghosts. The first night after she heard of this seemingly sudden death she could not sleep, and made one of her women sit up. She tried to cure her insomnia by reciting her favourite stories, recounting them in the way that children require from their nannies. That night, however, nothing brought sleep; her woman, thinking that she was asleep, was tiptoeing away from her bed but the slight noise on the floor roused the Queen, who cried, 'Where are you going? Stay; go on with your story.' As it was past two in the morning, this woman, whose name was Boirot and who was somewhat naïve said, 'What can the matter be with Your Majesty tonight? Are you feverish? Shall I call the doctor?' 'O no, no, my good Boirot, I am not ill; but that poor Madame de Châteauroux—if she were to come again!' 'Jesus, madam,' cried the woman who had lost all patience, 'if Madame de Châteauroux should come again, it will certainly not be Your Majesty that she will be looking for.' The Queen burst into a fit of laughter at this observation; her agitation subsided, and she soon fell asleep.

Bereft of his public mistresses and not content with the girls at the Parc-aux-Cerfs Louis was an easy prey for the pretty Madame le Normant d'Etioles, a Parisian bourgeoise who was thrust at him by her perspicacious family. She became his mistress after the Ball of the Clipped Yew Trees given in honour of the dauphin's second marriage in 1745 and her reign, as Madame de Pompadour, lasted for twenty years until her death. Le Roy, a gamekeeper at Versailles, was among those who were in favour of her:

Her eyes had a particular attraction, perhaps owing to the fact that it was difficult to say exactly what colour they were; they had neither the hard sparkle of black eyes, nor the dreamy tenderness of blue; nor the special delicacy of grey; their indeterminate colour seemed to lend them to all forms of seduction and shades of expression. Indeed her expression was always changing, though there was never any discordance between her various features; they all unfolded the same thought, which presupposes a good deal of self-control, and this applied to her every movement. Her whole person was half way between the last degree of elegance and the first of nobility.

Madame de Pompadour was installed at Versailles, in small warm rooms which Louis loved to visit. Her personal maid, ear glued to keyhole, has left a reasonably well-authenticated account of life there:

I was for a long time about the person of Madame de Pompadour, and my birth procured for me respectful treatment from herself, and from some distinguished persons who conceived a regard for me. I soon became the intimate friend of Dr Quesnay, who frequently came to pass two or three hours with me.

The King was in the constant habit of seeing me. He talked without any constraint

Madame de Pompadour in 1753 by François Boucher.

when I was in the room.

The King was very fond of having little private correspondences, very often unknown to Madame de Pompadour: she knew, however, of the existence of some, for he passed part of his mornings in writing to his family, and also to some obscure persons. 'It is, doubtless, from such people as these,' said she to me, one day, 'that the King learns expressions which perfectly surprise me. For instance, he said to me yesterday, when he saw a man pass with an old coat on, *"il y a là un habit bien examiné"*. He once said to me, when he meant to express that a thing was probable, *"il y a gros"* [meaning, probably, a big bet]; I am told this is a saying of the common people, meaning, *il y a gros à parier*.' I took the liberty to say, 'But is it not more likely from his young ladies at the Parc, that he learns these elegant expressions?' She laughed, and said, 'You are right; *il y a gros*.' The King, however, used these expressions designedly, and with a laugh.

An event, which made me tremble, as well as Madame, procured me the familiarity of the King. In the middle of the night, Madame came into my chamber, *en chemise,* and in a state of distraction: 'Here! Here!' said she, 'the King is dying.' My alarm may easily be imagined. I put on a petticoat, and found the King in her bed, panting. What was to be done?—it was an indigestion. We threw water upon him, and he came to himself. I made him swallow some Hoffman's drops, and he said to me, 'Do not make any noise, but go to Quesnay; say that your mistress is ill; and tell the doctor's servants to say nothing about it.' Quesnay, who lodged close by, came immediately, and was much astonished to see the King in that state. He felt his pulse, and said, 'The crisis is over; but, if the King were sixty years old, this might have been serious.' He went to seek some drug, and, on his return, set about inundating the King with perfumed water. I forgot the name of the medicine he made him take, but the effect was wonderful. I believe it was the *drops of General Lamotte*. I called up one of the girls of the wardrobe to make tea, as if for myself. The King took three cups, put on his dressing-gown and his stockings, and went to his own room, leaning upon the doctor. What a sight it was to see us all three half-naked! Madame put on a robe as soon as possible, and I did the same, and the King changed his clothes behind the curtains, which were very decently closed.

Madame called me, one day, into her closet, where the King was walking up and down in a very serious mood. 'You must,' said she, 'pass some days in a house in the avenue of St Cloud, whither I shall send you. You will there find a young lady about to lie in.' The King said nothing, and I was mute from astonishment. 'You will be mistress of the house, and preside, like one of the fabulous goddesses, at the *accouchement*. Your presence is necessary, in order that everything may pass secretly, and according to the King's wish. You will be present at the baptism, and name the father and mother.' The King began to laugh, and said, 'The father is a very honest man;' Madame added, 'beloved by everyone, and adored by those who know him.'

The King said, 'Guimard will call upon you every day, to assist you with his advice, and at the critical moment you will send for him. You will say that you expect the sponsors, and a moment after you will pretend to have received a letter, stating that they cannot come. You will, of course, affect to be very much embarrassed; and Guimard will then say, that there is nothing for it but to take the first-comers. You will then appoint as godfather and godmother some beggar, or chairman, and the servant girl of the house, and to whom you will give but twelve francs, in order not to attract attention.'

'Guimard,' continued the King, 'will tell you the names of the father and mother; he will be present at the ceremony, and make the usual presents. It is but fair that you also should receive yours;' and, as he said this, he gave me fifty *louis*, with that gracious air that he could so well assume upon certain occasions, and which no person in the kingdom had but himself. I kissed his hand and wept. 'You will take care of the *accouchée*, will you not? She is a good creature, who has not invented gunpowder, and I confide her entirely to your direction; my chancellor will tell you the rest', he said, turning to Madame, and then quitted the room. 'Well, what think you of the part I am playing?' asked Madame. 'It is that of a superior woman, and an excellent friend,' I replied. 'It is his heart I wish to secure,' said she; 'and all those young girls who have no education will not run away with it from me. I should not be equally confident were I to see some fine woman belonging to the court, or the city, attempt his conquest.'

I asked Madame, if the young lady knew that the King was the father of her child? 'I do not think she does,' replied she; 'but, as he appeared fond of her, there is some reason to fear that those about her might be too ready to tell her; otherwise,' said she, shrugging her shoulders, 'she, and all the others, are told that he is a Polish nobleman, a relation of the Queen, who has apartments in the castle.' This story was contrived on account of the *cordon bleu*, which the King has not always time to lay aside.

Madame de Pompadour said to me, 'Be constantly with the *accouchée*, to prevent any stranger, or even the people of the house, from speaking to her. You will always say that he is a very rich Polish nobleman, who is obliged to conceal himself on account of his relationship to the Queen, who is very devout. You will find a wet-nurse in the house, to whom you will deliver the child. Guimard will manage all the rest. You will go to church as a witness; everything must be conducted as if for a substantial citizen. The young lady expects to lie in in five or six days; you will dine with her, and will not leave her till she is in a state of health to return to the Parc-aux-Cerfs, which she may do in a fortnight, as I imagine, without running any risk.' I went, that same evening, to the avenue de St Cloud, where I found the abbess and Guimard, an attendant belonging to the castle, but without his blue coat. There were, besides, a nurse, a wet-nurse, two old menservants, and a girl, who was something between a servant and a waiting-woman. The young lady was extremely pretty, and dressed very elegantly, though not too remarkably. I supped with her and the mother-abbess.

The next day, I talked to her in private. She said to me, 'How is the Count?' (It was the King whom she called by this title.) 'He will be very sorry not to be with me now; but he was obliged to set off on a long journey.' I assented to what she said. 'He is very handsome,' said she, 'and loves me with all his heart. He promised me an allowance; but I love him disinterestedly; and, if he would let me, I would follow him to Poland.' She afterwards talked to me about her parents.

'My mother,' said she, 'kept a large grocer's shop, and my father was a man of some consequence; he belonged to the Sixth Corps, and that, as everybody knows, is an excellent thing. He was twice very near being head-bailiff.' Her mother had become bankrupt at her father's death, but *the Count* had come to her assistance, and settled upon her sixty pounds a year, besides giving her two hundred and forty pounds down. On the sixth day, she was brought to bed, and, according to my instructions, she was told the child was a girl, though in reality it was a boy; she was soon to be told that it was dead, in order that no trace of its existence might remain for a certain time. It was eventually to be restored to its mother. The King gave each of his children four or five hundred a year. They inherited after each other as they died off, and seven or eight were already dead. I returned to Madame de Pompadour, to whom I had written every day by Guimard. The next day, the King sent for me into the room; he did not say a word as to the business I had been employed upon; but he gave me a large gold snuff-box, containing two *rouleaux* of twenty-five *louis* each.

This little adventure, which initiated me into the King's secrets, far from procuring for me increased marks of kindness from him, seemed to produce a coldness towards me; probably because he was ashamed of my knowing his obscure amours. He was also embarrassed by the services Madame de Pompadour had rendered him on this occasion.

The Count of St Germain, who wished to have it believed that he had lived several centuries, often visited Madame de Pompadour. One day, at her toilet, Madame said to him, in my presence, 'What was the personal appearance of François I? He was a king I should have liked.' 'He was, indeed, very captivating,' said St Germain; and he proceeded to describe his face and person as one does that of a man one has accurately observed.

Some days afterwards, the King, Madame de Pompadour, some lords of the court, and the Count of St Germain, were talking about his secret for causing the spots in diamonds to disappear. The King ordered a diamond of middling size, which had a spot, to be brought. It was weighed; and the King said to the Count, 'It is valued at two hundred and forty pounds; but it would be worth four hundred if it had no spot. Will you try to put a hundred and sixty pounds into my pocket?' He examined it carefully, and said, 'It may be done; and I will bring it to you again in a month.' At the time appointed, the Count brought back the diamond without a spot, and gave it to the King. The King had it weighed, and found it but very little diminished. The King sent it to his jeweller by Monsieur de Gontaut, without telling him anything of what had passed. The jeweller gave three hundred and eighty pounds for it. The King, however, sent for it back again, and kept it as a curiosity. He could not overcome his surprise, and said that Monsieur de St Germain must be worth millions, especially if he had also the secret of making large diamonds out of a number of small ones.

Louis found himself in much the same position as his great-grandfather in connection with his foreign policy, and although he reached the height of his popularity with the French victory at the battle of Fontenoy in 1745 it then declined sharply. Madame de Pompadour was deeply involved in the politics of the reign and her expensive tastes and Louis's increasing womanising helped to turn the tide against him. He had fallen in public esteem by the outbreak of the Seven Years War in 1756 but it was temporarily halted when he was attacked and nearly assassinated by Damiens in 1757. Louis's family and one of the court factions saw the occasion as yet another one to rid him of his mistresses. Dufort de Cheverny:

The King, in bed, calmly but sadly reflected on life. Obsessed by his family and his children, he remembered the incident at Metz although the others had forgotten it. He was very afraid but did not show it. He was afraid that his private life would cost him the friendship of his people. Opposed by all the *Parlements* in the country since they had united, the tale told about the assassin caused him bitter moments. He thought he could not go out without risking his life, that he would have to lead a constricted life unable to satisfy his tastes which were far from over and that he might have to part from the woman who had such a hold on him and in whom he confided a large part of the government and the boredom his wholly respectable family caused him.

He spent eight days in this uncertainty shut up behind his bed-curtains. On the ninth the doctors and surgeons told him he had nothing to fear. When his soup was called for, he opened the curtains but said not a word. The first time that we were able to see him, this handsome man simply looked at us miserably as if to say, 'Look at your King whom a poor man wanted to kill—he is the most unhappy man alive.'

From that day mass was said with the door open. He was not allowed to miss one and he appeared to be overcome with devoutness. The family, in command, certain that communications had been broken and that the King did not speak to anyone in the private rooms, thought themselves strong enough to take action. Madame de Pompadour must be sent away. They thought that if he saw her all his good intentions would melt away.

His good intentions did melt away and Madame de Pompadour was reinstalled. Madame Campan has a rather more light-hearted tale about the incident:

I often heard Monsieur de Lasmartres, groom and master of the hunt, say how on news of the assassination attempt he rushed to the King. I cannot repeat the expressions he used to reassure the King but the story he told was a constant source of amusement in his circle. He was an old soldier who had behaved with extreme bravery. Nothing could induce him to moderate his expression nor his freedom of speech and he would not conform to court usage. The King was very fond of him. Monsieur de Lasmartres had a thunderous voice. When he arrived in the King's room he found all the princesses there, in tears. 'Sire, send out these weepers,' he said and the King told them to go. 'Now,' he said, 'your wound is nothing; your clothing took the brunt.' And, baring his own breast, he said, showing the King four or five large scars, 'Look, that's what matters. I've had these for thirty years. Cough.' The King coughed. And then taking the chamber pot with the briefest order he told the King to use it. The King did as he was told. 'It is nothing,' said Lasmartres; 'forget it, in four days we shall be hunting again.' 'But what if the knife was poisoned?' 'A load of rubbish,' said he; 'if it was, your waistcoat and shirt would have cleaned it off.' The King was reassured and spent a good night.

Louis's foreign policy was unsuccessful and the French defeat at the end of the Seven Years War led to the loss of virtually all her overseas possessions. By the Treaty of Paris in 1763 France lost Canada, all her territories east of the Mississippi, everything in India except for five trading posts, Senegal and the Windward Isles.

Madame de Pompadour died in 1764 and the King was ageing. He was not as ready to be amused as he had been, and the contradictions of his character puzzled Dufort de Cheverny:

The King's study was attended by a group of mostly young men, all of whom were high-spirited for the King liked amusing people. We were all waiting for the King to go to bed officially, an occasion when one could be noticed if one wished. The King had a white angora tom-cat, of an incredible size, gentle and very friendly. The King always came in to his private rooms at half past midnight. It was not yet midnight when Champcenetz said, 'Do you know I can make a cat dance for several minutes?' We all laughed, and took bets on it. Champcenetz took a flask from his pocket, stroked the cat and poured the water of a thousand flowers liberally over its four paws. The cat went back to sleep, and we thought we had won. Suddenly the spirits of wine began to take effect, and the cat leaped up and, farting, jumped on to the King's table, hissing, capering and dancing in the air. We were all laughing immoderately when the King arrived like a bombshell. He asked us what the joke was. 'Nothing, Sire, we were telling stories,' said Champcenetz. At that moment the wretched cat started its dance again and ran about like a mad creature. The King looked icily at us. 'Gentlemen,' he said, 'what is going on? Champcenetz, what have you done to my cat? I want to be told.' The enquiry could not be gainsaid. Champcenetz hesitated, but then told the truth, while the cat kept up its caperings. We smiled at the tale, to see how the King would take it but he scowled. 'Gentlemen,' he said, 'I will leave you here but if you wish to amuse yourselves, see that it is not at the expense of my cat.' It was said so drily that since then no one has made the cat dance again.

The King also had a King Charles spaniel, who went to the King only. I think he was flattered to think that this animal was perhaps the only person to love him for himself.

Another day he was a little better disposed towards us. We were dining at Fontainebleau with Lebel, his first valet, who towards the end of his life was responsible for all his pleasures. Lebel greatly liked women of uncertain virtue and those sent to him by the procuresses of Paris were not amateurs. We were six. Two of these women joined us and it was a jolly party. St Vigor took one of the women who was playing at being tiresome onto his knee and pretended to spank her. She pretended to be cross and we were all laughing when we heard the door open and saw the King come half through it. When he saw what was causing our mirth he was highly amused and shutting the door he said, 'Gentlemen, I won't disturb you; assume I have not seen you.' It was the signal for us to withdraw and we went to the ceremony of him going to bed, and nothing was ever said about the incident.

A friendly man and a good talker, no one enlivened conversation more than he by the variety of questions he asked. The role of king is difficult, he cannot imitate anyone, he has always to be himself; and the only questions asked of him are favours. So he has to make all the running himself and in the way that he chooses. The only subjects open to him are the field of knowledge, the arts or hunting, for if he mentions politics or people, the word goes round. He did not care for intellectual matters although he was tolerably educated and whether from choice or skill he always brought the talk round to the hunt of the day or the morrow.

I have asked myself a hundred times why a king so gifted with such a social conscience and such good qualities should have been so unmoved by the death of people in his circle. I have been able to find only one answer. A king has always a moving picture before his eyes; his entourage changes every three months, like a magic lantern. Equally, for everyone around him who dies, there is a position to be filled and he makes someone happy so that by continual change he forgets the dead very quickly.

The King in private was the most friendly and best of men, as a friend, as a father, he ought to have been loved, esteemed and revered. He lacked nothing that all kings do not lack—that of getting on with other men. Accustomed from the moment of their birth to

Engraving of Louis XV, by Madame de Pompadour herself, of a cameo by Jacques Guay, a jeweller from Marseilles whose work she collected and left to the King.

deference, adulation even, I think they believe themselves to be above other human beings.

Lebel arranged for the bored Louis to spy on a party at Versailles at which Madame du Barry, a former prostitute, was dining. It was not long before she was installed as reigning mistress. The Duchess of Northumberland on a visit to Versailles, reported:

I own I expected her to be much handsomer. She had nothing on her head, but 7 fine Diamond Pins, a *negligée* of Chintz with very little gold. She is rather of a tall, middle size, full breasted, and is pretty but not to be call'd handsome, very like the print but not so well, & has a strong Look of her former profession. Her Complexion is fair & clear & her skin very smooth but her Bloom is entirely gone off, she wears Rouge but in a very small Quantity & of a faint Colour. Her Face is oval, rather long, her Forehead high but her Hair, which is very fine & in great quantity, grows very well upon it.

Her Eyes are of a lively light Blue & she has the most wanton Look in them that I ever saw. Her Eyebrows are well form'd, and so is her Nose; her mouth is pretty, her Lips very red & her Teeth fine, but she has a kind of artificial smirk which also savours strongly of her old trade. Her Chin is very pretty, her Voice loud, her Air very good, & her manner obliging & civil, but vulgar. Her Behaviour extreamly free & chearful, Her Disposition Benevolent, good-natured, generous and charitable, but her Temper I imagine as warm as her Constitution, her Language very rough & indelicate when she is angry.

Madame du Barry by Vigée Lebrun.

Madame du Barry, who survived Louis's death, to end ignominiously on the guillotine in 1793, was ill-received by Louis's family, including the dauphine, his grand-daughter-in-law, Marie-Antoinette. Madame Campan, who went to court as the reader to the King's daughters and stayed on when Marie-Antoinette became queen, brought a fresh, if rather frightened eye to bear on the King:

One day at the château of Compiègne, the King came in while I was reading to Madame. I rose and went into another room. Alone, in a room with no exit and with no book other than that of Massillon [a fashionable preacher], which I had been reading to the princess, light and gay as one is at fifteen, I was amusing myself with swinging round, with my court hoop, and suddenly kneeling down to see my rose silk petticoat parachuting round me. In the middle of this serious exercise His Majesty came in followed by the princess. I wanted to get up; my feet got in the way and down I fell in the middle of my aerated dress. 'Daughter,' said Louis XV, bursting into laughter, 'I advise you to send back to the convent a reader who makes cheeses.'

Louis XV had the most imposing presence. His eyes remained fixed on you all the time he was speaking; and in spite of the beauty of his features, he inspired a sort of fear. I was very young, it is true, when he first spoke to me; if it was gracious, you shall judge. I was fifteen. The King was going out to hunt, and was followed by a large crowd. He stopped in front of me and said, 'Mademoiselle Genet, they tell me you are very learned, and understand four or five foreign languages.' 'I know only two, Sire,' I answered trembling. 'Which are they?' 'English and Italian.' 'Do you speak them fluently?' 'Yes, Sire, very fluently.' 'Quite enough to send a husband mad.' After this pretty compliment the King went on; his followers saluted me, laughing; and, for my part, I remained motionless with surprise and confusion for some moments on the spot where I stood.

She continues:

The King thought of nothing but the pleasures of the chase; one might have thought that the courtiers amused themselves in inventing epigrams when one heard them say quite seriously on those days when the King did not hunt that 'the King does nothing today'.

Small journeys were also of great importance to the King. On the first day of the year he wrote down in his almanac the days for going to Compiègne, to Fontainebleau, to Choisy, etc. The weightiest matters, the most serious events never disturbed his schedule.

Louis XV saw very little of his family; he went every morning to the rooms of Madame Adelaide by a private staircase. He often brought and drank there coffee that he had made himself. Madame Adelaide pulled a bell which warned Madame Victoire of the King's visit; Madame Victoire in rising to go to her sister's rooms rang for Madame Sophie who in turn rang for Madame Louise. The princesses' rooms were very large and Madame Louise's were at the far end. This youngest daughter was deformed and very short; the poor princess had to run with all her force to join the daily meeting, but, having so many rooms to cross, she frequently, in spite of her haste, had only just time to embrace her father before he set out for the chase.

Each evening at six Mesdames interrupted my reading to accompany the princes to Louis XV; this visit was called the King's *débottée* [unbooting] and was marked by a kind of etiquette. Mesdames put on an enormous hoop, which supported a petticoat ornamented with gold or embroidery; they fastened a long train round their waists; and hid the undress of the rest of their clothing by a long cloak of black taffeta which wrapped them up to the chin. In an instant the whole palace, normally empty, was in a ferment. The King kissed each princess on the forehead, and the visit was so short that the reading which it interrupted was frequently resumed at the end of quarter of an hour.

In the summer the King sometimes came to the princesses before the time of his *débottée*. One day he found me alone in Madame Victoire's closet and asked me where '*Coche*' was. When the King had gone I asked Madame of whom he spoke. She told me that it was herself and very coolly explained to me that, being the fattest of his daughters, the King had given her the familiar name of *Coche* [old sow], that he called Madame Adelaide *Loque* [rag], Madame Sophie *Graille* [scrap] and Madame Louise *Chiffe* [stuff]. People intimate with the King observed that he knew a great number of such words; it was thought he picked them up from his mistresses or that he amused himself with finding them in dictionaries. If this loose style of speaking betrayed the habits and taste of the King, his manners did not. His walk was easy and noble, he had a dignified carriage of the head, and his look, without being severe, was imposing; he combined great politeness with a truly regal demeanour, and gracefully saluted the least bourgeoise whom curiosity led into his path.

He was very expert in a number of pointless matters which only occupy the attention if there is nothing better; for instance, he was very adroit at knocking off the top of an egg with a single stroke of his fork; so he always ate eggs when he dined in public, and the gapers who came on Sundays to watch him dine returned home less struck with his fine figure than with the dexterity with which he broke his eggs.

Louis XVI

Louis XVI was born on 23 August, 1754 at Versailles. He acceded to the throne on 10 May, 1774 and was crowned at Rheims on 11 June, 1775.
He married, on 16 May, 1770, Marie-Antoinette of Austria (1755–1793).
He reigned for eighteen years and died, aged thirty-eight, by execution in Paris on 21 January, 1793. He was buried immediately afterwards in the cemetery of the church of the Madeleine and so much quicklime was put into the grave that only with difficulty were any traces of it found on exhumation in 1815.

When Louis XV died there were still plenty of malcontents but their weapons had become books and plays. There were complaints about everything, the government, war, alliances, and principally and as usual, taxes.

The new king, Louis XV's grandson, acceded to the throne with the best intentions in the world. He wished to implement the reforms which Voltaire and Rousseau had made fashionable. Unfortunately he was very young and had little experience. He had a weak character and in his desire to do the right thing he lacked resolution, and to that extent laid the path for the Revolution.

As a young man he expressed pious hopes:

I know that I owe to God, by choosing me to reign, to the memory of my ancestors, to come out of my childhood, and to make myself worthy of the throne upon which I may one day sit. And that to do this, I must forget nothing which will make me a truly pious prince, good, just and resolute; that I can only acquire these qualities by attention to work, and I resolve to devote myself entirely to it.

He was pleased to make epigrams:

I would like Seneca, if he had practised his principles; but his life belied his precepts; he was a deceitful philosopher.

I cannot convince myself that the harangues of Livy were ever delivered on the battlefield; they are too long.

Tacitus was daring; I like and admire him.

If Rousseau, who was a melancholic, had suspected the evil which would one day result from his writings, I am certain that he would never have let them see the light of day. In this he is unlike Voltaire, who would have held forth even if he had known he would overthrow the state. His pride exceeded even his sensibility.

Louis married Marie-Antoinette in 1770 but it was not until four years later that the royal couple set a new fashion for conjugal manners:

At the period of his grandfather's death, still not having consummated his marriage, Louis began to be exceedingly attached to the Queen. As the first period of so deep a mourning did not allow hunting, he suggested that they should go for walks in the gardens at Choisy; they went out like husband and wife, the young King giving his arm to the Queen, and accompanied by a very small suite. The influence of this example had such an effect upon the courtiers that the next day several couples, who had long, and for good reasons, been disunited, were seen walking on the terrace with the same apparent conjugal intimacy. Thus they spent whole hours, braving the intolerable wearisomeness of their protracted *têtes-à-têtes,* out of mere obsequious imitation.

The young Queen found the etiquette at the French court stifling and although at first she accepted it, her desire to lead a more informal life was ultimately damaging to the untouchability of the French monarchy.

Dressing the Queen was a masterpiece of etiquette; everything was done in prescribed form. The *dame d'honneur* and the *dame d'atours* if they were there together, assisted by the first *femme de chambre* and two ordinary women, were responsible for the main work but even that service had its distinctions. The *dame d'atours* put on the petticoat and handed the gown. The *dame d'honneur* poured out the water for her hands and put on her shift. When a princess of the royal family happened to be present while the Queen was dressing, the *dame d'honneur* yielded this act, but not directly; in such a case the *dame d'honneur* handed it to the first *femme de chambre* who, in her turn, handed it to the princess of the blood. Each of these ladies observed these rules rigidly as of right.

One winter's day it happened that the Queen, who was entirely undressed, was going to put on her shift; I held it ready unfolded for her; the *dame d'honneur* came in, slipped off her gloves, and took it. A scratching was heard at the door; it was opened, and in came the Duchess of Orléans: her gloves were taken off, and she came forward to take the garment; but as it would have been wrong in the *dame d'honneur* to hand it to her she gave it to me and I handed it to the princess. More scratching; it was Madame the Countess of Provence; the Duchess of Orléans handed her the shift. All this while the Queen kept her arms crossed upon her bosom, and appeared to feel cold; Madame observed her uncomfortable situation, and merely laying down her handkerchief without taking off her gloves; she put on the shift, and in doing so knocked the Queen's cap off. The Queen laughed to conceal her impatience, but not until she had muttered between her teeth, 'how disagreeable, how tiresome'.

All who knew the Queen's private qualities knew that she deserved both attachment and esteem. She was kind and patient to excess in her relations with her household, she was considerate to all around her and interested herself in their affairs and even in their pleasures.

Marie-Antoinette painted by Vigée Lebrun who became a great friend of hers.

Louis XVI in 1775 by Duplessis. Because Duplessis's painting of Marie-Antoinette on horseback, when she was still dauphine, for her mother was so successful, Louis marked him out for painting his portrait. Here Louis wears the Orders of the St Esprit and the Golden Fleece.

The Queen possessed in a high degree two valuable qualities—temperance and modesty. She only ate chicken, roasted or boiled, and she drank water only. She showed no particular partiality for anything except her morning coffee, and a sort of bread to which she had been accustomed in her infancy in Vienna.

Her modesty in every particular of her private toilet was extreme. She bathed in a long flannel gown, buttoned up to the neck; and, while her two bathing women assisted her out of the bath she made one of them hold a sheet in front of her so that they could not see her.

Louis's good intentions included publicising potatoes at the behest of Parmentier, for he helped Parmentier convince the French that potatoes did not cause leprosy and wore a potato flower in his buttonhole. He also had himself and his family vaccinated with Jenner's new vaccine, but such gestures were not a substitute for firm government.

Louis himself neither in his person nor his beliefs was able to sustain Louis XIV's concept of the monarchy, although he was clearly a nicer, if duller, person:

The features of Louis XVI were noble enough, though somewhat melancholy; his walk was heavy and ignoble, his person greatly neglected; his hair, however great the skill of his hairdresser, was soon in disorder. His voice, without being harsh, was not agreeable; if he grew animated in speaking he often got above his natural pitch, and became shrill. His teacher had given him a taste for study. The King had continued to teach himself; he knew the English language perfectly; I have often heard him translate some of the most difficult passages in Milton's poems. He was a skilful geographer, and was fond of drawing and colouring maps; he was well-versed in history but had not perhaps sufficiently studied the spirit of it. He appreciated good drama and was a competent judge of it.

This prince combined with his attainments the attributes of a kind husband, a tender father and an indulgent master. Unfortunately he enjoyed the mechanical arts too much: masonry and lock-making so delighted him that he allowed into his private apartment a common locksmith with whom he made keys and locks; and his hands, blackened by that sort of work, were often, in my presence, the subject of remonstrances and even sharp reproaches from the Queen who would have chosen other amusements for him.

Austere and rigid with regard to himself alone, the King observed the laws of the church scrupulously, always fasting on the appointed days. He did not require the Queen to emulate him for, though sincerely pious, the spirit of the age had disposed him to toleration. Modest and simple in his habits, his ministers [Turgot, Malesherbes and Necker] judged that a prince of such character would willingly sacrifice the royal prerogative to the solid greatness of his people. His heart, in truth, disposed him towards reforms; but his principles, his prejudices and his fears, and the clamours of pious and privileged persons, intimidated him, and made him abandon plans which his love for the people had suggested.

People tended to agree about the King's character:

The only passion which Louis XVI ever discovered was for the chase. This occupied his mind so much that, in going up to his small apartments at Versailles, after the 10th of August, I observed, in the staircase, six paintings, which contained the representation of all his chases, both when he was dauphin and king. In these paintings were exhibited the number, the kind, and quality of the game which he had killed in each department of the chase, with the particulars of every month, every season, and every year of his reign.

The King was born with a weak and delicate constitution; but, when he reached the age of twenty-four, his temperament amended so much, that he afterwards became even robust. At court, they related of him some particular feats of strength, which he inherited from his mother, a descendant of the house of Saxony, so famous for vigour of constitution through successive generations.

Louis XVI was distinguished by such a peculiarity of character, that it may, in some measure, be said, there were in him two men; a man who *knows,* and a man who *wills.* The former of these qualities was very extensive and various. The King was perfectly well versed in the history of his own family, and that of the first houses of France.

His memory was stored with an infinity of names both of persons and places. It was astonishing also with respect to quantities and numbers. He was one day presented with a long account, in the statement of which the minister had placed an article of expenditure, which had been inserted in the account of the preceding year. 'Here is a double entry,' said the King: 'bring me the account of last year, and I will show you that this article is mentioned in it.'

When the King was thoroughly acquainted with all the particulars of an affair, and discovered any violation of justice, he was severe even to a degree of brutality. A flagrant act of injustice made him overleap the ordinary bounds of his character: he would then insist upon being obeyed that moment, both to make sure of the atonement, and to prevent any similar misconduct in future.

But in the great affairs of state, the King who *wills,* who *commands,* was not to be found in this monarch. Louis XVI was, upon the throne, nothing superior to those private persons whom we meet with in society, so weak in intellectual faculties, that nature has rendered them incapable of forming an opinion. In the midst of his pusillanimity, he placed his confidence entirely in a particular minister, and, although among the variety of opinions delivered in his cabinet-council, he well knew which was the best, he never once had the resolution to say, 'I prefer the advice of such a one.' Here lay the copious source of national misfortune.

But despite playing at being locksmiths or dairymaids, as Marie-Antoinette enjoyed, the external life of the court before 1789 was dazzling. A young lady-in-waiting, Madame de Gouvernet, later Madame de la Tour du Pin, recollected it many years later:

It would perhaps be of interest to describe the Sunday courts over which that unfortunate Queen presided so brilliantly.

A few minutes before midday, the ladies entered the salon next to the Queen's bedchamber. They all stood, except the elderly ones, who in those days were treated with great deference, and those of the younger ladies who were thought to be pregnant. There were always at least forty people present, often more. Sometimes, we were very closely packed, for our paniers took up a great deal of room. Ordinarily, when the Princess of Lamballe, mistress of the household, arrived, she went straight into the bedchamber where the Queen was dressing. She usually arrived before the Queen had begun her toilette. A few minutes later, a footman advanced to the door of the bedchamber and called in a loud voice for '*le service*'. The four ladies on duty that week, and all those who had come, as was customary, to wait on the Queen between their periods of duty, would then enter the bedchamber.

As soon as the Queen had greeted each of us in her charming, kindly way, the door was opened and everyone admitted. We stood to the right and left of the room in such a manner as to leave a clear space at the door and in the centre of the room. Often when there were many ladies in attendance, we stood in rows two or three deep. But the first arrivals would withdraw skilfully towards the door leading to the card-room, through which the Queen had to pass on her way to mass. To this salon a few privileged gentlemen who had either been received earlier in private audience or who were to present visitors from abroad were often admitted.

Thus it happened one day that the Queen, stopping unexpectedly to say a word to someone, saw me in the corner of the doorway shaking hands with the English ambassador. She had never seen this English form of greeting before and found it very amusing. As jokes do not die easily at court, she never failed to ask the ambassador on the many occasions when we were both present, 'Have you shaken hands with Madame de Gouvernet?'

This tragic Queen still betrayed, even then, a few trifling and very feminine jealousies. She had a very lovely complexion and a radiant personality, but she showed herself a little jealous of those young ladies who could bring to the hard light of noon a seventeen-year-old complexion more dazzling than her own. I was one of them, and once when she was passing through the door, the Duchess of Duras, who was always very kind and helpful to me, whispered in my ear: 'Do not stand facing the windows.' I understood what she meant and followed her advice. But this did not prevent the Queen from sometimes passing remarks which were almost cutting about my liking for bright colours and for the poppies and brown scabious which I often wore.

These Sunday morning audiences lasted until forty minutes past noon. Then the door opened and the footman announced: 'The King!' The Queen, who always wore court dress, would go to meet him with a charming air of pleasure and deference. The King would incline his head to the right and to the left, and speak to a few ladies whom he knew, though never to the young ones. He was so short-sighted that he could not recognise anyone at a distance of more than three paces. He was stout, about five foot six or seven inches tall, square shouldered and with the worst possible bearing. He looked like some peasant shambling along behind his plough; there was nothing proud or regal about him. His sword was a continual embarrassment to him and he never knew what to do with his hat, yet in court dress he looked really magnificent. He took no interest in his clothes, putting on without a glance whatever was handed to him. His coats were made of cloths suited to the various seasons, all very heavily embroidered, and he wore the diamond star of the Order of the Holy Ghost. It was only on his feast day, or on days of gala or great ceremonial that he wore the ribbon over his coat.

When the Queen returned to Paris, she gave up her boxes at the theatre, an expression of resentment which, though very natural, was most unfortunate. It made the people of Paris more hostile than ever towards her. This ill-starred princess either did not know how to consider people's feelings or was not prepared to do so. When she was displeased, she allowed it to be evident, regardless of the consequences, and this did great harm to the King's cause. She was gifted with very great courage, but little intelligence, absolutely no tact and, worst of all, a mistrust—always misplaced—of those most willing to serve her.

The French were anxious to efface the indignities of the Treaty of Paris and to avenge themselves on the English. When the American colonies revolted against George III it gave both the French king and Frenchmen an opportunity to further the cause of liberty and hinder the English at the same time. But supporting the Americans and war was expensive and since none of the ministers of finance Louis appointed seemed to be able to solve the problems of bankruptcy and discontent he called the Estates General—who had not met since 1614—together.

Rumours that Louis wished to dissolve the meeting he had called, impelled by his by now unpopular Austrian queen, only resulted in the determination of the third estate to remain assembled. Louis was not prepared to use force to break up the meetings and his conciliatory attitude is clear in his address to the National Assembly—as it had now become—on 15 July, 1789:

I have called you together to consult you on the most important affairs of state and there are none more urgent and which affect me more than the disorder which reigns in the capital.

The head of the nation comes to the heart of his representatives to make known his distress, and to invite it to find the means of restoring law and order. I know that unjust accusations have been made; I know too that someone has dared to say that your own persons are not safe; do I have therefore to reassure you about the equally unjust rumours about myself?

Well, I, who am at one with my nation, it is I who put my trust in you; help me at this juncture to maintain the well-being of the State. It is what I expect from the National Assembly. It is you, the representatives of my people, met here together for our common good, who offer me this hope. Certain of the devotion and loyalty of my subjects, I have ordered the troops to evacuate Paris and Versailles, and I authorise you—indeed I beg you—to make my views known throughout the capital.

When Louis returned to Versailles from hunting on 14 July—the day of the 'fall' of the Bastille—and heard the news he asked the Duke of Liancourt if it was a revolt. 'No, Sire,' was the reply, 'it is a revolution.'

By 17 July the royal family's attitude was less sanguine, as Madame Campan's report of the King's visit to Paris shows:

His departure on 17 July for Paris caused equal grief and alarm to his friends, in spite of his calm. The Queen restrained her tears and shut herself in her private room with her family. She sent for several persons belonging to her court; their doors were locked. Terror had driven them away. The silence of death reigned throughout the palace; they hardly dared hope that the King would return.

It was gone four when the King, who had left Versailles at ten in the morning, reached the hôtel de ville. Everyone knows that it was then that the King received the tricoloured cockade which he put in his hat.

His return to Versailles filled his family with inexpressible joy; in the arms of the Queen, his sister and his children, he congratulated himself that no accident had happened; and he repeated several times, 'Happily, no blood has been shed, and I swear that never shall a drop of French blood be shed by my order'; a humane wish but too openly avowed in such factious times.

The revolt against the King went slowly, for at first the Parisians believed that at Versailles he was surrounded by false counsellors and that all would be changed if he were to live in Paris. Escorted by a mob suffering from hunger, since grain was scarce, the royal family was moved to Paris and took up residence in the Tuileries. A year later on the anniversary of the taking of the Bastille Louis presided over a Festival of Federation at the Champ de Mars and revolution and royalty seemed to march together.

For a time the King reconciled himself to the new constitution but when he was asked to approve the civil constitution of the clergy his conscience would not allow him to do so. His attempted escape with the Queen and his children on 21 June, 1791 was foiled at Varennes and from then on his downfall was certain. His brothers, Louis, Count of Provence and Charles, Count of Artois, who were to be kings after Napoleon's fall, had left France in 1791, and his two surviving aunts, 'Mesdames' (Adelaide and Victoire) left their château at Bellevue early in 1791 for Rome. It is with Christian charity and resignation that he wrote to them in 1792:

We have sustained with grief, my dear aunts, your parting from us but it was necessary for your peace of mind and happiness. No less has it deprived me of the consolation I would have derived in your affection for me. Staying in the capital of the Christian world you enjoy the benefits of a true religion. Pray fervently for me to the King of kings, that the troubled sky should be calm again, that He will restore the good old days to France and to the French the confidence they owe me, and that in the heart of discord, happiness should reign again. Then I will be able to say I have lived long enough.

Your last letters reached me ten days later than usual; this was because the post is disorganised. Since everything is disorganised letters are no more certain than events themselves. My children languish, the Queen finds physical strength through her spirit, and I in my resignation to the decrees of providence.

Farewell, dear aunts, the distance that separates us has no effect on my tender affection for you.

Madame Campan records the Queen's views about her husband's character during their imprisonment:

She [Marie-Antoinette] spoke to me of the King's want of energy, but always in terms expressive of her veneration for his virtues and her attachment to him. 'The King,' said she, 'is not a coward; he has a great deal of passive courage, but he is cowed by an awkward shyness, a mistrust of himself, which comes from his education as much as from his disposition. He is afraid to command, and, above all things, dreads speaking to an assembly of people. He lived like a child, and always ill at ease under the eyes of Louis XV, until the age of twenty-one. This constraint confirmed his timidity.'

Cléry, the King's valet, has left an account of the royal family's life in the Temple, which contrasts strangely with their court life at Versailles:

The King generally rose at six o'clock in the morning. He shaved himself; I did his hair and dressed him. He immediately went to his study, which was very small and under constant supervision by a guard. His Majesty prayed on his knees for five or six minutes and then read until nine o'clock. During this time, having done the room and laid the table for luncheon, I went to the Queen's suite; she opened her door only when I arrived to prevent the municipal guard from entering her room. I dressed the young prince's hair and I arranged the Queen's toilet and then went to the rooms of Madame Royale and Madame Elisabeth for the same purpose. It was then that I could inform the Queen and the princesses of what I had learned. I would make a sign to show that I had something to say to them and one of them would then distract the attention of the municipal officer by talking to him.

At nine o'clock the Queen, her children and Madame Elisabeth went up to the King's room for luncheon. At ten the King and his family went down to the Queen's room and spent the day there. He had taken in hand the education of his son; made him recite passages from Corneille and Racine, gave him geography lessons and taught him how to draw maps. The boy's precocious intelligence responded well to his father's loving care. His memory was so good that he could mark in the departments, districts, towns and courses of rivers—the new geography of France. The Queen, in her turn, looked to the education of her daughter, and lessons went on until eleven o'clock. The rest of the morning was spent sewing, knitting or embroidering. At mid-day the three princesses went into Madame Elisabeth's room to change out of their morning clothes—unaccompanied by a guard.

At one, if the weather was fine, the royal family were allowed out into the garden, accompanied by five guards. I was allowed to go with them and I played games with the young prince.

At two we went back into the tower where I served dinner, and every day at the same time Santerre, the brewer, commander-in-chief of the Paris National Guard came to the Temple with two of his aides. He inspected all the rooms; sometimes the King spoke to him; the Queen never. After the meal the royal family went to the Queen's room and played a game of piquet or backgammon.

At four the King took a short nap, surrounded by the princesses who read in silence. When he awoke conversation was resumed, and the King listened to me giving the prince writing lessons and under his direction I copied from the works of Montesquieu and other famous writers. After this I took him to Madame Elisabeth where we played ball or shuttlecock.

At the end of the day the royal family sat round the table, the Queen read aloud—from history books or some other well-chosen text for the edification or amusement of the young but from time to time parallels with her own unhappy situation caused her grief. Then Madame Elisabeth would read until eight o'clock. I served supper to the young prince in her room in the presence of the family—while the King tried to divert the children. After supper I undressed the dauphin, the Queen recited his prayers with him and I took him to his room. It was then that I could pass on the day's news to the Queen for although no papers were allowed in the Temple, a crier came each evening at seven and I managed to remember all he said.

At nine the King dined while either the Queen or Madame Elisabeth stayed with the dauphin. Then he would go to the Queen's room, give her and his sister his hand in a gesture of farewell, receive the embraces of his children and go to his room. He would read until midnight. The Queen and the princesses went to their suite.

Edmund Burke, the English politician and political writer, wrote in 1790, in his Reflections on the Revolution in France, *of Marie-Antoinette:*

I hear, and I rejoice to hear, that the great lady, the other object of the triumph, has borne that day (one is interested that beings made for suffering should suffer well), and that she bears all the succeeding days, that she bears the imprisonment of her husband, and her own captivity, and the exile of her friends, and the insulting adulation of addresses, and the whole weight of her accumulated wrongs, with a serene patience, in a manner suited to her rank and race and becoming the offspring of a sovereign distinguished for her piety and her courage: that, like her, she has lofty sentiments; that she feels with the dignity of a Roman matron; that in the last extremity she will save herself from the last disgrace; and that, if she must fall, she will fall by no ignoble hand.

It is now sixteen or seventeen years since I saw the Queen of France, then the dauphiness, at Versailles; and surely never lighted on this orb, which she hardly seemed to touch, a more delightful vision. I saw her just above the horizon, decorating and cheering the elevated sphere she just began to move in,—glittering like the morning-star, full of life, and splendour, and joy. O! what a revolution! and what a heart must I have to contemplate without emotion that elevation and that fall! Little did I dream when she added titles of veneration to those of enthusiastic, distant, respectful love, that she should ever be obliged to carry the sharp antidote against disgrace concealed in that bosom; little did I dream that I should have lived to see such disasters fallen upon her in a nation of gallant men, in a nation of men of honour, and of cavaliers. I thought ten thousand swords must have leaped from their scabbards to avenge even a look that threatened her with insult. But the age of chivalry is gone. That of sophisters, economists, and calculators, has

Drawing of Louis XVI, in charcoal heightened by water-colour, made during the King's last days in captivity. Ducreux had been commissioned by Choiseul to go to Vienna to paint Marie-Antoinette in 1769 and became a court painter. Despite this he was allowed into the Temple to make this drawing.

succeeded; and the glory of Europe is extinguished for ever. Never, never more shall we behold that generous loyalty to rank and sex, that proud submission, that dignified obedience, that subordination of the heart, which kept alive, even in servitude itself, the spirit of an exalted freedom. The unbought grace of life, the cheap defence of nations, the nurse of manly sentiment and heroic enterprise, is gone! It is gone, that sensibility of principle, that chastity of honour, which felt a stain like a wound, which inspired courage whilst it mitigated ferocity, which ennobled whatever it touched, and under which vice itself lost half its evil, by losing all its grossness.

The Princess of Lamballe, who became Marie-Antoinette's chief lady-in-waiting, after a certain amount of opposition, went to England for a time during the troubles but faithfully returned to Paris and was with the Queen from 20 June to 20 August, 1792. She obtained permission to go to the Temple with her but was sent to the Petite Force prison on 3 September. She was asked to repeat vilifications against the Queen but shouting 'No, never', her attackers murdered her there and then. Louis XVI had tried to save her.

Madam, you have found at the court of St James a welcome, a peaceful people who are proud of the laws which protect them, a monarch dear to the English nation, and worthy, by his virtues, of their love. You ought to be happy, and yet you wish to sacrifice your happiness for us, you wish to return to us to share our burdens and those of the Queen. Your devotion is too noble and too generous but I beg you not to do so for a little longer. It would show us how much you love us if you were to keep yourself for happier days, if we may still hope for them. The present is frightful, what will our future be? God and the wicked only know. We certainly would greatly like to see you but we would be selfish in our love for you if we did not counter your tender sentiments by the most urgent prayer that you should not expose yourself at a time when every crime goes unpunished and all excesses are approved. I send you our most tender greetings and most sincere devotion.

On 10 August, 1792 the monarchy was abolished, and Louis was to be known as plain Louis Capet.

After the French victory over the invading Prussians at Valmy on 20 September, 1792 and their victory over the Austrians at Jemappes in November, the Republic was threatened with a coalition of such strength that in a gesture of revolutionary defiance Danton cried, 'Let us throw them the King's head'.

The voting which resulted in his execution was as follows:
The Convention consisted of 749 members:

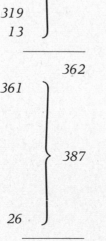

Absent on purpose	*15*	
through illness	*6*	*28*
with no reason	*1*	
Non-voting	*6*	

Leaves to vote 721
Clear majority 311

Votes

For irons	*2*	
For detention and banishment at the peace, or for banishment immediately, or for solitary confinement and hard labour	*319*	*334*
For death with stay of execution	*13*	
		362
For death	*361*	
For death, asking in accordance with the motion of Mailhe—a discussion on the point of knowing if it was consonant with public interest that it should be deferred or not and declaring their wish independent of this demand	*26*	*387*
		749

The King was condemned and the execution fixed for 21 January, 1793. Cléry takes up the story of the last day of his life:

I heard five strike and lit the fire. The noise woke the King and he told me to draw the curtains. I dressed him and did his hair. He removed a note from his watch, put it in his waistcoat pocket and put the watch on the chimney-breast. Then, removing a ring from his finger, which he contemplated for some time, put it in the same pocket with the note, changed his shirt for a white one he had worn the previous evening, and I passed him his jacket. He took out of its pockets his wallet, his lorgnette, his snuff-box and other small personal belongings. He also put his purse on the chimney-breast—all in silence and in the presence of the guards. While he was doing this, I had placed a commode in the centre of the room and prepared it for an altar upon which to say mass, all the necessary objects having been brought at two in the morning. When everything was ready I told the King who asked me if I knew how to serve at mass. I said I did not know all the responses by heart. He opened the book he held in his hand and gave it to me, taking another book himself. In the meanwhile the priest was dressing. I had put an armchair in front of the altar and a large cushion on the ground for the King. However he made me remove it and went himself to his room to get a smaller one, decorated with horsehair, the one he normally used for his prayers. The priest entered, the guards withdrew and mass started at six. The King heard mass in an attitude of saintly prayer, took communion, and then went to his room.

At seven he came out and called me; 'Give this note to my son,' he said, 'and this ring to the Queen; tell her that I part with it in sorrow. This packet contains hair from each member of my family—give her that too. Tell the Queen, my dear children and my sister that I promised to see them this morning but I wished to spare them the anguish of separation and how much it pains me to go without their last embrace.' He dried his tears and added in mournful tones, 'I bid you to make my farewells'. Then he left me. A quarter of an hour later he reappeared. 'Ask,' he said, 'if I may have a pair of scissors.' I asked the guards; 'Do you know what he wants them for?' 'No.' 'We must know.' I knocked at the King's door and asked him. He replied, 'So that Cléry may cut my hair.' One of the guards went away to seek permission and came back half an hour later refusing it. The King explained that he would not touch the scissors but no permission was forthcoming. Then they told me to accompany the King and prepare him for the scaffold.

At nine, Santerre came in accompanied by seven or eight guards, with ten gendarmes and lined them up. Hearing this noise the King emerged again from his study. 'You have come for me?' he asked Santerre. 'Yes.' 'One moment, I beg you.' He went back into the room, came out again followed by his confessor and holding his will in his hand. 'I ask you to give this to the Queen, my wife,' he said to Jacques Roux, the foremost guard. 'Nothing to do with me,' he replied, 'I am here to conduct you to the scaffold.'

I was behind the King, and as he turned to me I offered him his frock coat. 'I do not need it,' he said, 'just give me my hat.' I gave it to him and he shook my hand for the last

Colour wash drawing of Louis's head being displayed to the populace, 21 January, 1793.

time. 'Gentlemen, I hope you will allow Cléry to remain with my son; he is used to him,' he said, and to Santerre, 'Let us go.'

They were the last words he spoke in the room.

Louis mounted the steps of the scaffold fearlessly and turned to address the people he thought he had served so well. But the drums rolled out and drowned his words and seconds later the Terror had claimed its most distinguished victim.

Marie-Antoinette remained in the Temple until she was transferred on 1 August, 1793 to the Concièrgerie. She was taken before the public prosecutor for questioning on 12 October and her formal trial, starting at eight o'clock on the morning of 15 October, lasted almost uninterrupted for twenty hours. She was found guilty by a unanimous verdict and went to the guillotine on 16 October.

The Moniteur*—the official newspaper of the day—reported the event:*

At five o'clock, the call to arms was sounded in all sections. At seven o'clock, the whole armed force was ready; at ten o'clock, a large number of patrols made the rounds in the

Pen and ink drawing of Marie-Antoinette on her way to the scaffold, 1793, by David. David was a leading Revolutionary, and a deputy who had voted for the death of Louis XVI.

streets. At eleven o'clock, Marie-Antoinette, the widow Capet, wearing a white, quilted gown, was taken to the scaffold in the same way as other criminals [i.e. in an open cart] accompanied by a constitutional priest dressed as a layman, and escorted by a large number of *gendarmerie* detachments on foot and on horseback. Marie-Antoinette, all along the way, appeared to regard with indifference the armed forces forming a double line along the streets through which she passed. Her face showed neither despondency nor pride, and she appeared insensible to the cries of 'Long live the Republic', 'Down with tyranny' which she heard all the way. She spoke very little to her confessor; her attention was caught by the tricolour flames in the rue du Roule and the rue St Honoré. She also noticed the signs placed on the frontispieces of the houses; on arriving at the square of the Revolution, she looked towards the national gardens [the Tuileries garden]; signs of keen emotion were then noticed on her face; she then climbed the scaffold with considerable courage. At a quarter past twelve, her head fell and the executioner showed it to the people amidst long drawn out cries of 'Long live the Republic'.

Epilogue

Long live the Republic!

The monarchy was abolished on 10 August, 1792.
A provisional government ruled from 10 August to 20 September, 1793.
The (first) Republic was proclaimed on 21 September, 1792.
Louis XVI was executed on 21 January, 1793.

Louis's son, 'Louis XVII', born in 1785, was still alive and imprisoned in the Temple with his sister, though in separate quarters. Years later she wrote of her life then, and has left this heart-rending account of her brother's last days:

For some time my brother complained of pain in his ribs; on 6 May he ran a high temperature, had a violent headache and the pain in his ribs. He couldn't stay in bed because he suffocated. My mother was very worried and asked the guards for a doctor. They said my brother's illness was not serious. My aunt helped my mother nurse him and sent me to her bed so that I should not be infected. He was feverish for several days after which Thierry, a prison doctor, came to visit him. When he came in the morning my brother's temperature was not high, but my mother persuaded him to come back in the evening when he saw for himself how ill he was and indeed he convinced the guards that his condition was serious. He had the honesty to consult Brunier about medicines since he had been our doctor since childhood and those prescribed made some improvement in my brother's condition. After a few days he was better though lack of air and exercise did not improve matters which were bad enough anyhow for a boy of eight.

On 3 July the Convention decreed that my brother should be removed from us to a more secure lodging in the tower and only on threats from the guards to kill both him and me did my mother allow him to be taken from her. She was prostrated by the separation and reached the depths of despair when she learned that my brother had been entrusted to Simon, the cobbler. She asked endlessly and in vain to be allowed to see her son. The guards were taken from us and we were shut in night and day seeing them only three times a day when they brought food. We had no servants; my aunt and I made the beds and looked after my mother. Simon maltreated my brother so badly that we dared not tell my mother.

Bust of Louis 'XVII', 1790, by Deseine.

At two in the morning on 2 August they woke us to tell us that the Convention had decreed that my mother was to be moved to the Concièrgerie to undergo trial. Every day we heard my brother being made to sing the Marseillaise and to swear against God, his family and the aristocracy by Simon whose ill-treatment made him ill again. He gave him disgusting food and made him drink a lot of wine which he hated, so that his health deteriorated even more.

On 19 January we heard a great noise in my brother's room and thought he was being removed but we learned later that it was Simon leaving. He had to choose between becoming a guard or looking after my brother and chose the former. They had the cruelty to leave my brother alone; an unheard-of barbarity to abandon a child of eight who was ill and to leave him locked in a room with no recourse for help other than a bell he was too frightened to use, preferring to go without rather than to ask his gaolers for the slightest thing. He was in a bed which had not been changed for six months and which he had no strength to make. He was infested with fleas and bugs; his shirt and stockings had not been changed for a year and his excrement had not been removed during the whole of that period. His window was bolted and barred and was never opened and his room stank. It is true that my brother neglected himself; he ought to have taken more care of himself and at least washed himself since he was given water to do so. But he was dying of fright. He spent his days doing nothing and he was given no light so that his morale and his physique deteriorated. It is not surprising that he became terribly depressed; the length of time he survived in good health and resisted such cruelty proves the strength of his constitution.

On 9 Thermidor [July 27–28, 1794, for even the calendar was changed] Robespierre was overthrown by the Convention. His friends the Jacobins tried in vain to defend him. Attacked by a pistol shot in the face he was taken bleeding to the guillotine to which he had sent so many. The Terror was over. The little boy was better looked after; Madame Royale continues:

My brother continued in his insalubrious state, visited only at mealtimes. He had one guard only, who was honest enough to dare speak of the harshness of his treatment which simply resulted in his dismissal. Later that month the Convention sent a deputation to consider my brother's condition, and at last took pity on him, requiring that he should be better treated. He was given another bed, made to take baths, and was deloused, but he was still left alone. At the beginning of November a commissar called Gomier came, and took care of my brother, saw that he had a light in the evenings and even spent some time with him. He soon saw that his knees and wrists were swollen and he thought that he might be rickety. He told the Committee who allowed my brother into the garden for some exercise. During the winter his fever returned and he was always cold. He did not want to walk and could barely do so. His illness grew worse and his knees swelled even more. I went up to see him in the spring but he weakened gradually and his spirits sank. Dessault, the doctor sent in by the Committee, undertook to cure him even though he knew how ill he was but Dessault died and Dumangin and Pelletan, who succeeded him, could hold out no hope. My brother had great difficulty in taking the medicines prescribed but at least was not in great pain, it was rather a slow deterioration, and he died of it on 9 June, 1795, at the age of ten and two months. I do not think he was poisoned.

The rise and fall of Napoleon Bonaparte—who took the bee as his symbol—plays no part in the history of the French monarchs. Proclaimed Emperor in 1804, the conqueror of Europe until the Russian fiasco, he was beaten at the battle of Leipzig, forced back to Paris, and abdicated in 1814.

Louis XVIII—born on 17 November, 1755 at Versailles—brother of Louis XVI, was called to the throne on 6 April, 1814. He reigned for ten years, with the exception of the 'Hundred Days', until his death, aged sixty-eight, on 16 September, 1824 in Paris. He was buried at St Denis.

Louis XVIII by Marigny after Gérard.

Charles X by Gérard.

He was succeeded by his brother Charles X—born on 9 October, 1757 at Versailles—who had himself crowned with full panoply at Rheims on 29 May, 1825. He abdicated on 2 August, 1830. He died aged seventy-nine at Goritzia, where he was buried, on 6 November, 1836.

He was the last King of France.

Sources

It would be a labour of supererogation to list all the works I have consulted in order to make this anthology but I am very grateful to all those authors who have quoted their references in enough detail for me to have been able to track them down. I have failed in only four cases and for these I have therefore had to use the secondary sources which are acknowledged.

For the linking passages, I have found Jacques Bainville's *Petite Histoire de France* (Tours, 1934) invaluable, and I could not resist including some of his simplistic and delightfully nationalistic views.

I am indebted to the following publishers for permission to quote from their publications:
J. M. Dent & Sons Ltd for permission to quote an extract from Dante's *La Divina Commedia,* translated by Thomas Okey, Temple Classics Series; an extract from *Memoirs* by Cellini, translated by Anne Macdonell; and an extract from Edmund Burke's *Reflections upon the Revolution in France,* Everyman's Library.

Thomas Nelson & Sons Ltd, for permission to quote an extract from *Miniatures of French History* by Hilaire Belloc.

Penguin Books Ltd, for permission to quote an extract from Joinville and Villehardouin's *Chronicles of the Crusades* (The Life of Saint Louis), translated by M. R. B. Shaw and an extract from Froissart's *Chronicles,* translated by Geoffrey Brereton.

Duckworth and Company Ltd, for permission to quote an extract from *St Francis to Dante* by G. C. Coulton.

Harvill Press Ltd, for permission to quote an extract from *Memoirs of Madame de la Tour du Pin* translated by F. Harcourt.

PAGE 20: Voltaire, *Oeuvres Complètes,* 1785, Vol. 21, *Siècle de Louis XIV,* p. 80.

PROLOGUE: Hilaire Belloc, *Miniatures of French History,* London, 1925, pp. 68–73.

HUGH CAPET: Richer, *Histoire* edited by A-M. Poinsignon, Rheims, 1855, pp. 371, 373, 375, 377; p. 103; p. 503.

ROBERT: Helgald, *Vie du Roi Robert* in *Collection des Mémoires relatifs à l'histoire de France depuis la fondation de la monarchie française jusqu'au 13e siècle* edited by M. Guizot, Paris, 1825, Vol. 6, pp. 365–6. Richer, *op. cit.*, pp. 377, 469, 471, 503. Ralph Glaber, *Chronique* in Guizot, *op. cit.*, p. 246. Helgald, *op. cit.*, pp. 368–9, 392–3. Glaber, *op. cit.*, pp. 283–5.

HENRI I: Continuation of Aimoin in *Les Grandes Chroniques de France* edited by Jules Viard, Paris, 1930, Vol. 5, pp. 69–71. Orderic Vitalis, *Histoire de Normandie* in Guizot, *op. cit.*, Vol. 26, p. 74.

PHILIPPE I: Henry of Huntingdon, *The History of England,* Appendix B *Epistola de contemptu mundi* edited by Thomas Arnold, Rolls Series, Vol. 74, London, 1879, p. 312. William of Malmesbury, *Gesta Regum Anglorum* edited by T. D. Hardy, English Historical Society, London, 1840, p. 631. Orderic Vitalis, *op. cit.,* Vol. 27, p. 341; p. 342. William of Malmesbury, *op. cit.,* p. 632. Orderic Vitalis, *op. cit.,* Vol. 28, pp. 248–9. Suger, *Vie de Louis-le-Gros* in Guizot, *op. cit.,* Vol. 8, pp. 46–7. Procès-verbal from Register B of fabric deliberations and the parish accounts for 1823–24 of St Benoît-sur-Loire, f.11 in *Le Règne de Philippe I* by Augustin Fliche, Paris, 1912, p. 560; pp. 561–2.

LOUIS VI: Beryl Smalley, *Historians in the Middle Ages,* London, 1974, p. 76. Suger, *op. cit.*, pp. 3, 4–5; pp. 8, 132, 151–9.

LOUIS VII: Guillaume de Nangis, *Chronique* in Guizot, *op. cit.*, Vol. 13, pp. 35–40. Walter Map, *De Nugis Curialium* in *Anecdota Oxoniensa*, Vol. 4, 14 edited by M. R. James, Oxford, 1916, p. 216. Continuator of Suger, *Vie de Louis-le-Jeune* in Guizot, *op. cit.*, Vol. 8, pp. 217–18; p. 219. Walter Map, *op. cit.*, p. 216.

PHILIPPE II: Rigord, *Vie de Philippe-Auguste* in Guizot, *op. cit.*, Vol. 11, pp. 9–10. Païeu Gâtineau, *Chronique de Tours* in *Recueil des Historiens des Gaules et de la France* edited by M. Bouquet: Vol. 18, edited by M. J. J. Brial, Paris, 1822, p. 304. Chroniclers quoted in *Histoire de France* edited by E. Lavisse: Vol. 3, part 1 by A. Luchaire, Paris 1901, pp. 282–3. Rigord, *op. cit.*, pp. 30, 47–8; p. 112. Guillaume le Breton, *La Philippide* in Guizot, *op. cit.*, Vol. 12, p. 108. Rigord, *op. cit.*, pp. 140–1. Philippe Mouskes, *Chronique Rimée* in *Chroniques Belges* edited by Baron de Reiffenberg, Brussels, 1838, Vol. 2, p. 355. L'Anonyme de Béthune, *Chronique Française* (BN. nouv. acquis. fr. 6295) in *Recueil des Historiens,* Vol. 24, ii, edited by L. Delisle, Paris, 1904, p. 768. Guillaume le Breton, *Vie de Philippe-Auguste* in Guizot, *op. cit.*, Vol. 11, pp. 301–3. Gilles de Paris, *Carolinus* quoted in Luchaire, *op. cit.*, pp. 280–1. Guillaume le Breton, *op. cit.*, pp. 348–9.

LOUIS VIII: Guillaume de Nangis, *op. cit.*, pp. 116, 118–20. Nicolas de Bray, *Vie de Louis VIII* in Guizot, *op. cit.*, Vol. 11, pp. 378–9. Guillaume de Puyslaurens, *Chronique,* in Guizot, *op. cit.*, Vol. 15, pp. 274–5. A. Lenoir, Notes historiques sur les exhumations faites en 1793 dans l'abbaye de Saint-Denis (Musée des Monum. franç., Vol. 2, cxxiv–cxxv) quoted in *La Vie et Règne de Louis VII* by Ch. Petit-Dutaillis, Paris, 1894, pp. 435–6.

LOUIS IX: Geoffroy de Beaulieu, *Vie de Louis IX* in *Recueil des Historiens,* Vol. 20 edited by P. C. F. Daunon and J. Naudet, Paris, 1840, pp. 6–7. Robert de Sorbon, *De Matrimonio* quoted in *Notices et extraits de quelques manuscrits latins de la Bibliothèque Nationale* by M. B. Hauréau, Paris, 1890, Vol. 1, pp. 197–8. Fra Salimbene, *Monumenta Historica ad provincias Parmensem et Placentinam pertinentia*. Parma, 1857, translated by G. C. Coulton in *From St Francis to Dante,* London, 1908, pp. 139–42. Joinville, *The Life of St Louis* translated by M. R. B. Shaw, London, 1936, pp. 204–5; pp. 315–16; pp. 325–6; pp. 331, 336–7. Louis IX, 'Enseignements' quoted in *La Vie en France au Moyen Age* by Ch-V. Langlois, Paris, 1928, Vol. 4, pp. 35, 37–9. Joinville, *op. cit.*, pp. 167–8, 177. Voltaire, 'Essai sur les moeurs et l'esprit des nations', *op. cit.*, Vol. 17, p. 154.

PHILIPPE III: Geoffroy de Beaulieu, *op. cit.*, p. 7. Joinville, *op. cit.*, p. 171. Guillaume de Nangis, *Vie de Philippe III* in *Recueil des Historiens,* Vol. 20, p. 467. 'Le Mercure de France', August, 1718 quoted in *Le Règne de Philippe III le Hardi* by Ch-V. Langlois, Paris, 1887, footnote, p. 6. Guillaume de Nangis, *op. cit.*, p. 491; p. 495. Anonymous Chronicler in *Recueil des Historiens,* Vol. 21 edited by J. D. Guigniaut and J. N. de Wailly, Paris, 1855, pp. 94–5; p. 102. Dante, *La Divina Commedia,* Purgatory, canto vii, translated by Thomas Okey, London, 1933, pp. 80–1.

PHILIPPE IV: William the Scot, *Chronicle* in *Recueil des Historiens,* Vol. 21, p. 205. Guillaume de Nangis, *Chronique* in Guizot, *op. cit.*; Vol. 13, pp. 307–8.

LOUIS X: Guillaume de Nangis, *op. cit.*, pp. 301–2; pp. 316–17.

PHILIPPE V: Guillaume de Nangis, *op. cit.*, pp. 302–3; pp. 353–4.

CHARLES IV: Guillaume de Nangis, *op. cit.*, pp. 355–6, 368, 388; p. 389; p. 391.

PHILIPPE VI: Jean Froissart, *Chronicles* selected, edited and translated by Geoffrey Brereton, London, 1968, p. 55; pp. 77–93.

JEAN II: Froissart, *op. cit.*, pp. 138–43; pp. 168–9.

CHARLES V: Froissart, *op. cit.*, p. 181. Christine de Pisan, *Le Livre des Fais et Bonnes Meurs du Sage Roy Charles V* edited by S. Solente, Paris, 1936, pp. 48–9, 82–5.

CHARLES VI: Froissart, *op. cit.*, pp. 252–7; pp. 358–9; pp. 361–72; pp. 392–8. Charles VI letter to Charles, Duke of Lorraine, 25 March 1422 (BN. fs Moreau 1425) in *Choix de Pièces Inédites relatives au Règne de Charles VI* edited by L. Douët d'Arcq, Paris, 1863, pp. 412–13.

CHARLES VII: Philippe de Vigneulles, *Chronique* edited by Charles Bruneau, Metz, 1929, Vol. 2, pp. 196–9. Thomas Basin, *Histoire de Charles VII* edited by Charles Samaran, Paris, 1944, Vol. 2, pp. 279–82. *The Secret History of Louis XI, King of France* otherwise called *The Scandalous Chronicle* in Philip de Comines, *Historical Memoirs*, London, 1817, pp. 559–60.

LOUIS XI: *Scandalous Chronicle*, pp. 560–2. Comines, *op. cit.*, pp. 55–7, 190, 219. Louis XI letter to Jacques de Beaumont, Seigneur de Bressuire, 4 November quoted in Brantôme, *Oeuvres Complètes* edited by Ludovic Lalanne, Paris, 1866, *Grands Capitaines François*, Vol. 2, pp. 338–9; p. 334. Comines, *op. cit.*, pp. 340–5. *Scandalous Chronicle*, pp. 639–40. 'Henry VII', Francis Bacon, *The Moral and Historical Works* edited by Joseph Devey, London, 1852, p. 478.

CHARLES VIII: Comines, *op. cit.*, p. 378. Brantôme, *op. cit.*, pp. 283–5, 319. Zaccaria Contarini, 1492 in *Le Relazioni degli Ambasciatori Veneti al Senato* edited by Eugenio Albèri, Florence, 1853, Series 1, Vol. 3, pp. 15–16. Zaccaria Contarini and Francesco Cappello quoted in *La Diplomatie Vénitienne; les Princes de l'Europe au XVIe siècle* by Armand Baschet, Paris, 1862, pp. 320–1. Charles VIII letter to Jean Bourré, Seigneur du Plessis, 4 December 1497 (BN. ms. fr. 6602. f. 147). in *Lettres de Charles VIII Roi de France* edited by P. Pélicier, Paris, 1905, Vol. 5, p. 156. Comines, *op. cit.*, p. 439; pp. 543–8.

LOUIS XII: Domenico di Trevisan, 1502 quoted in *I Diarii* by Marino Sanuto edited by Nicolò Barozzi, Venice, 1880, Vol. 4, p. 332. Antonio Loredan, 1498 quoted from Sanuto, *op. cit.*, Vol. 2, suppl. f. 47–125 in Baschet, *op. cit.*, pp. 355–6. Brantôme, *Vie des Dames Illustres Françoises et Etrangères*, Paris, 1823, Vol. 5, pp. 196–7; pp. 1–3, 5–6. Louis XII letter to Thomas Wolsey, Archbishop of York, 5 September 1514 (Cotton Caligula D. vi. Brecq. Vol. lxxxv) in *Collection des Documents Inédits* edited by M. Champollion-Figeac, Paris, 1847, Vol. 2, pp. 544–5. Letter from Mary to Louis XII, September 1514 (Cotton Vitell, C.xi.f.156^{v}., Brecq. Vol. lxxxv), Champollion-Figeac, *op. cit.*, pp. 545–6. Fleurange, *Mémoires* in *Nouvelle Collection des Mémoires pour servir à l'Histoire de France* edited by J. F. Michaud and J. J. F. Poujoulat, Paris and Lyon, 1850, Vol. 5, pp. 44–5. Brantôme, *Gr. Cap. Fr.*, Vol. 2, pp. 364, 368.

FRANÇOIS I: Fleurange, *op. cit.*, p. 47. François I letter to Charles V October 1525 in *Anthologie de la Correspondence Française* edited by André Maison, Paris, 1969, Vol. 1, p. 30. Brantôme, *op. cit.*, Vol. 3, pp. 243–5, 124, 105, 118. Benvenuto Cellini, *Memoirs* translated by Anne Macdonell, London, 1903, reprint 1948, pp. 254–9. Marino Cavalli, 1546 in Albèri, *op. cit.*, Series 1, Vol. 1, pp. 236–9.

HENRI II: Matteo Dandolo, 1542 in Albèri, *op. cit.*, Series 1, Vol. 3, p. 46. Matteo Dandolo, 1547 in Albèri, *op. cit.*, Series 1, Vol. 2, pp. 171–3. Brantôme, *Gr. Cap. Fr.*, Vol. 3, pp. 276–9. Brantôme, *Dames Illus.*, pp. 33–4. Chateaubriand, *Oeuvres Complètes: Etudes ou discours historiques*, Brussels, 1835, Vol. 3, pp. 248–9. Marino Cavalli, 1546 in Albèri, *op. cit.*, Series 1, Vol. 1, p. 242. Henri II letters to Diane of Poitiers, 1547 quoted in *Henri II: His Court and Times*, by H. Noel Williams, London, 1910, pp. 253–4. Lorenzo Contarini, 1551 in Albèri, *op. cit.*, Series 1, Vol. 3, p. 78. Brantôme, *Vie des Dames Galantes*, Paris, 1822, pp. 429–30. Brantôme, *Gr. Cap. Fr.*, Vol. 3, pp. 272–3. Girolamo Lippomano, *Chronicle* quoted in Baschet, *op. cit.*, p. 493.

FRANÇOIS II: Giovanni Capello, 1554 in Albèri, *op. cit.*, Series 1, Vol. 1, pp. 280–1. Brantôme, *Dames Illus.*, pp. 82–6. Renauld de la Beaulne, Funeral Oration quoted in *De Vita et Rebus Gestis Serenissimae Principis Mariae Scotorum Reginae, Franciae Dotoriae* by S. Jebb, London, 1725, Vol. 2, pp. 685–6.

CHARLES IX: Giovanni Michiel, 1561 in Albèri, *op. cit.*, Series 1, Vol. 3, pp. 429–30. Giovanni Correr, 1569 in Albèri, *op. cit.*, Series 1, Vol. 2, p. 205. Letter from Catherine de Medici to Charles IX, 1563 in *Archives Curieuses de l'Histoire de France* edited by L. Cimber and F. Danjou, 1st series, Vol. 4, Paris, 1835, pp. 246–7. Charles IX letter to M. de Fourquevaux, 28 September, 1567, in *Lettres de Charles IX à M. de Fourquevaux* (1565–72) edited by M. l'abbé Douais, Montpellier, 1897, pp. 119–20. Brantôme, *Gr. Cap. Fr.*, Vol. 4, pp. 239–40, 250. Brantôme, *Dames Illus.*, pp. 293–7. Charles IX letter to the Comte de Matignon, 29 May, 1574, Maison, *op. cit.*, pp. 102–3. Brantôme, *Gr. Cap. Fr.*, Vol. 4, pp. 268–71. Pierre de l'Estoile, *Journal* edited by Louis-Raymond Lefèvre, Paris, 1943, p. 7.

HENRI III: Alvise Contarini, 1572 in Albèri, *op. cit.*, Series 1, Vol. 2, pp. 256–7. Giovanni Michiel, 1575 in Albèri, *op. cit.*, Series 1, Vol. 2, pp. 305–6. L'Estoile, *op. cit.*, pp. 50–1, 64–5, 93, 142, 180, 188–9. Francesco Morosini, 1574 in *Histoire de la Chancellerie Secrète* by Armand Baschet, Paris, 1870, p. 571. Giovanni Michiel, 1575 in Albèri, *op. cit.*, Series 1, Vol. 2, p. 363. Lorenzo Priuli, 1582 in Albèri, *op. cit.*, Series 1, Vol. 2, pp. 423–5. 'Seditions and Troubles', Bacon, *op. cit.*, p. 38. Henri III quoted in *A History of France* by André Maurois, translated by Henry L. Binsse, London, 1966, p. 164.

HENRI IV: A Bordeaux magistrate, 1567 quoted in *Mémoires* by M. le duc de Nevers, Paris, 1665, Vol. 2, pp. 585–6. The Duke of Sully, *Memoirs*, London, 1856, Vol. 4, pp. 129–33; p. 134. Pierre Matthieu, *Histoire de Henry IIII*, Paris, 1631, Vol. 2, p. 837. *Mém. pour l'Histoire de France*, Vol. 2, p. 277 quoted in Sully, *op. cit.*, footnote p. 128. Henri IV letters to Gabrielle d'Estrées in *Lettres Intimes de Henri IV* edited by L. Dussieux, Paris, 1876, 4 February, 1593, p. 173; 10 February 1593, p. 175; 17 February 1593, p. 176; 20 April 1593, p. 181; 18 December 1594, p. 209; end 1594, p. 214; 22 October 1597, p. 274; 12 September 1598, p. 287; Gabrielle d'Estrées letter to Henri IV, October 1592, p. 172; Henri IV letter to his sister Catherine, 15 April 1599, p. 305; Henri IV letter to Henriette d'Entragues's father, 1 October 1599, p. 311; Henri IV letters to Henriette d'Entragues, 21 April 1600, p. 331; 4 October 1601, p. 355; 8 October 1601, pp. 356–7; April 1604, p. 396. Henri IV to Sully in *Mémoires des Sages et Royalles Oeconomies*, Amsterdam, 1638, Vol. 2, p. 329 translated by Desmond Seward in *The First Bourbon*, London, 1971, p. 170. Sir George Carew, *A Relation of the State of France*, London, 1749, pp. 491–2. Jean Richer, 1610 quoted in Dussieux, *op. cit.*, p. 11. Hardouin de Péréfixe, *Histoire du roi Henry le grand*, Paris, 1662, pp. 404–5. L'Estoile, *op. cit.*, Vol. 3, pp. 75–6, 91.

LOUIS XIII: Jean Héroard, *Journal sur l'enfance et la jeunesse de Louis XIII* 1601–28 edited by E. Soulié and E. de Barthélemy, Paris, 1868, 30 July 1606, Vol. 1, p. 202; 26 January 1610, Vol. 1, p. 423; 13 October 1614, Vol. 2, pp. 161–2; 21 December 1614, Vol. 2, p. 168; 26 January 1612, Vol. 2, p. 98; 21, 22 and 25 November 1615, Vol. 2, pp. 185–6. Ce qui c'est passé lors de la consommation du marriage du roi (BN. ms. fonds Dupuy) quoted in *Le Roi chez la Reine* by Armand Baschet, Paris, 1866, pp. 197–9. Héroard, *op. cit.*, 6 November 1614, Vol. 2, pp. 166–7; 25 January 1619, Vol. 2, p. 230. Le sieur de Bellemaure, Le Pourtrait du Roy sent to the sieur de Mirancourt, 20 September 1618 in *Archives Curieuses*, 2nd series, Vol. 1, 1837, pp. 401–15. Mme de Motteville, *Mémoires* in *Mémoires pour servir*, Paris, 1851, Vol. 10, pp. 11–14.

LOUIS XIV: Mme de Motteville, *Mémoires sur Anne d'Autriche et sa cour* edited by M. F. Riaux, Paris, 1891, Vol. 1, p. 51. Mlle de Montpensier, *Mémoires* edited by A. Chéruel, Paris, 1891, Vol. 3, p. 352. Mme de Brégis in *La Galerie des Portraits de Mlle de Montpensier* edited by E. de Barthélemy, Paris, 1860, pp. 2–4. M. Martinet in Montpensier, *op. cit.*, pp. 5–10. J. B. Priuli Visconti, *Mémoires sur la cour de Louis XIV* edited by Jean Lemoine, Paris, 1908, pp. 44–6. Voltaire, *op. cit.*, Vol. 21, pp. 81–2. Mme de Montespan, *Memoirs,* London, 1895, Vol. 1, pp. 56–7. Voltaire, *op. cit.*, p. 139. Louis XIV, *Mémoires* edited by Charles Dreyss, Paris, 1860, Vol. 2, p. 570. Louis XIV, *op. cit.*, pp. 518–20, 250–1. Visconti, *op. cit.*, pp. 31–5. *Saint-Simon at Versailles* selected and translated by Lucy Norton from the *Memoirs,* London, 1958, pp. 245–52. Voltaire, *op. cit.*, p. 100. Mme Campan, *Mémoires sur la vie privée de Marie Antoinette,* London, 1823, Vol. 1, pp. 373–4, Voltaire, *op. cit.*, p. 153; pp. 163–8. Saint-Simon, *Historical Memoirs* edited and translated by Lucy Norton, London, 1968. Vol. 2, pp. 468–96.

LOUIS XV: Elisabeth Charlotte, 'Madame', letter to the Raugravine Luise von Degenfeld, 26 March 1722, in *Letters from Liselotte* edited and translated by Maria Kroll, London, 1970, p. 240. Cha Séphi, *Mémoires secrètes pour servir à l'histoire de Perse* quoted in *Mistress of Versailles* by Agnes de Stoeckl, London, 1966, p. 1. Duc de Luynes, *Mémoires sur la cour de Louis XV* edited by L. Dussieux and E. Soulié, Paris, 1861, Vol. 1, August 1737, p. 326; September 1737, p. 346; 5 December 1737, p. 411; 8 December 1737, pp. 412–13; 24 December 1737, p. 426. Marquise du Deffand, *Lettres à Horace Walpole,* Paris, 1812, Vol. 4, pp. 449–50. Marquis d'Argenson, *Journal et Mémoires* edited by E. J. B. Rathery, Paris, 1862, Vol. 4, 19 March 1743, pp. 52–3; 19 May 1743, p. 64; 'le Roi', pp. 162–8. Luynes, *op. cit.*, Vol. 6, 26 August 1744, pp. 39, 46–7; September 1744, p. 85. Mme Campan, *op. cit.*, Vol. 1, pp. 414–15. Le Roy quoted in *Mme de Pompadour* by Nancy Mitford, London, revised edition 1968, p. 39. Mme du Hausset, *The Private Memoirs,* London, 1895, pp. 2–3, 16–17, 38–9, 73–8, 81–6, 153–4, 157–8. J. N. Dufort, Comte de Cheverny, *Mémoires sur les règnes de Louis XV et Louis XVI et sur la Révolution* edited by Robert de Crevecoeur, Paris, 1886, Vol. 1, pp. 184–5. Mme Campan, *op. cit.*, Vol. 1, pp. 381–3. Dufort de Cheverny, *op. cit.*, pp. 124–5, 93, 320. Duchess of Northumberland, *The Diaries of a Duchess* edited by James Grieg, London, 1926, pp. 116–17. Mme Campan, *op. cit.*, Vol. 1, pp. xxix, 2–5.

LOUIS XVI: Louis Auguste, dauphin, Réflexions sur mes entretiens in *Oeuvres de Louis XVI* edited by C. Moussy, Paris, 1865, p. 191; pensées sur quelques auteurs, pp. 24–5. Mme Campan, *op. cit.*, Vol. 1, pp. 75–6; pp. 84–6, 91–2; pp. 111–13. John Lewis Soulavié, *Historical and Political Memoirs of the reign of Lewis XVI,* London, 1802, Vol. 2, pp. 30–1, 35–7. Mme de la Tour du Pin, *Memoirs* edited and translated by Felice Harcourt, London, 1970, pp. 70–2, 139. Louis XVI address to the National Assembly, 15 July 1789, Moussy, *op. cit.*, pp. 222–3. Mme Campan, *op. cit.*, Vol. 2, pp. 54–7. Louis XVI letter to Mesdames, 25 March 1792, Moussy, *op. cit.*, pp. 173–4. Mme Campan, *op. cit.*, Vol. 2, pp. 217–18. Cléry, *Journal,* Paris, 1825, pp. 23–30. Edmund Burke, *Reflections upon the Revolution in France* (1790) London, 1912, pp. 72–3. Louis XVI letter to the Princesse de Lamballe, 1790, Moussy, *op. cit.*, pp. 128–9. Voting at the Convention, Moussy, *op. cit.*, p. 444. Cléry, *op. cit.*, pp. 142–51. *L'Ancien Moniteur,* new impression, Paris, 1841, Vol. 18, p. 219.

EPILOGUE: Mme Royale, *Récit des Evénements arrivés au Temple,* Paris, 1825, pp. 214–20, 242–3; pp. 249–56.

CAPTION SOURCES: p. 31 Robert II: Ralph Glaber in Guizot, *op. cit.*, p. 203. p. 41 Louis VI: Walter Map, *op. cit.*, p. 211. p. 52 Philippe II: Chronicler quoted in Paul Guth, *La Douce France,* Paris, 1968, Vol. 1, p. 555. p. 68 Philippe III: Arch. Nat. J.218. no. 79 (*Doc. Inéd.*, Mélanges, 1, 554) quoted in Charles V. Langlois, *op. cit.*, p. 7, f. 6. p. 70 Philippe IV: Villani in Muratori, Vol. 9, p. 473 quoted in Edgard Boutaric, *La France sous Philippe le Bel,* Paris, 1861, p. 417. p. 112 Charles VII: Gérard (Philippe) de Vigneulles, *Chronique,* edited by C. Bruneau, Metz, 1927–9, p. 205. p. 191 Louis XIII: Soulavié, *op. cit.*, p. 7. p. 201 Louise de la Vallière: Visconti, *op. cit.*, p. 39. p. 205 Louis XIV: Fénélon to Louis, 1692 quoted in Philippe Erlanger, *The Age of Courts and Kings,* London, 1967, p. 213. p. 218 Marie Leczinska: President Hénault, *Mémoires,* p. 217 quoted in Luynes, *op. cit.*, p. 26.